The Poetic Theology of Love

Cupid in Renaissance Literature

Thomas Hyde

Newark: University of Delaware Press
London and Toronto: Associated University Presses

Associated University Presses
440 Forsgate Drive
Cranbury, NJ 08512

Associated University Presses
25 Sicilian Avenue
London WC1A 2QH, England

Associated University Presses
2133 Royal Windsor Drive
Unit 1
Mississauga, Ontario
Canada L5J 1K5

The paper used in this publication meets the
requirements of the American National
Standard for Permanence of Paper for Printed
Library Materials Z39.48-1984.

Library of Congress Cataloging-in-Publication Data

Hyde, Thomas, 1948–
  The poetic theology of love.

  Bibliography: p.
  Includes index.
  1. Cupid (Roman deity) in literature. 2. Love in
literature. 3. Literature, medieval—History and
criticism. 4. European literature—Renaissance, 1450–
1600—History and criticism. I. Title.
PN57.C85H94   1986   809.1'9351   84-40368
ISBN 0-87413-273-8   (alk. paper)

Printed in the United States of America

For Martha, Emily, and Andrew

Contents

Acknowledgments   8

A Note on Sources   9

1   The Poetic Theology of Love   13

2   Medieval Developments   29

3   The *Vita Nuova* and the *Trionfi*   45

4   Renaissance Poetry   72

5   Renaissance Mythographers and Neoplatonists   87

6   Spenser's Minor Poems   111

7   *The Faerie Queene*   143

Epilogue   180

Notes   183

Bibliography   195

Index   209

Acknowledgments

For help of various kinds including generous readings of my manuscript, I am grateful to my colleagues Thomas M. Greene, Giuseppe Mazzotta, George Hunter, Louis Martz, and Lawrence Manley, as well as to A. Bartlett Giamatti, who supervised the dissertation from which this book partly derives. The patient and helpful staffs of the Sterling and Beinecke libraries deserve thanks, as, for different reasons, do two endowed Yale funds. A Morse Fellowship gave me time off from teaching during which parts of this book were written, and a grant from the A. Whitney Griswold Fund supported preparation of the manuscript. Marina Leslie helped check references. The dedication records my deepest hopes and joys.

A Note on Sources

In the interests of brevity, notes contain only shortened references to works that are accompanied by full documentation in the bibliography. Similarly, the editions of works cited in the notes are those appearing in the bibliography, unless specifically noted.

I have used the common abbreviations for scholarly journals and titles of works, including *LCL* for the volumes of the Loeb Classical Library and *PL* and *PG* for those of the *Patrologiae cursus completus, Series Latina* and *Graeca.* I/j and u/v are modernized. Translations, unless otherwise noted, are my own.

The Poetic Theology
of Love

1

The Poetic Theology of Love

"WHAT is Love?" begins Plotinus in *Enneads* 3.5, "a god, a demon or a passion of the mind? Or is it, perhaps, sometimes to be thought of as a god or demon and sometimes merely as an experience?" The first of Plotinus's questions, "What is Love?" is perennial; most of us find occasion enough to ask it in our own experience. His other questions are possible answers to the first, and they too have perennial interest if old literature still speaks to our present case. We must ask "What is Love?" when we read *Anna Karenina* or *Lady Chatterley's Lover*, just as when we read the *Roman de la rose* or the *Vita Nuova* or *The Faerie Queene*. For more recent works we can eliminate the first two of Plotinus's answers and assume that love is a human experience, while in medieval and Renaissance literature we meet Love as a god or demon at every turn and must entertain all three. But how seriously must we entertain them? This question about the poetic theology of love is the central issue of this book.

As Plotinus suggests, his three answers usually reduce to two: is love a superhuman power ("god or demon") or a human emotion—a divine cause or a human effect? Both alternatives inhere in Eros or Cupid or Amor—his names are usually interchangeable—who began his long literary career in Hesiod as a deified abstraction and remained throughout the Middle Ages and Renaissance an amphibious figure, alternately or simultaneously both mythical deity and personified passion. Though Plotinus presented them disjunctively, his alternatives may seem unprofitable if not impossible to keep distinct. Faced with specific poems, how could one tell the difference? Should we say that the troubadours, who give Amors only arrows, are using the personification, while Petrarch uses the mythical deity because he gives him wings also and makes Venus his mother? The distinction seems trivial, and some of the last generation's best scholarship on allegory and poetic theology has taught us to suspect it even in theory. E. H. Gombrich has argued, for example, that in the Renaissance, as in antiquity, "no real distinction can be made between the Gods conceived as demonic beings and their role as personifications and metaphors."[1] At the same time theorists of allegory have been concerned to break down C. S. Lewis's distinction between allegory as representation of the facts of individual psychology and symbolism as representation of an invisible, ideal world which individual experiences are supposed merely to copy. Rosemond Tuve, for example, urged it as "an extraordinary merit of allegory" that it does not specify the locus of its action as psychic or cosmic, and Angus Fletcher argues for the demonic aspect of all allegory.[2] What used to be seen, and often disparaged, as only a mode of representation has in the past twenty years recovered its ontological basis and its animating demons.

The light of these developments has cast into shadow some aspects of the god of love's poetic career, however, precisely by collapsing the distinctions between Plotinus' alternatives, "a god, a demon, or a passion of the mind," and therefore by failing to follow the hint when Plotinus turns from ontology to epistemology: "Or is it, perhaps, sometimes *to be thought of* as a god or demon and sometimes merely as an experience?" Two passages will suffice to indicate the importance of the distinct ontologies and the poetic use of the shift to epistemology. Midway through her consolation, Philosophy sings for Boethius a song probably more imitated than any other passage of the *Consolatio*. It describes the "love which rules the earth and the seas, and commands the heavens"—in other words, love as the cosmic force or divine agent of universal concord. The idea goes back to Empedocles, but Philosophy ends her song with a pessimistic, Judaeo-Christian twist:

> Hic [Amor] sancto populos quoque
> iunctos foedere continet,
> hic et conjugii sacrum
> castis nectit amoribus,
> hic fidis etiam sua
> dictat jura sodalibus.
> O felix hominum genus,
> si vestros animos amor
> quo caelum regitur regat![3]

(Love holds together peoples joined by a sacred pact; he makes good the holy rites of marriage with chaste loves; he imposes, too, his laws on true friends. O happy race of men, if that love by which the heavens are ruled rules also your souls.)

In a song celebrating the power that unifies and harmonizes the universe, the last sentence comes as a shock, since it implies disunity between the two loves and implies another between the macrocosm and the microcosm, the heavens and men's souls. Cosmic or divine love (apparently) rules some human souls, where it produces *sacred* marriages and *true* friends. The love that usually rules men's souls, however—the love that Plotinus would call "a passion of the mind"—does not produce such happy effects, never rules the heavens, and on both accounts cannot be called a god. The Fall, which caused this disjunction, lies beyond Philosophy's ken, and so she gives no explanation of whether or what relation persists between divine and human love. She simply teaches that the two not be confused so that the prevalence of unholy marriages and false friends will not convince men that malevolent or capricious powers govern the universe.

There is another danger, opposite to despair, in collapsing the distinction between Love as a god and love as "merely an experience." Chaucer's Troilus, who imitates Philosophy's song but omits her pessimistic conclusion, might illustrate the delusive hope that can come from attributing one's own passion to the Love "that of erthe and se hath governaunce" (3.1744). An exchange from the tragedy *Octavia*, however, will cast this danger into sharper focus. The play was thought to be by Seneca until the nineteenth century, perhaps because he appears in it as a character. In the following dialogue, Seneca tries to dissuade his former pupil from marrying Poppaea:

Seneca: Recedet a te (temere ne credas) amor.
Nero: Quem summovere fulminis dominus nequit,
caeli tyrannum, saeva qui penetrat freta
Ditisque regna, detrahit superos polo?
Seneca: Volucrem esse Amorem fingit immitem deum
mortalis error, armat et telis manus
arcuque sacras, instruit saeva face
genitumque credit Venere, Vulcano satum.
vis magna mentis blandus atque animi calor
Amor est; juventa gignitur, luxu otio
nutritur inter laeta Fortunae bona;
quem si fovere atque alere desistas, cadit
brevique vires perdit extinctus suas.
Nero: Hanc esse vitae maximam causam reor,
per quam voluptas oritur; interitu caret,
cum procreetur semper humanum genus
Amore grato, qui truces mulcet feras.
hic mihi jugales praeferat taedas deus
jungatque nostris igne Poppaeam toris

(553–71)

(Seneca: Do not believe blindly; Love will depart from you.
Nero: What? He whom the lord of lightning cannot banish? The tyrant of heaven who enters the raging seas and the realm of Dis and drags the gods from the sky?
Seneca: It is a mortal delusion that feigns Love to be a god, winged and inexorable, arms his sacred hands with bow and arrows, furnishes his blazing torch, and believes him Vulcan's offspring, born of Venus. This "Love" is a mighty power of the mind and a seductive warmth of the spirit. It is born of youth, nursed by licentious idleness among the happy gifts of Fortune. If you refuse to foster or feed it, it declines, and its force quickly dwindles and dies.
Nero: I believe him to be the chief source of life, through which pleasure

takes its being. He is immortal, since pleasing Love, who soothes even savage beasts, forever regenerates the human race. May this god bear before me the wedding torches and with his fire yoke Poppaea to my bed.)

To counter Nero's identification of his own passion with the Love that rules the heavens, Seneca the philosopher goes further than Philosophy herself went in Boethius; he denies the divinity of love altogether. Love is only a *vis magna mentis*, which men have personified and imagined to be a god. Seneca does not give the grounds for his position, but his argument clearly involves an epistemological skepticism that reduces the object of belief to a projection onto the cosmos of the subject's internal state—that is, a skepticism about allegory or poetic theology. Not yet suicidal, Seneca cannot question the genuineness of Nero's belief in Cupid, but only its veracity. Therefore he speaks as if Nero were a victim of popular and poetic fictions and warns him to be less credulous. But credulity may be feigned. Licentiousness can masquerade as patience or even piety simply by asserting that a god is the irresistible cause of our passions. Divine compulsion justifies self-indulgence, as a passage from a genuine Senecan tragedy makes explicit:

> Deum esse amorem turpis et vitio furens
> finxit libido, quoque liberior foret
> titulum furori numinis falsi addidit.[4]

(Base and servile lust feigned love to be a god and, in order to be less restrained, has given passion the title of an unreal divinity.)

This categorical denial of Love's divinity is an extreme position and perhaps a rhetorical one, directed to the particular credulity or bad faith of the dramatic situations. Not even the choruses of *Octavia* or *Hippolytus* accept it, and the plays themselves affirm Plotinus's alternatives, but like Plotinus they affirm them disjunctively. A metaphysician can explain easily enough the relationships among these alternatives, as Plotinus himself goes on to do in the tractate which his questions introduce, but the ethical philosopher must take account of the practical consequences when people act according to their belief in these ideas or feign belief in order to justify their actions. If Love is "sometimes to be thought of as a god or demon and sometimes merely as an experience," we must be able to tell the difference in order to avoid either disobeying a divine impulse or making an idol of our own desires. If the Eros or Amor or Cupid who appears in literature also is sometimes to be thought of as a god or demon and sometimes merely as an experience, then readers and poets (who "read" the tradition whenever they write a poem) need to tell the difference too. Otherwise they risk errors analogous to those of literary characters: either too skeptically spurning poetic theology as empty fables (and so missing its divine truths) or, like Nero, too credulously accepting fictions that may be dangerous (and so deluding themselves or others). The distinction between Cupid as a god and Cupid as a passion of the mind may now seem less trivial and critically unprofitable.

There is an opposite danger, however; the distinction may seem too easy. If, as I have argued, the divinities of poetic theology can be understood too complacently or credulously by those learned in Neoplatonic or High Renaissance cosmology and literary theory, they are more easily and more often understood too skeptically by ordinary or amateur readers. W. H. Auden makes a good spokesman for this position: "It is as meaningless to ask whether one believes or disbelieves in Aphrodite or Ares as to ask whether one believes or disbelieves in a character in a novel; one can only say that one finds them true or untrue to life. To believe in Aphrodite or Ares merely means that one believes that the poetic myths about them do justice to the forces of sex and aggression as human beings experience them in nature and their own lives."[5] Orthodox monotheists will be obliged to disagree on doctrinal grounds, of course, but Auden's skeptical account of fictive deities must be rejected even on literary grounds alone. Aphrodite is unlike a character in a novel precisely because she is a divinity; her divinity makes what logicians call a truth-claim. According to Cedric Whitman, Homer's gods are "symbolic predicates of action, character, and circumstance," but their divinity is not therefore neutral or transparent. Their involvement adds "an aspect of the absolute and irreversible" to the hero's action. "The divinity, by his very presence, removes the aspect of chance or accident from . . . persons and events, and casts them in the shape of ineluctable reality."[6] That ontological effect—being cast "in the shape of ineluctable reality"—in turn has ethical consequences. A fiction in which a divinity appears is therefore less like a novel than like a forgery (say, the Donation of Constantine) which, if taken for true, becomes an immediate constituent of the "reality" within which people see their duties and choices and determine their actions. That is why literary criticism begins with attempts to refute or explain away the divinity of Homer's gods and why biblical prophets condemn false prophets without asking whether they are true or untrue to life. A divinity claims to be more real than life; it presents itself as the Archimedean point and asks us to judge whether life is true or untrue to it. In a fiction, then, Aphrodite does not merely "do justice" to the force of sex in the sense of "represent it accurately"; she justifies it.

It might be objected that these are practical or affective replies to Auden's argument, which merely circumscribes a divinity's inherent truth-claim within the fictive world of the poem and maintains a clear boundary between that fictive world and the Real World of the reader. Auden implies, moreover, that the boundary is passable only in one direction; art imitates the world as we already know it. But of course we do not already know the world; we read at least partially in order to know it better. The boundary between fictive and real worlds is seldom clear and allows a lively commerce of concepts, images, and categories in both directions. The liveliest commerce occurs where fictions try seriously to export goods to the real world, but even within this didactic sector commerce is restricted or complicated at some points more than others. This book is about a crucial point on the boundary between fictive and real worlds, the point at which the poetic theology of love confronts the logical implications of divinities and the theological and ethical tradition that includes both Genesis and Plato and that still controls the preconceptions of most readers. The important point to urge against Auden, however, is that readers' preconceptions and whatever view of reality they represent do not *by themselves* fix the boundary between fictive and real worlds or manage the commerce over it. Every work of fiction draws the boundary anew, even if only by retracing the lines temporarily fixed in extra-literary traditions. The greatest works may not win more ground for literature, but they seldom merely occupy what ground there is. Instead, they reconstitute literature itself by opening its boundaries to radical questioning. To neglect this questioning is to miss an essential aspect of literature and, in particular, to miss a major function of the poetical gods.

Another objection to Auden's skepticism is more obvious and more purely or conventionally literary. When Auden identifies Aphrodite and Ares as "the forces of sex and aggression as human beings experience them," he apparently assumes a one-to-one correspondence between the deities of a fictional world and the forces of the real one, so that each mythological figure will be translatable without reference to other figures or to the specifics of plot and theme. But if a poem creates a fictional world, it does more than simply achieve a measure of autonomy from the real world and its customary terminology. It organizes a cosmos in which parts have meaning only as they function in relation to other parts and to the whole. A skepticism based on understanding mythology as a simple code will inevitably distort its meanings in particular contexts and miss its subtleties.

The poetic theology of love is both more complex and more ambiguous than others because the fictional or figurative cosmos it implies shares so many terms and images with the real cosmos explicit in Christian theology. In the one Love is a god; in the other God is love. This correspondence has made commerce between fictional and real worlds easy, but also dangerous. Plotinus's distinction between Love as a god and love as a passion of the mind becomes both harder and more crucial because a Christian can cite Scripture to identify his own passion with the love that rules the heavens, where Nero could cite only poets whose authority was disputed even by pagan theologians. In a Christian poem, Amor or Cupid can be a partial manifestation, a figure or image of the love that is God, but only if readers never confuse or forget the hierarchical relation between the figure and fact, between the fictive world and the real one. If readers do forget that hierarchical relation, then the partial manifestation ceases to point to the whole reality; the sign becomes an obstacle to signification rather than its instrument; Cupid becomes once again a pagan god, an idol. Reading or writing poetic theology always combines recognition or education with temptation, and the combination is usually put to poetic use.

Cupid's meaning thus depends upon the fictional status of the poems in which he appears, but at the same time he is one of the ways that poems constitute themselves as fictions. This circular acquisition of meaning is no doubt a special case of the hermeneutic circle, and it implies that except in particular contexts Cupid's meaning always remains indeterminate. He never becomes an unambiguous term in an iconographical language, despite what often seem the best efforts of commentators and mythographers to reduce poetic theology to a lexicon of fixed meanings. The important point to make here, however, is that Cupid's indeterminate status carries with it the potential for two kinds of poetic structure. It makes possible irony or satire when a poem leads its readers to understand Cupid differently than do its speaker or characters. The dreamer of the *Roman de la rose,* for instance, takes Love to be a god, while the poem encourages its readers to see him as a passion of the mind. Cupid's indeterminacy also has a narrative or dramatic potential, since the disjunction between meanings that is simultaneous in irony can occur sequentially in a plot. A poem's speaker or characters can recognize that Cupid is not what they had thought. In the *Vita Nuova,* for example, Dante finds that the poetic theology of his own early works may do dangerously more than justice to the force of love. Therefore he demythologizes Amore by explaining that what he had thought a god is really just an emotion. Later he will work out the conditions under which his emotion is a trace of providential design and therefore a sign of God. Recognition can also work the opposite way, as when Giuliano de Medici in Poliziano's *Stanze per la giostra* meets the god he has scorned as merely a passion. This kind of recognition obviously figures the experience of falling in love, but, as I have argued above, its obviousness does not make it a neutral or transparent trope. It presents falling in love in "the shape of ineluctable reality" and can for that reason mark a crisis in the work's figuration. Even within a single poem, then, Love is "sometimes to be thought of as a god or demon and sometimes merely as an experience." The distinction is not merely a nicety of literary representation, extrinsic to poems themselves and irrelevant to their interpretation. It is often crucial because it implicates the status of the poetic fiction itself for poets, for characters in poems, and for readers outside them.

Cupid plays so many roles in so many different kinds of literature, not to mention in all sorts of visual arts and hybrid forms like emblem books, parlor games, and pageantry, that even to undertake a catalogue of his appearances would be a mad endeavor. Selection of works to illustrate his poetic theology is therefore bound to seem arbitrary. It is less arbitrary than it seems. Cupid's roles in all the arts are so various that it makes little sense to speak of them all together as constituting a tradition. His tradition would be nearly coextensive with the Western Tradition itself and hardly more manageable as the subject of a book. In this Cupid differs from other mythological figures like Ulysses or

Prometheus or Orpheus. Still, the chaotic variety of Cupid's appearances in all the arts does contain traditions which center on single attributes, motifs, or conceits as they recur and evolve through a historical sequence of works. Erwin Panofsky traces one such tradition when he shows how Cupid grew blind during the Middle Ages, and other traditions have been catalogued in older studies of sources and influences like Neilson's *Origins and Sources of the Court of Love* or Hutton's "The First Idyl of Moschus in Imitations to the Year 1800." The poetic theology of love is another such tradition. It does not include all of Cupid's appearances in the arts, but only those that employ seriously his single most important or intrinsic attribute: divinity. But to use Cupid's divinity seriously is, as I have argued, to question whether it is a fact, a figure of speech, or a delusive fiction and, as artist, to abide the answer. I ignore, therefore, or rather use only for contrast, the myriad works of art in every age that use Cupid ornamentally, frivolously, or facilely. What kind of works are left?

Cupid's appearances in the visual arts are often enough ornamental, frivolous, or facile, but I shall say little even about those that are not and should begin by explaining what justifies this omission. The term "poetic theology" owes much of its present currency to art historians like Edgar Wind who find its ideas illustrated in the great works of High Renaissance mythological art. But it is *poetic*, not artistic, theology and applies directly to the supposed texts illustrated in works of art, but only indirectly to the works of art themselves. "The crucial difference" between the text and its illustration, as E. H. Gombrich defines it, ". . . lies of course in the fact that no verbal description can ever be as particularized as a picture must be. . . . The same text can be illustrated in countless ways. Thus it is never possible from a given work of art alone to reconstruct the text it may illustrate."[7] The artist must add visual particularities that the text omits, but he must omit textual particularities that he cannot depict. Among these textual particularities is precisely Cupid's uncertain ontology as a god, a demon, or a passion of the mind and the ambiguous figurality that follows from it. A painting or a statue may be able to suggest both of these, and I shall mention a few that do, but it cannot depict them and so must always leave undetermined the ironies or the recognition that a poet can enforce. Though they often illustrate episodes from the poetic theology of love, paintings cannot depict the ambiguous status of poetic theology itself, which always underlies and often animates those episodes.

This limitation of the visual arts will emerge more clearly if we turn briefly from poetic theology to the theology that Christians take to be non-poetic or literal. An artist can represent the true God, of course, but he cannot represent Him truly, and this limitation leads to the prohibition or destruction of images in the more austere periods and movements of the Judaeo-Christian tradition or in less austere ones to an insistence that images are not to be taken as true representations. According to the Council of Trent, for example, "If ever the histories and stories of holy Scripture should happen to be expressed or depicted, as for the unlearned multitude is useful, let the people be taught that the Deity is not therefore depicted as if He could be seen with the bodily eyes or expressed in colors or pictures."[8] But the unlearned multitude cannot be taught not to take paintings as portraits of God by the paintings themselves, because paintings—or any other kind of visual art—cannot successfully represent themselves as representations except by recourse to language or through conventions that are precisely what the unlearned need to learn in the first place. Half-figures or busts, for example, may conventionally indicate man's partial knowledge of God, but paintings using this convention cannot at the same time teach it.[9] And if a Renaissance artist, following ancient ideas of negative or aniconic representation rather than his own age's emphasis on pictorial illusion, used incongruities in order to show that his painting was not a likeness, he risked condemnation for heresy. A fifteenth-century archbishop of Florence, later canonized, judged that "painters who paint things contrary to the faith are also reprehensible, as when they make the image of the Trinity one person with three heads, which in the nature of things is a monster."[10] Jan van Eyck risked similar misunderstanding when he painted the central panel of the *Adoration of the Mystical Lamb*, which is formally indistinguishable from depictions of the Hebrews worshipping the golden calf. St. Augustine preferred the arts of time to the arts of space precisely for these reasons—because the former can encourage and nearly compel a dialectical or interpretive movement from sensible exteriors to intelligible interiors.[11]

To return to Cupid, we can see the sensible exteriors of the visual arts becoming a figure for fiction itself in the long tradition of poems coupled with or describing pictures of Cupid. In the *Octavia*, we remember, Seneca taught Nero that "a mortal delusion" fashions Love as a winged god, and Propertius, in *Elegies* 2.12, describes a painting as a way of indicating the fictiveness of conventional images of Cupid:

> Quicumque ille fuit, puerum qui pinxit Amorem,
> nonne putas miras hunc habuisse manus? . . .
> idem non frustra ventosas addidit alas,
> fecit et humano corde volare deum:
> scilicet alterna quoniam jactamur in unda,
> nostraque non ullis permanet aura locis.
>
> (1–2, 5–8)

(Whoever first painted Love as a boy, do you not think his hands had wonderful skill? . . . With good reason, too, he gave him airy wings, and made the god flit about human hearts, for truly we are always tossed on a shifting sea, and our breeze never lasts in any one quarter.)

However appropriate in general, the conventional fiction is untrue in Propertius's case, and he goes on to correct it. "Sed certe pennas perdidit ille suas"; Love has lost his wings, since he never flies forth from Propertius's

Andrea Alciati, *Emblemata*. Padua: Tozzius, 1618.

bosom (14). A painter might represent Propertius's constant love more accurately, then, by omitting the wings, but without recourse to language he could not show that he was representing an individual case of love or that all such representations are only fictions.

An emblem of Alciati illustrated here makes the same limitations of the visual arts explicit. It depicts a naked youth lacking wings, blindfold, or bow and arrows and carrying a shield with a device of a fruit transfixed by an arrow. Unidentifiable without the title "In Statuam Amoris," the image hardly specifies the meaning of its departure from convention even with it.

Perhaps the lack of wings, blindness, or bow and arrows makes this an image of divine love, constant, clear-sighted, and benevolent. But then should not divine love have wings to soar above the earth? In fact, Alciati's verses make clear that the title means "Against the Image of Cupid" as well as "On the Image of Cupid." The verses mock all of Cupid's usual attributes beginning with his divinity:

Quis sit Amor, plures olim cecinere Poetae,
Eius qui vario nomine gesta ferunt.
Convenit hoc, quod veste caret, quod corpore parvus,
Tela alasque ferens, lumina nulla tenet.
Haec ora, hic habitusque Dei est. Sed dicere tantos
Si licet in vates, falsa subesse reor. [12]

(Many poets have sung who is Love and told his deeds under various names. But they agree on this: that he lacks clothes and that he is small in body, has darts and wings, and cannot see. These are the attributes and this the condition of a god! But if to say so much be permitted to poets, I think it at bottom to be false.)

The mockery has a moral purpose as the verses make clear at the end:

At tu ne tantis capiare erroribus, audi:
Verus quid sit Amor, carmina nostra ferent.

(But so that you will not be possessed by such errors, listen: our songs will tell what love truly is.)

After twenty-nine lines spent dispelling the errors of poetic tradition, the poem begins again; "Quis sit Amor?" becomes "Verus quid sit Amor?"—depersonifying love by shifting to the neuter pronoun. In truth, Alciati concludes, "Love is pleasing work, wantoness in idleness, and its sign is a punic apple on a black shield" (Jucundus labor est, lascivia per otia: signum / Illius est nigro punica glans clypeo). Pleasing work and wantoness in idleness are hard to depict, however. The heraldic sign, which signifies the act of libido according to one annotator, is the poet's one concession to the illustrator, who, despite the neuter pronoun, has had to add the youthful figure and an arrow transfixing the fruit, presumably to retain some vestige of Cupid's usual features. It is not surprising that *nostra carmina*, rather than *nostra pictura*, will tell the truth about love. And how could one illustrate a still less compromising answer to the question "What is Love?" like that once attributed to Dante: "Io dico che Amor non è sustanza, / nè cosa corporal ch'abbia figura" (I say that Love is not a substance or a thing that has bodily shape)? [13]

Artists did use Cupid, of course, in works with a moral purpose not unlike Alciati's or Seneca's: to reprove the love he represents. A painting like Guido Reni's *Sacred and Profane Love* shows clearly enough the victory of divine love, but it cannot show this victory as a recognition or undoing of a popular error, because that error is precisely the figuration that the painting employs. Countless cassoni decorations modeled on Petrarch's *Trionfi* show Cupid similarly bound, but they necessarily ignore what will be a major topic of Chapter 3 below—the poetic means by which Petrarch exposes Amore as his own passion deified by his fixated imagination. An artist can make Cupid look like a peas-

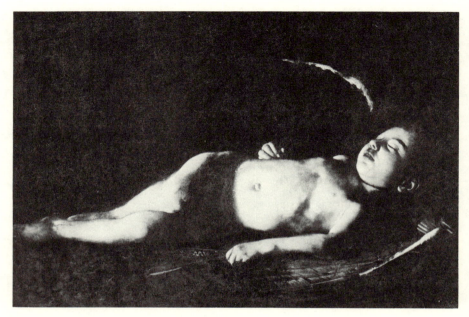

Caravaggio, *Sleeping Cupid*. Palazzo Pitti, Florence. Photo: Alinari.

ant, as Caravaggio does here, but he cannot inquire, as a poet can, whether Cupid looks like a peasant because he images a common passion or because he is a rough god. Visual art can reprove or subordinate or de-idealize, but it cannot demythologize.

I have stressed the incapacity of the visual arts to enforce movement from the exterior fictions of poetic theology to its interior truths, but there are other reasons perhaps as important to account for the fact that an extensive, though necessarily amateur, survey of the visual arts fails to turn up more than a few isolated analogues for the central and animating concerns of the poetic tradition. Artists who worried that images of Cupid unavoidably give substance to a potentially delusive fiction probably avoided Cupid altogether. Those who do depict Cupid, if they thought about it at all, could calm their worries by regarding themselves as craftsmen. If someone is deluded by a depiction of poetic theology, let the blame fall upon the patron who commissioned the work, on his humanist advisors who provided the program for it, or on the deluded himself; all of them ought to know better. If, with few exceptions, artists lacked the prestige of poets, they also lacked the responsibilities.

Still, as the Renaissance proceeded, artists did experiment with the limitations of pictorial and plastic form and manipulated their conventions for purposes of wit or in defense of truth. Few of these experiments seem to bear upon Cupid, but I should like to mention one that does because it shows that even

Vermeer, *A Young Woman Standing at a Virginal*. Reproduced by courtesy of the Trustees, The National Gallery, London.

when an artist succeeds in suggesting the ambiguities of poetic theology, he will not use them dialectically as a poet will. Like many other late Renaissance paintings (Velasquez' *Las Meninas* being the best known example), Vermeer's *Young Woman Standing at a Virginal* uses a painting-within-the-painting to comment on the scene it depicts.

Cupid's determined gaze and the trump card he holds up to view help to interpret the young woman's interested and open gaze outward at the viewer. Just as his nakedness contrasts with her elaborate dress, his presence lays bare tensions or expectations that underlie the conventional scene and have interrupted the lady's playing. But, of course, Cupid is not really present; he is represented in, and perhaps therefore as, a product of human art. So instead of his usual arrows and torch, he holds a playing card, an attribute that signifies victory only within the rules of a game that, unlike war, is also fictive. Vermeer succeeds in depicting Cupid, then, without giving delusive substance to his fictional divinity. The painting has the skeptical component that I have identified in the poetic theology of love, but does it have the other necessary component, the mythopoeic? Does Cupid merely illustrate a Dutch domestic scene, or can we see the domestic scene as illustrating the true, though figurative, power of the god of love? Probably not the latter. The frame of the painting-within-the-painting too successfully isolates its subject; Cupid comments upon, but does not cause, the lady's state of mind. And for either lady or viewer, belief in Cupid is not at issue. One can imagine a painting after Vermeer's in which the viewer could not tell whether an armed Cupid was present or only represented, hovering in front of the wall or painted on it. If the lady glanced toward Cupid while gesturing to the viewer, such a painting might engage both the skeptical and mythopoeic components of poetic theology. I have not discovered such a painting, but even if one or several do exist, the generalization would still hold that Cupid's uses in the visual arts intersect but do not significantly overlap the subject of this book.

If the poetic theology of Cupid always raises the question of his ontological status and attends to the consequences of the answer, then it will exclude not only the visual arts in general, but also a great many literary works. Short poems, for example, may allude to Cupid's figural ambiguity, but seldom have space to unfold its potential. Especially in the fifteenth century, when the *Greek Anthology* and *Anacreontea* gain almost sovereign influence, the Cupid who appears in sonnets and other short lyrics tends to be an ornament or mythological plaything. The texts in which poetic theology does operate are mostly longer narrative or discursive works like the *Roman de la rose*, the *Vita Nuova*, or *The Faerie Queene*, which create a fictional world with sufficient detail and integrity to make Cupid a force, perhaps a god, and therefore to call both characters and author to a reckoning. In these poems, Cupid gains a prominence he never had in antiquity.

The nature of poetic theology determines the procedure appropriate to demonstrate it or at least to illustrate its usefulness. If Cupid's role in a poem simultaneously reflects and helps to define the poem's specific claims for itself as a fiction, then it will emerge only through a critical reading of the poem. This reading will often range beyond the incidents in which Cupid appears because he accumulates meaning functionally, like a chess piece whose meaning derives from its position on the board and the rules that govern its movements: "the meaning of a piece is its role in the game."[14] On the other hand, it need not be a full-scale reading since Cupid's role, however, crucial, seldom engages all of a poem's patterns of significance, especially when the poem is a major work like the *Roman de la rose* or *The Faerie Queene.* The sequence of readings that make up this book record the diversity of Love's pageants in European poetry as well as the nature of the poetic theology that underlies them and shapes their significance. Like the rules of chess, the logic of poetic theology remains constant even while its exemplars evolve in new directions and with new emphases. That evolution too emerges in this book's sequence of readings and, given the nature of poetic theology, can only emerge from such a sequence.

Some mythological figures make significant appearances in literature ranging from Homer to Joyce, Aeschylus to Gide. Cupid is not one of these figures. His major roles define a broad movement in post-classical literary history, very nearly the tradition that C. S. Lewis surveyed in *The Allegory of Love,* but I do not claim that the texts treated in this book constitute a tradition in themselves or that every author knew or was influenced by the authors who precede him in my sequence. I do claim that these texts fairly *represent* a tradition, and when appropriate I shall indicate other texts that might illustrate the same or similar uses of Cupid. My aim has been to show how the poetic theology of love works, to explore the logic that governs Cupid's potential meanings, rather than to write a comprehensive history of the tradition. Such a comprehensive history may not be desirable in the first place. In *Theory of Literature,* Wellek and Warren protested that "various versions of a story have no . . . necessary connexion or continuity. . . . To trace all the differing versions of, say, the tragedy of Mary Queen of Scots throughout all literature might well be a problem of interest for the history of political sentiment, and would, of course, incidentally illustrate changes in the history of taste—even changing conceptions of tragedy. But it has itself no real coherence or dialectic. It presents no single problem and certainly no critical problem" (p. 260). The poetic theology of Cupid does present a single problem and, as I have argued, a critical one, but Wellek and Warren's other objections potentially apply, especially since poems that illustrate Cupid's poetic theology do not fall into a single generic tradition such as that of the Renaissance epic. Therefore I have not thought it worthwhile to diffuse the focus of this book by pointing out, except incidentally, general and well-known developments in the history of style and ideas that may be visible in Cupid's various appearances.

One general development comes clear in and indeed determines Cupid's career, however, and deserves to be better known. That is precisely the ambiguity of poetic theology itself, which can come about only when poets are considered in some sense *theologi* in a literary tradition in which Scripture provides an ultimate example of textual truth and therefore an ultimate model of poetic authority. The relation between literature and Scripture is never static, and tension within it—between confidence in fiction as a necessary veil for truth and mistrust of it as deceit or delusion—animates the literary career of Cupid, where it poses again and again the question with which I began: "What is Love? A god, a demon, or a passion of the mind?" Better-known developments like the taste for mythological ornament, the cult of courtly love, or the rediscovery of ancient Neoplatonism play their parts, of course, but they too submit to the logic of poetic theology. They too gain life and form from the tradition they join.

2
Medieval Developments

POETICA *Theologia* was to have been the title of a book by Pico della Mirandola expounding the secrets of ancient hermetical tests; it was to have been a work of interpretation. The poetic theology of love begins much earlier, not in medieval works of interpretation, but in fictions that make love a god and place him in a fictive world in which his divinity is constitutive rather than merely a local trope for the force of erotic desire. Though such stories multiply almost beyond reckoning during the late Middle Ages, a few will suffice to illustrate the essential development. I single out a dialogue from Andreas Capellanus's *De amore*, Alain de Lille's *De planctu naturae*, and the *Roman de la rose* because they are among the earliest and most influential, and because they clearly exhibit characteristic medieval phases in the logic governing that complex figure, both personification and deity, the god of love. The god of love, with his classical avatars Cupid and Amor, is ubiquitous in medieval literature, however, and preliminary notice of some of his other roles will help to contrast and clarify the development of his poetic theology.

Medieval handbooks of mythology and commentaries on classical texts share the goal of translating the delusive fictions of the pagan poets into a world-view acceptable and meaningful to Christian readers. It is not surprising that the poetic theology of love does not develop in works dedicated to explaining away the divinity of the old gods, undoing the cosmologies they helped to constitute, making them safe as mere figures of speech. Still, the career of Amor or Cupid in medieval mythography and commentary evolves in parallel and enabling ways with the development of his roles in mythopoeic fictions. If mythographers explain away his divinity, they also allow him increasingly positive significances and thereby make him increasingly ambiguous as a mythological sign. Both tendencies encourage development of his poetic theology.

The Cupid whom the Middle Ages inherited from the Roman poets already occupied a limbo between true divinity and personification. He was a "paramythical figure" whose wings, torch, and arrows were less mythical attributes than "metaphorical accessories," each standing for a negative quality of erotic passion.[1] In the hierarchy of love supposed to range from the mystical bond of the Trinity to the sexual instinct of beasts, Cupid conventionally stood toward the bottom as the patron and sign of "carnal concupiscence."[2] About 1100, however, this quasi-lexical convention begins to collapse under pressure from renewed debate about love as a natural impulse, from the fashions still passing under the name "courtly love," and from the proto-humanism of the twelfth-century renaissance. Less defensive in the face of paganism than Lactantius or even Augustine, twelfth-century commentators found themselves unwilling to understand the poetical gods only as cautionary examples or personified sins, tending instead to seek new and positive undermeanings in the body of philosophical and theological thought.[3] As the prestige of the classics rose, so did the number and extravagance of Christianizing allegories. Rising prestige of the classics helped to transvalue all the gods, but especially Amor or Cupid, who also benefited from the centrality of love in Christian theology and from the ambiguity of the common nouns from which his names derive.

The distinction between two kinds of love—*eros* and *agape, cupiditas* and *caritas*—for example, leads to a distinction between two Loves, as in the twelfth-century Third Vatican Mythographer: "Likewise there are two Loves, one good and chaste by whom wisdom and virtues are loved, the other unchaste and evil by whom we are inclined to vice."[4] The new *in bono* reading does not replace the old *in malo* reading, but joins it, doubling the god of love, half redeeming him, but at the same time making him thoroughly equivocal. In the thirteenth and fourteenth centuries, doctrinal allegories raise Cupid's station still higher. Before 1318, Francesco Barbarino, for example, re-interprets Cupid as *Amor Divino*, inverting the moral significance of every attribute. Among its multiple interpretations of the Apollo and Daphne myth, the early fourteenth century *Ovide moralisé* reads Cupid as the love of God the Son, the good archer whose darts are the commandments of the law. The English Franciscan John Ridewall could see even the Incarnation as the work of Cupid, so that Christ himself illustrates the Virgilian commonplace, "Omnia vincit amor."[5]

If doctrinal allegorizing helps to transvalue the mythology of love, so does the lexical ambiguity of the Latin nouns *amor* and *cupido*. Because of the god of love's double status as both deity and personification, allegoresis worked easily in reverse, generating mythological beings, attributes, and even incidents from abstract concepts or relations. Cupid grows blind during the Middle Ages, for instance, because several classical phrases describe love as blind.[6] In his *Genealogia deorum gentilium* 1.15, Boccaccio can cite Aristotle's categorization of love (*Nic. Eth.* 8.2) as evidence that Antiquity recognized three Cupids, although the passage lacks any trace of mythology. On the model of Apollo and Daphne and in order to illustrate "Omnia vincit amor," mythographers add a contention between Pan and Cupid to the Syrinx episode of *Metamorphoses* 1—a bit of mythological midrash repeated so often as to appear part of the Ovidian text.[7] Given this easy interchangeability between image and concept, the god of love comes inevitably to encompass the range of meanings denoted by *amor* and *cupido*. Of the two names, he was mostly known throughout the Middle Ages by the more ambiguous, *amor,* which could denote every force of nature and every impulse of the human soul. *Cupido,* too, was equivocal. Even St. Augustine did not restrict it to cupidity, and many exegetes followed Origen's less categorical view of the Scriptural vocabulary of love.[8] Taking the poets *in bono,* then, the devout reader could see the god of love standing for Christ or for the love of God more easily than other mythological types such as Hercules or Orpheus. As a personification he may have seemed less tainted by polytheism, and his name includes the love that Scripture identifies with God (1 John 4.8).

But in a severer mood or for a different purpose, the same devout reader might read *in malo,* making Cupid once again a demon of fornication or sign of fleshly lust. Far from creating a system or language of mythological signs, these late medieval commentators and mythographers dismantled one, loosening conventional correspondences between myths and meanings, multiplying interpretations, and enveloping Cupid and the other gods in ambiguities. Not until the Renaissance do mythographers attempt to reduce these ambiguities to order and reconstitute what they begin to think of as the *system*—which is to say the theology and cosmos—of the ancient gods.

The ambiguities that invest the mythology of love in the late Middle Ages are part of a much larger and older conflation of pagan and Christian love imagery instanced and authorized by the Song of Songs and rationalized by its commentators. For a variety of reasons, this conflation enjoyed a resurgence beginning in the twelfth century. Commonplaces like Virgil's "Omnia vincit amor" and Ovid's "Militat omnis amans" were turned to purposes of Christian devotion.[9] Adapting the title of Ovid's licentious book, a Christian writer could wittily declare, "Ars est artium ars amoris." Pagan love symbols largely supplant the *misericordia* in thirteenth century iconography as images for *caritas.*[10] A schoolman and antihumanist like Hugh of St. Victor could borrow Cupid's snares and arrows for his *De laude charitatis* and even echo the notorious argument Nero made in the *Octavia* to justify his lust: "You [caritas] have drawn Him [Christ] to you bound in your chains; you have drawn Him to you wounded by your arrows. A man ought to be ashamed to resist you when he sees that you have triumphed even over God."[11]

For reasons not long to seek, the poetic theology of love develops in the twelfth and thirteenth centuries alongside such Christian appropriation of the myths and imagery of pagan love poetry. When in the *Vita Nuova* Dante uses Biblical echoes and theological commonplaces to describe his *dio d'amore,* he simply reverses the process of appropriation. But there is a deeper reciprocity between the two processes. Neither doctrinal allegorizing of pagan texts nor cloaking of Christian themes in pagan imagery necessarily betray some heterodox syncretism or naturalism, but both do promote radical ambiguity of those texts and images. That ambiguity is acceptable because writers and readers are presumed to share a fundamental faith (a view of history, a cosmology, an ethical standard), which determines what is meaningful and how, and which thus ensures that pagan integuments stay subservient to Christian meanings. Even while pagan myths and images tolerate this subservience and gain currency from it, however, they can resist conversion and harbor apostasy. To varying degrees, they can still evoke a non-Christian cosmology and so challenge the very presumption of faith upon which their currency depended.[12] When texts pose this challenge within themselves, enacting or elaborating the potential for apostasy of their own myths and images, the result is poetic theology. The late medieval mythographers and commentators who help to make the god of love and the rest of erotic mythology so ambiguous do not take this step. Still less do writers and artists who merely ornament their works with pagan allusions or iconography. But their confident embrace of ambiguity does give both occasion and importance to fictions that test the dangers of that confidence—that is, to the characteristic ironies and defenses of the medieval poetic theology of love.

Before turning to our first instance of poetic theology, it is worth noting that discursive modes like mythography and commentary are not alone in demythologizing the god of love and treating him as a simple personification, though one with equivocal meanings. Many medieval fictions and lyric poems do the same. In Chrétien de Troyes, for example, lovers feel Love's arrows, darts, lance, and sword; they join his army, camp, and court; they struggle in his snares and bonds; but they never actually *see* him. They go to his school, but never hear him speak. Like the authors of the slightly earlier narrative poems *Pyramus et Tisbé* and the three *romans antiques* (the *Thèbes, Enéas,* and *Troie*), indeed like Ovid in the *Ars amatoria* which he translated, Chrétien personifies Love without mythologizing him or incarnating him as a character.[13] Though once called "li deus d'Amors" (*Yvain* 5371), he is never actually present in the romances and never signals a divine intervention in the action. Instead, Amors represents a subjective emotion, chiefly to be apostrophized in lovers' monologues. When Lancelot deliberates whether to mount the cart, Amors can contradict Reason, but the passage is not a *debat* and lacks completely the fictional trappings, the mythopoeia, that the debate would have a century later in the *Roman de la rose*. Chrétien's Amors is morally less equivocal than in later mythography, but his meaning remains ambiguous, dependent upon literary context rather than lexical or iconographical convention. Though never reaching so high as *caritas* or so low as lust, he ranges widely between. He represents Lancelot's irrational and perhaps degrading passion as well as the love that leads to marriage in both *Cligés* and *Yvain*. He can also represent emotions having nothing to do with erotic love. When Yvain and Gawain do battle, each unaware of the other's identity, Amors stands for their chivalric *amicitia* subjected by circumstance to irrational Hate. Love is indeed blind, the narrator comments, if it cannot recognize its object (*Yvain* 6053–56).

Chrétien's use of Amors may derive from that of the early Provençal troubadours, and together they exemplify what might be called the lyric use of personified Love. Like Chrétien, the troubadours employ Amors exclusively as a personification, seldom calling him the god of love or mentioning mythological genealogies or incidents.[14] The troubadours, too, personify Love without incarnating it. Thus the grammatical peculiarity that turned Latin *amor* feminine in Provençal did not make Amors female because the early troubadours do not make the word flesh sufficiently for its sex to be meaningful.[15] To borrow an Aristotelian distinction, troubadour Amors represents the formal cause of love as much as the efficient cause. Perhaps this is only to say that troubadour songs are indeed lyrics, recounting subjective experience and setting that experience, however conventional or fictive it may have been, in a courtly and social context rather than a cosmological one. The troubadour claimed none of the epic poet's sway over the gods, even in the form of mythological allusion or ornament, and did not pretend to reveal divine agents behind the story of his passion, as Virgil, for example, had recorded Cupid's part in the tragedy of Dido. The troubadour saw himself, not as a *vates,* but as a composer and singer of songs; he imagined no new model of the cosmos, but sought to divert or embellish or honor the human world he lived in.

Though not a mythological or fictive deity, Amors or "Fin'Amors" does have in the troubadour lyrics what had been Cupid's Ovidian weaponry, but his darts and arrows are also demythologized in a way that helps to make Amors himself even more indeterminate than he became for later mythographers. When not simply projections of the pangs and joys of love, Love's darts and arrows represent glances from the lady's eyes or beams from her bright countenance. Uc Brunec's version of this conceit is typical, though his philosophical language is not:

> Amors, que es us esperitz cortes,
> Que no s laissa vezer mas per semblans,
> Quar d'huelh en huelh salh e fai sos dous lans,
> E d'huelh en cor e de coratge en pes.[16]

(Love is a courteous spirit who lets himself be seen only in his semblance, for he shoots his sweet arrows from the eyes to the eyes, and passes from the eyes to the heart and from the heart to the thoughts.)

This little allegory of enamorment became for four centuries one of the hardest-worked conceits in love poetry. Although differing widely from mythographical *in bono* and *in malo* readings, it still represents a rationalistic interpretation of Cupid's mythological attributes. In its emphasis on the eyes as the sources of love, the conceit derives from the Platonic definition of love as desire for beauty as filtered through speculations, both ancient and medieval, on the psychology, physiology, and even physics of love.[17] Within this allegory of enamorment, Amors is necessarily an indeterminate figure. He can merge indistinguishably with the lady as the source of the lover's wounds, yet he makes his seat within the lover's heart or mind.[18] His power is as indeterminate as his ontological status. According to Aimeric de Peguilhan, "True love . . . does not and cannot have in himself force or power or any authority either small or large unless the eyes and the heart give it to him."[19] Unlike a god's, Love's power is derivative and contingent.

Despite attempts by some thirteenth-century troubadours to preserve the traditions they inherited by systematizing them in allegorical arts of love, "troubadour love" remains far from uniform and the figure who personifies it far from unambiguous. The tradition itself—upwards of four hundred troubadours who constantly distinguished among different varieties of love, debated these distinctions with each other, and revised both their opinions and their vocabulary—works against uniformity.[20] In the tradition as a whole, Amors ranges as widely as he would in later mythography, from erotic desire to chaste devotion to the Virgin. After the Albigensian Crusade, he clearly stands for *caritas*.[21] Even in individual poems, Amors is often ambiguous. Widespread use of religious imagery in profane *cansos d'amore* and erotic imagery in religious poems makes interpretation difficult, an effect cultivated in the *trobar clus* style. Jaufré Rudel's "amor de lonh" does not submit to specification, for example, nor do stanzas like Marcabru's "Ai! fin'Amors, fons de bontat."[22]

Ambiguities like these do not constitute a poetic theology of love, but they do contribute essential materials for the development of one. By making many troubadour songs equivocal about the nature and value of love itself, they made misinterpretation inevitable and provoked both poetic quarrels among troubadours and controversies with civil and ecclesiastical authorities. These controversies were the keener because so much troubadour poetry implicitly displaces ordinary social or religious norms while purporting to set up norms of *cortezia* in which conduct becomes a form of poetry and poetry an ideal of conduct.[23] Poetic theology sharpens both the problematic of reading and the normative professions of troubadour poetry by making Amors into a god and the poetic art of love into a pseudo-scripture.

The poetic theology of love emerges in twelfth-century Latin poetry, whose clerical authors drop the courtly and feudal imagery of Provençal lyric in favor of pseudo-sacred fictions, often those of antique myth. Gone from these poems is the troubadour's fealty to the lady he called "midons," replaced by a simulated neo-pagan cult of Cupid and Venus. These Latin poems are all in a general sense arts of love, and they draw heavily from Ovid, but evolve toward poetic theology less by imitating Ovid than by reinventing him as a parody of Christian ideas and forms. Ovid never presented himself as a *theologus* or *vates;* he never pretended to poetic authority derived from access to divinely sanctioned truths. Instead, he subjected the divinities themselves to playful travesty in poems that claim little in the way of truth of authority. Medieval

Latin poems, however, often treat Ovid as a founding prophet and his works as the scriptures of a religion of love. To choose one example of dozens, the well-born nuns of *The Council of Love at Remiremont* (ca. 1150) begin their liturgy with the gospel of Ovid, *doctor egregius.* This was a kind of poetic authority unknown to Ovid. Whether for the sake of satirical exaggeration or wish fulfillment in an erotic never-never land, poems like the *Council* or the *Altercatio Phyllidis et Florae* obviously depart from actual social conditions or beliefs, but their poetic theologies nevertheless ironically make a kind of truth-claim and pretend to a kind of authority. A similar claim is implicit even in lyric prayers to Cupid for aid in overcoming a lady's resistance, but the workings of poetic theology are clearest when they are neither lyric nor satirical, but rhetorical—that is, when participants in a debate or dialogue appeal to the god of love to judge their differences. Most such *judici d'amor* take up the perennial question of whether clerks or knights make better lovers, but poetic theology becomes more complex and urgent when, to persuade his reluctant lady, an eager lover enlists the god of love on his side and cites his scriptures. Andreas Capellanus, in his prose treatise *De amore,* offers an early and influential example of this debate.

Except in the fifth dialogue of the eight presented as models of amorous persuasion, Andreas follows Ovid in producing a serio-comic art of love without a theology of love. Like his fellow townsman and contemporary, Chrétien de Troyes, Andreas speaks easily of Love's arrows, darts, soldiers, snares, chains, and so forth, but, everywhere except in that fifth dialogue, leaves Love himself a disembodied personification, a mere sign for the complex of emotions defined at the outset as "a certain inborn suffering" derived from meditation on the beauty of the opposite sex and striving for sexual fulfillment.[24] In the fifth dialogue, differentiated like all eight according to the social class of the lover and lady, a nobleman woos a noblewoman, and, though he has no more success than the men of the other dialogues, his casuistry takes a different form. When the lady refuses to give him hope, he resorts at first to fiction and then to poetic theology.

Men say that Love's palace has four gates, the nobleman reports; Love uses the eastern gate himself; ladies who accept only worthy lovers use the southern; those who cannot say no to anyone use the western; and cruel ladies who spurn all offers of love use the northern gate. These last are cursed ("maledictae"), the nobleman declares, being placed on the left hand of Love. The lady remains unmoved by a curse derived from the seating habits of courtly society and unpersuaded by the fable itself. In one manuscript, she complains that the nobleman has made it up.[25]

Failing, then, with his emblematic fable, the nobleman turns to poetic theology. Once he lost his way in a wood, he reports, and chanced upon the entourage of Love. At first he did not recognize the god, who looked like a king crowned with a golden diadem and led an army of ladies grouped into the same three classes as in the first fable. But a lady of the miserable third class identified the god and explained that these were dead ladies, rewarded or punished according to their actions toward lovers while in life. The nobleman says he followed this gothic triumph of Love until it came to Love's afterworld, divided into three concentric circles in which the three classes of dead ladies receive their just deserts. "Lest anything should be lacking to this extraordinary parody of the Christian afterworld," wrote C. S. Lewis, "the story ends with a remarkable scene in which the mortal visitor is brought before the throne, presented with a list of the commandments of Love, and told to report on earth this vision which has been allowed him in order that it may lead to the 'salvation' of many ladies."[26]

Andreas's dialogue with its two fables makes almost a miniature history of the development of poetic theology as a process of rhetorical escalation. The first fable called Love "deus," but in no way realized his deity and failed to persuade the lady. Perhaps, then, a full-blown theophany will impress her. The nature of Love's curse changes accordingly from disfavor under courtly protocol to eternal punishment. To buttress the rhetorical pressure of these changes, the nobleman also escalates the truth-claim of his fable. For the first fable he alleged only the authority of rumor ("Men say that . . ."), but poses in the second, not merely as an eyewitness, but as a prophet divinely commanded to report what had been revealed to him. He aims obviously to deny the lady any grounds for further argument by replacing ordinary ethical norms and their ultimate religious sanctions with a new set of commandments and a new eschatology. Even while making such claims for itself, however, the nobleman's poetic theology remains, in the context of the whole dialogue, a second effort, a secondary fiction obviously elaborating the fable that precedes it. The lady herself glances at this secondariness when in her politely ironic reply to the second fable she returns to the imagery of the first. Too courteous to give the lie direct, she raises the question of veracity, only to describe exactly the response the nobleman might have hoped for. "If these things which you say are true," she says, it is glorious to serve Love and dangerous to rebel, but "true or false, the story of those terrible punishments frightens me so that I do not wish to be a stranger to Love's service." Like many later heroines of courtship comedy, however, she is toying with her pursuer and proceeds to reject his suit on the authority of his own tale—his first tale. Since she would join Love's service, she tells him, she must "follow in every respect the custom of the ladies at the southern gate," which includes inquiring carefully into the worth of every lover before accepting him. Understandably let down, the man complains of her "bitter" reply as the dialogue ends.

To say that the fifth dialogue represents a double abuse of fiction may be to take Andreas's comic treatise too seriously, but it will help to get at some further implications of its poetic theology. The second fable is an abuse of fiction first in its palpable design on the lady. It tries to induce her to specific actions and thus differs markedly from poems like Guido Cavalcanti's famous "pastorella," in which a chance encounter with a shepherdess proves so rapturous that it playfully climaxes in a vision of the god of love. In Cavalcanti's poem, a fictive theophany crowns the deed; it is not invoked to instigate or justify action and is not part of an effort at seduction. Later versions of Andreas's fable, which range from close imitations to distant variations on the same theme, differ from the original in a similar fashion. Most of these versions occur as inset fables in rhetorical or dramatic contexts, and in their contexts all these versions are used to convert cruel beauties from genuine hardness of heart; none is abused to seduce the innocent.[27]

None of these later versions of the fable, moreover, includes a god of love who rules an afterworld of his own or hands down commandments to supplant the biblical ones. That fact points to the second abuse of fiction in Andreas's dialogue. Fictions and lies both recount things not true, but, according to an ancient distinction, fictions differ in not affirming them to be true. "Now for the Poet," wrote Sidney, "he nothing affirmes, and therefore never lyeth. For, as I take it, to lye is to affirme that to be true which is false."[28] The nobleman's fable strays beyond the bounds of fiction in part because he explicitly affirms its truth, but, even if he had not posed as an eyewitness and prophet of a new revelation, Love's divinity alone, as realized within the fiction, would advance a truth-claim. Like all poetic theology, the fable implicitly claims for itself the status of Scripture. That claim makes poetic theology equivocal and unstable. Reading it becomes a moral problem, a temptation.

For a Christian, writer or reader, any divinity except the One God must be figurative or frivolous; it must mean something else or mean nothing at all. To the noble lady, who is the primary reader included within the dialogue, the god of love seems to mean nothing at all. Sure of her place in a comedy, she laughs off the man's urgings to take Love's divinity literally and does not bother to inveigh against his abuses of fiction. But later readers illustrate clearly the unstable tone of the poetic theology which for most of them formed the crux of Andreas's treatise. An anonymous thirteenth-century translator took Andreas's subject figuratively, identifying it as love of the Virgin. Drouart la Vache laughed or at least smiled when he read the *De amore* in 1290, but in 1277 the bishop of Paris was not amused. He condemned the book. At least metaphorically, the bishop took the *De amore* as a counter-scripture and Andreas as a false prophet, coaxing "Let us go after false gods . . . and let us serve them."[29] The controversy continues to this day. For some, Andreas's book is a scholar's attempt at Ovidian humor; for others, it codifies "the heresy of courtly love"; for still others, it satirizes erotic obsession by pretending to tout it as a religion.[30] That a work of modest literary merit could have produced such varying interpretations over such a length of time may help to suggest the ambivalence, the peculiar instability, and also the force of its poetic theology.

The poetic theology of Andreas's dialogue could be comic because the lady was in a double sense too good a reader to be seduced by it, but also because she did not try to expose or correct the nobleman's abuses of fiction. The problem of reading implicit in poetic theology therefore remained submerged in Andreas's comedy. That problem becomes fully explicit, however, in another roughly contemporary dialogue, the *De planctu Naturae*, of the Chartrian poet-theologian Alain de Lille. The *De planctu* is particularly worth notice because its duplicitous mythopoeia is no longer the *ad hoc* invention of a would-be seducer, but the common inheritance of antique myth. Seduction remains at issue for Alain, however, but now it is the capacity of the mythical gods to seduce readers by upsetting the proper subservience of *integumenta* to meaning. That capacity was strengthened by the tendency, especially at Chartres, to draw analogies between poets and prophets, poetry and Scripture—a positive counterpart, perhaps, to the mock canonization of Ovid in satirical poems. Alain has cosmological and ethical aims in the *De planctu*, but first he must reduce the risk of seducing unwary readers, which he does by including a very unwary reader as narrator of the dream vision. Alain's dreamer proves confused just where Andreas's noblewoman had been steadiest—on the gods of erotic myth.

Alain's prosimetrum begins with a prologue in elegiacs deploring sexual corruption. Nature herself then appears to the dreamer, and, after pages of allegorical stage-setting, she takes up his complaint, rattling off a list of examples culled from Ovid—Helen, Pasiphae, Myrrha, Medea, Narcissus. These examples raise a doubt in the narrator. "I wonder as I consider the fictions of the poets," he says, why Nature mentions only human offenders when we read that the gods shared the same vices.[31] Didn't Jupiter make the Phrygian boy his bedfellow? Inheriting their father's lewdness, didn't Apollo and Bacchus seduce mortal women under false pretenses? Shocked, Nature reproves these questions as "unworthy of doubt." Is he so ignorant as to put faith in poetic fictions? Does he not know that some poets tell lies in order to corrupt their readers? All stories "either that there are gods, or that they wanton at the sports of love" are not only false, Nature proclaims; they transgress the limits of fiction (Moffat, 40–41). Poets are permitted outer falsities ("exterioris falsitatis") in which to convey a sweet kernel of truth ("nucleum veritatis"), but tales of the gods' adulteries are the opposite of such poetic fictions; they are naked falsehood ("nudam falsitatem"), without even a covering of truth. For that reason, Nature explains, she mentioned only mortal offenders and passed over these myths in silence.

As in Andreas's dialogue, deity is the crux of the problem because within a fiction a deity constitutes a truth-claim, supplanting the reality principle by which a reader discerns literal from figurative, true kernel from counterfeit husk. In repudiating these myths, Alain's Nature follows a tradition beginning before Plato that attacked these stories as both blasphemous and corrupting. Men cannot be wicked if they imitate the gods; therefore either the gods themselves are wicked or poets are lying about their misdeeds in order to give a fictive sanction to human lust. Early Christian apologists wavered between the two explanations, but a consensus emerged from late antiquity that the *amores deorum* were lies told by the poets.[32] Abelard, Albricus, and many others were still making the same point in the twelfth century, and so, on the other side, were scholarly lovers who cited Jupiter for precedent and urged their ladies or fellows: "Imitemur superos."[33]

In Nature's repudiation of these myths as empty of truth and dangerous to readers, the *De planctu* makes explicit several essential problems of poetic theology, but it is helpful here because it also illustrates the uses of contradiction in redeeming even such myths. Only a few lines after repudiating all tales "either that there are gods, or that they wanton at the sports of love," Nature begins her own myth of divine adultery. What are we to make of so conspicuous an inconsistency? Is her earlier repudiation a hypocritical disclaimer or ineffective gesture? I submit that the contradiction serves to exemplify the fallen state of human discourse, which serves Nature throughout as both matter and metaphor, and to warn against the deceptiveness and duplicity of all myths and fables.[34] It works as an "alienation device" to assure that readers will not take the gods of Nature's fable literally. The contradictory fables of Andreas's dialogue served a similar purpose, nor is this function a medieval oddity. Perhaps the chief modern theory of metaphor takes some self-contradictoriness to be essential in all figurative expression as the necessary cue to read figuratively.[35]

In addition to Nature's conspicuous inconsistency, Alain places another hedge against misinterpretation of his poetic theology—the hierarchical cosmos within which he allows the ancient gods their scope. Deriving ultimately from Plato's *Timaeus,* this cosmology helped to justify poetic use of the pagan gods throughout the Middle Ages. In her fable of divine adultery, Nature traces human vices back to Venus, whom she, as the "vicar" of God, had appointed to be "subvicar" in charge of procreation. Human sexuality fell with Venus when she left her fruitful work with husband Hymen and son Cupid to take up with Antigamus ("Enemy of marriage"). The gods of this fable, as creatures of the One God, have only a circumscribed divinity—that is, only a figurative divinity. ("Circumscribed divinity," in the Judaeo-Christian scheme of things, is exactly the sort of self-contradiction that calls for figurative reading.) Moreover, the divinity of Venus, Hymen, and Cupid makes them appropriate figures for human love that accords with the divine purpose. To adopt a distinction from Alain's first metrum, their divinity is a *translatio* bearing some resemblance to its figurative meaning, rather than a *tropus,* whose lack of resemblance makes it easy to abuse (ll. 23–24). Venus, Hymen, and Cupid, fixed in a hierarchical relation to literal Deity as deputies of the deputy of the Creator, can appear in Nature's fable without subverting the semantic hierarchies that must govern reading.

These two tactics—the prefatory repudiation and the explicit subordination of fabulous deities to the true God—do not exhaust the dangers of poetic theology or Alain's efforts to control them. The obtuse dreamer again interrupts Nature's myth, now to question her about Cupid, whose authority over men, he says, is proved by experience: "Though various authors have pictured his [Cupid's] nature under the covering wrap of allegory (sub integumentali involucro aenigmatum); they have yet left us no marks of certainty" (Moffat, 45). The dreamer wants a definitive account to settle all the uncertainties and ambiguities that make Cupid unreliable as a lexical sign or object of belief, but Nature refuses to play mythographer. Her reply in fact criticizes the complacency, the neglect of danger, implicit in the mythographical accounts discussed earlier in this chapter. The dreamer has failed to see that Cupid is not something wrapped in an allegory; he is himself the wrapper. He is himself an *involucrum*, or *integumentum*, and so Nature rebukes the dreamer for continuing to believe in her fables instead of attending to their significance. Moreover, although he has taken the letter of her hierarchical cosmology and restricts Cupid to ruling only mortals, he has missed the spirit, for his question tends to the same abuse as his earlier question about the adulteries of the gods. If Love is an external power which no mortal, however wise or courageous, can resist or avoid, then no mortal can be held morally responsible for his passions. The Virgilian logic becomes inescapable: "Omnia vincit Amor: et nos cedamus Amori" (*Ecl.* 10.69). Thousands of literary lovers besides Nero in the *Octavia* have resorted to pleading compulsion. Even hedged about as it is, Nature's fable seems to confirm Cupid's irresistible sway over mortals and therefore lends itself to abuse as easily as do myths in which the gods set wanton examples for mortals to imitate.

After rebuking the misreading implicit in the dreamer's question, Nature answers it with a mocking account of Cupid, which became better known than the *De planctu* itself after Jean de Meun reproduced it in his portion of the *Roman de la rose*. Stuffed with oxymora that outdo even the most excessive later Petrarchism, Nature's "Descriptio Cupidinis" (met. 5) is a kind of counter-mythography, mocking the dominion of Cupid while demythologizing him by using *Cupido* and *furor* interchangeably. Toward the end, she turns to the ethical issue—that is, to the relationship between Cupid, the putative mythical cause, and *furor*, the psychological effect—which Virgil formulated most succinctly: "Do the gods put this fire in our minds . . . or does his own furious desire (cupido) become for each man a god?" (*Aen.* 9.184–85). In Virgil, the question does not call for an answer, since love, whether a god or passion, is an irresistible power for Nisus. In Alain, Nature also proclaims Love's omnipotence, but then quickly denies it:

> Ipse tamen poteris istum frenare furorem,
> Si fugias, potior potio nulla datur.
> Si vitare velis Venerem, loca, tempora vita;
> Et locus et tempus pabula donat ei.
> Prosequitur, si tu sequeris; fugiendo fugatur;
> Si cedis, cedit; si fugis, illa fugit.

(Wright, 2:474)

(But you can bridle that madness yourself if you flee—no stronger medicine is needed. If you wish to avoid Venus, avoid her places and her times. Both place and time give her nourishment. She pursues you if you pursue her; by fleeing she is put to flight. If you retreat, she retreats; if you flee, she flees.)

These last lines of the "Descriptio Cupidinis" incongruously substitute Venus for Cupid as if to demonstrate once more the arbitrariness of Nature's mythological signs, but they also advance a subtler point. As in Aimeric de Peguilhan's song quoted above, Love has no power over a lover but what a lover allows, and Alain's rhetoric implies why this should be so. "Si cedis, cedit; si fugis, illa fugit." Love is merely an image, indeed a *mirror* image, of the lover's own desire, as suggested by exactly the syntactical mirroring that Ovid had used repeatedly to figure the predicament of Narcissus.[36]

His own furious desire can become for each man a god, then, but Nature stops short of out-and-out demythologization because, as she wittily explains in the following prose, she and Cupid are close kindred. She is no less a poetic figment than he, no less a figurative divinity, and her own fable implies, of course, that the God who has Cupid and Venus for his subvicars does indirectly put the fire of love in our minds. Nature's jocular speech has catered to the dreamer's puerile tastes in poetry, she says, but it has also mocked him out of childish misbelief in mythology. As Nature has trained the dreamer, Alain has been training the reader to use poetic theology rather than abuse it or be seduced by it, and the *De planctu* can now proceed without further dialectical corrective. The dreamer does not mistake again, but has become the alert reader too confidently presumed by the mythographers. In this new atmosphere of redeemed reading, it may be no surprise that Cupid, too, is redeemed. Nature goes on to report her own version of the mythographers' two Cupids in which Cupid becomes again true subvicar to God, while all the excesses and perversions earlier blamed on him Nature now attributes to Jocus, bastard son of Venus and Antigamus. Once again a conspicuous inconsistency exemplifies and counteracts the instability of poetic theology and of all human speech. By opening a rift in the fictive husk, it reminds Alain's readers to search within for the kernel of truth. There is, of course, far more to the *De planctu Naturae* than these strategies by which it avoids seducing its readers, but, for Cupid's career in medieval poetic theology of love, these strategies are paradigmatic. As we shall see, Alain's defensive dialectics represent a phase that recurs toward the beginning of other renascences of the mythical gods, before convention and consensus have reduced deities to cliché and made the gods entirely safe.

The *Roman de la rose* is too well known to need more than a brief outline of the way that it combines the poetic theologies of both Andreas Capellanus and Alain de Lille. Within the garden of Deduit so winsomely depicted in the original poem by Guillaume de Lorris, the lover-dreamer Amant experiences

the theophany only reported by Andreas's nobleman. He, too, meets the god
of love, swears his allegiance, and receives a set of commandments. He, too,
insists on the truth of his vision and of the verses in which he records it at
Love's command.[37] Indeed, he claims to comprehend the subject of Andreas's
whole treatise in this poem "Ou l'Art d'Amors est toute enclose" (38).

Despite these likenesses, the rhetorical situation in Guillaume's portion of
the *Roman* is both more complex and more one-sided than in Andreas's dialogue. Amant identifies his lady with the rose and addresses the entire poem to
her, but the poem does not include her response.[38] It does subsume her earlier
actions by analyzing them into allegorical parts—the rose itself, Biaus Sem-
blanz, Bel Acueil, Jalosie, Dangiers, and so forth—but the dream never becomes a vision of judgment on the lady as in Andreas's eschatological fable.
Rather than threatening her with Love's power, Amant emphasizes his own
painful experience in hopes of stirring her pity. The lady therefore stands
outside and detached from Guillaume's poetic theology which, by focusing
instead on Amant as reader and mythologizer of his own experience, sets the
direction for Jean de Meun's continuation of the poem, as well as for the
subjective emphasis that the poetic theology of love will take in Dante and
Petrarch.

If Guillaume refigured the troubadours' allegiance to fin'Amors into a delusive though guileless theology, Jean de Meun borrows Alain's mythology and
vastly expands his dialectics, but in order to make fun of erotic obsession and
also of poetic theology itself. Alain aimed to stabilize his mythological fiction
by incorporating a surrogate reader and correcting his mistakes. By the end of
their interchange about Cupid, Nature had recuperated both the dreamer-
reader and Cupid himself for purposes of receiving and conveying her doctrine.
By contrast, in his immense continuation, Jean depicts the failure of dialectical
strategies like Alain's. Jean's dreamer confronts, not one authority, but a conflicting multitude and cannot tell true from false. His misreadings of mythology prove incorrigible. He reproves Reason for questioning his allegiance to
the god of love, for example, and this allegiance takes precedence for him over
all other criteria, thus subverting proper hierarchies of meaning and value.
Jean's quarrel with Alain extends to specific figures and strategies. Nature and
Genius reappear, but have been morally degraded and poetically diminished.
When Reason recites a close translation of Alain's "Descriptio Cupidinis,"
Amant replies that her lesson contains so many contrarities that he can learn
nothing from it (4364–65). So much for the efficacy of Alain's demythologizing
contradictions.

In Jean's continuation, dialectics cannot redeem poetic theology, which becomes a self-validating delusion. Even the lady to whom Guillaume addressed
his poem disappears, collapsing the rhetorical situation and leaving Amant
enclosed within a poetic labyrinth which he cannot escape because he misreads
its figures. Jean, however, "likes to startle [actual readers] with a reminder that
we are living within a figure of speech."[39] Amant's chief delusion is his continuing belief in Love's divinity. Taken in by the paraphernalia of erotic religion,

Amant worships as a god a figure who lacks any essential attribute of divinity—omniscience, omnipotence, even immortality. The god of love's omnipotence was already ironic in Guillaume's poem, in which his attack on a castle could be repelled and the god himself fretted like a feudal baron and sputtered about punishing rebels if only he could get them back in his power (1960–68). Jean consistently sharpens Guillaume's ironies. Amant, for example, attributes omniscience to a god who fears being deceived (see 1955–93, 4190–91, 10318), and this sort of irony can become an outright joke, as when Cupid laments the death of Tibullus: "His death gave me such grief that before his tomb I dragged my wings, all torn because I had beaten them so in my sorrow." Jean is imitating Ovid (*Amores* 3.9), but he adds his own punch line: "My mother," Cupid says, "cried so for his death that she nearly died."[40] So much for divine *apatheia* and even immortality, the minimal qualification for deity even in ancient polytheism. Ironies like these keep readers of the *Roman* continually aware of the absurdity of Amant's devotion to a god who is himself subject to mortal frailties, who promises no peace in this life and has no power over the next—who is, in other words, no god at all, but a projection of Amant's own passion.[41]

Amant's behavior is subject to Jean's caustic satire, of course, as is nearly everything else, but despite its Juvenalian passages, I take the *Roman* as a whole to be more comic than cynical, for a reason that will become crucial for early and High Renaissance instances of the poetic theology of love. For all the explicit didacticism of the three medieval works I have taken as paradigms, only in the *De planctu Naturae* did learning actually occur. Nature succeeded in teaching the dreamer-narrator to avoid the errors and misconceptions that she repeatedly termed childish. His character or consciousness, such as it was, derived precisely from those childish errors, however, so that as he learned to read Nature's myths properly, he did not so much grow up as fade away, his function fulfilled. The dreamer-narrator of the *Roman* neither grows up nor fades away, but the later poem, even more insistently than the *De planctu*, associates the dreamer's folly with childishness and youth. At the outset, Amant places his dream-vision within his personal history; he had the dream in his "twentieth year, at the age when Love exacts his tribute from young people" (21–23). The garden of Deduit objectifies this association. Old Age, painted on the exterior wall, is excluded while Youth gambols in Love's throng within. At the fountain of Narcissus, Cupid lays his snares for the young—"damoiseles e damoisaus"—he wants no other birds (1593–94). Guillaume thus explicitly identifies the dream, the garden, and the god with youth.

In both parts of the poem, Reason takes up this identification in such a way as to qualify moral judgment on Amant and also to suggest the process of outgrowing illusion which has yet to take place at the poem's end. In Guillaume, Reason frames her judgment on Amant's folly with the generalization: "One should not be surprised when a young man commits folly" (3016–17). And in Jean, Reason interpolates a fable that asserts that Age will come to recognize and repent the delusions of Youth, but also clearly implies that the disillusioned rationality she recommends will come only as a sequel to the follies of youth.

The season of the poem, May—"that delightful time when every thing rouses itself with love" (84–85)—helps also to blunt its satirical and moral edge. Amant's experience appears as the typical and natural folly of "yonge, fresshe folkes, he or she, / In which that love up groweth with youre age," as the narrator of Chaucer's *Troilus* would phrase the commonplace (5. 1835–36). Troilus's youthful folly ended in death, of course, but the *Roman* implies strongly that Amant's will end comically with youth maturing into age, wisdom replacing folly, reality succeeding dream. The *Roman* does not advance a philosophic gradualism or a system of two truths, but rather accepts an inescapable relativism expressed most authoritatively in 1 Corinthians 13:11: "When I was a child I spake as a child, I understood as a child, I thought as a child: but when I became a man I put away childish things." A century earlier the Cistercian William of St. Thierry had seen the orthodox hierarchy of love as a sequence: "Just as with the waxing and waning of life the boy becomes a youth, the youth a man, and the man an elder, . . . so also with progress in virtue, will grows into love, love into charity, and charity into wisdom."[42] This transformation of the hierarchy of love into a sequence will become essential in later poetic theology of love from Dante to Spenser. In the *Roman de la rose*, it helps to explain why the most influential poem of the Middle Ages, for all its sharp satire, remains a comedy.

3

The *Vita Nuova* and the *Trionfi*

THE contrast between the twelfth-century works by Andreas and Alain and the thirteenth-century *Roman de la rose* shows the tendency toward increased exemplification of moral and philosophical themes that marks late medieval style in literature as well as in the visual arts. But beneath this contrast in styles, the three works share similar concerns and therefore similar uses of the god of love. All three are first-person narratives, but none is truly subjective. Though implicated in a vastly more complex argument, Jean's dreamer remains as typical and as anonymous as Andreas's hypothetical nobleman. Rather than records of subjective experience, all three works are arts of love, unfolding an essentially orthodox view of the proper place and nature of human love and moving their readers toward that view by making fun of typical errors and abuses. Much of the fun comes at the expense of the narrators of the *De planctu* and the *Roman de la rose* and of the men in Andreas's repertoire of arguments for would-be seducers. Alain's dreamer begins to recognize his errors under Nature's prodding, but the others remain insensate, subject to expanding ironic distance between them and readers not so dull. All three speakers mistake or misrepresent the ontological status of love, an error that becomes not merely an example of their other errors, but a figure for them. Put in another way, these speakers all take literally the poetic theology of the god of love; they misread the figurative expression. All three works share a dialectical pattern in which delusive belief in poetic theology is corrected or retracted or ridiculed, whether by speakers within the fictions, by the author himself as in *De amore*, Book 3, or by a later author.

Dante's *Vita Nuova* could hardly offer a greater contrast, even though it contains as explicit a retraction as any medieval poetic theology, and even though it comes little more than fifteen years later than Jean's portion of the *Roman de la rose* and from a pen that had already worked the material of the *Roman* into the sonnets of the *Fiore*.[1] Where the earlier works retracted or qualified their claims to truth, the *Vita Nuova* purports to copy faithfully a portion of the book of Dante's memory. Where the earlier works were didactic and ironic, the *Vita Nuova* is, or at least claims to be, autobiographical and

45

forthright. Where the earlier speakers were anonymous and exemplary, to be distinguished from their authors, Dante presents himself as a historical figure and moreover as the author of both the poems and prose that make up the work. Dante's genius accounts for much of this contrast, no doubt; so does Tuscany itself, where gothic style never dominated and the lyric traditions of Provence and the Two Sicilies still lived and mingled. But it would be a mistake to overdraw the contrast. The *Vita Nuova* contains lyric poems, but as a whole it is autobiographical rather than lyric. It records subjective experiences, but also searches among them and their poetic records for a shape and meaning not yet revealed. It presents to the reader a riddle in the process of solution.

The status of Amore is part of this riddle—indeed the central instance of the *Vita Nuova*'s urgent concern with the possibilities and risks of poetic representation.[2] The first poem of the sequence addresses Dante's fellow poets and lovers, asking them to interpret the enigmatic vision it describes of Amore as "a lord of fearful aspect" (3.3). Dante does not report these interpretations except to comment that all were wrong, but that comment points forward to what seems the *Vita Nuova*'s definitive account of Dante's own poetic theology in Chapter 25:

> Potrebbe qui dubitare persona degna da dichiararle onne dubitazione, e dubitare potrebbe di ciò, che io dico d'Amore come se fosse una cosa per sè, e non solamente sustanzia intelligente, ma sì come fosse sustanzia corporale: la quale cosa, secondo la veritate, è falsa; chè Amore non è per sè sì come sustanzia, ma è uno accidente in sustanzia. (25.1)

> (At this point someone may be puzzled whose every doubt deserves explanation, and his doubt may be this: that I speak of Amore as though it were a thing in itself, and not only an intelligent substance but indeed a corporeal one, which, in truth, is false; because Amore does not exist in itself as a substance, but is an accident in a substance.)

With all the precision of scholastic logic, Dante clears away the ambiguities of poetic theology. Love is not a god or demon, which are "intelligible" substances and subsist in themselves; it is only a passion of the mind, an accident that exists only as it occurs in the corporeal substances of human beings. But, as Dante goes on, poetic license and tradition justify the figure of speech or rhetorical ornament ("figure o colore rettorico") that speaks of a passion as a god, but only so long as the poet can do what Dante has just done: justify his usage by "divesting his words of such covering so as to reveal a true meaning" (25.10). Dante's love for Beatrice is the true meaning of which Amore is the fictive covering; the riddle of Amore's status and the *Vita Nuova*'s doubt about poetic figuration would seem to be resolved.

Yet the solution is disingenuous and poses a still deeper riddle. Though justifying Amore as a poetic figure, Chapter 25 has the effect of removing him from the rest of the *Vita Nuova*, in which he does not appear again as a being in itself. Beneath Dante's assertion of poetic license lies what was missing from the paradigmatic medieval works—an anagnorisis. Unlike Alain's interlocutor or Jean's dreamer, the author of the *Vita Nuova* is capable of self-correction. In Chapter 25 Dante recognizes that as a rhetorical figure Amore is not merely a color playing over an inviolate truth within, but threatens and distorts that very truth, just as Alain's Nature had insisted. Chapter 25 is usually seen as betraying Dante's embarrassment with a clichéd trope or as marking his conversion from troubadour love to Christian *caritas,* but neither view fully explains the complications of Dante's use of Amore, and both miss the way that his demythologization prepares for the later episode of the *donna gentile* where Dante dramatizes the peril of figuring love as a god—the same peril that we have seen satirized in the earlier works. The best approach to Chapter 25, however, is through the carefully planned ambiguities and conflicting clues by which Dante poses the chief questions of the poetic theology of love: "Is Love a god? Is he a personification?"

Is Love a god? Until Chapter 25, this question receives equivocal but insistent answers. Amore in the *Vita Nuova* is, first of all, a near descendant of the troubadour Amors. Like Amors, he is not a naked, winged infant and lacks any genealogical or narrative relationship to mythological deities. He lacks even Cupid's bow and arrows, which the troubadours, most of the poets of the *dolce stil nuovo,* and Dante himself in several of the *Rime* often preserve.[3] Although the *stil-novisti* often call Amore "lo dio d'amore," in the *Vita Nuova* he is only once called a god—in the portentous line upon Dante's first sight of Beatrice: "Ecce deus fortior me, qui veniens dominabitur michi" (2.4). But this line is spoken by Dante's "spirito della vita" in the depths of his heart; Amore is deified by an accident in a substance, a faculty of Dante's physiology, not by Dante himself or his soul or reason.[4] Amore may be a god to Dante's *spiriti,* but to Dante himself he is "lo mio segnore" (18.4) and holds his *segnoria* "through the power (vertù) which my imagination gave to him" (2.7). In another place, Amore rules Dante "through the power (vertù) of my most gentle lady" and, when Dante is separated from her, Amore looks as if he had lost his *segnoria* (9.3, 10). Dante's Amore appears to have no more *virtù* in himself than the Amors of Americ de Peguilhan, the Cupid of Alain de Lille, or the Dieu d'Amours of the *Roman de la rose.*

But if Dante avoids making Amore a god explicitly, he does invest him with a persuasive appearance of divinity in two visions and, by implication, in freeing him from the traditional association with madness and folly. In Chapter 2, he specifies that Beatrice's nobility restrains Love within the bounds of Reason, and the association of Love and Reason appears again with less qualification in Chapters 4 and 15, where Amore is "consigliato de la ragione" (15.8; 4.2). Dante's Amore, then, does not invert the proper hierarchy of human faculties. He is not the irrational passion of Cavalcanti, nor the Love which seized Lancelot, assaulted the dreamer of the *Roman de la rose,* and was to echo throughout Dante's account of the circle of carnal sinners who subjected reason to desire.[5] Amore's alliance with reason leaves the riddle of his status open for both Dante and the reader, just as Amors's antagonism to Reason in the *Roman de la rose* had settled some of the ironies of calling him a god.

The riddle deepens when two of the *Vita Nuova*'s visions invest Amore with an appearance of divinity far more compelling, because it follows a biblical model, than the explicit attributions of divinity in Andreas Capellanus or the *Roman de la rose*. The investiture begins with the vision of Chapter 3, the subject of the first poem of the *Vita Nuova*. While asleep, Dante had a marvelous vision:

> che me parea vedere ne la mia camera una nebula di colore di fuoco, dentro a la quale io discernea una figura d'uno segnore di pauroso aspetto a chi la guardasse; . . . e ne le sue parole dicea molte cose, le quali io non intendea se non poche; tra le quali intendea queste: "Ego dominus tuus." (3.3)

> (I seemed to see in my chamber a cloud the color of fire, within which I discerned the figure of a lord of aspect fearful to anyone who saw him, and in his words he said many things, of which I understood only a few; among those I understood were these: "Ego dominus tuus.")

The sonnet of Chapter 3, though not the prose, identifies the lord of fearful aspect as Amore. The model for Dante's *maravigliosa visione,* as Scherillo and others have noticed, is the theophany which opens the book of Ezekiel. Dante's Amore, infolded in Ezekiel's fiery cloud and speaking half echoes of Biblical phrases, hardly seems to lack *virtù,* but discrepancies complicate the effect of the Biblical allusions. The most important discrepancy, that Dante's vision occurs in a dream while Ezekiel's does not, is best discussed later. Dante's casual statement that he could understand only a few of his lord's words gains significance in contrast to Ezekiel's insistence that he hears and repeats every word.[6] "Ego dominus tuus" echoes, among many Biblical phrases, the first commandment, "Ego sum dominus deus tuus," but omits the crucial word *deus.* Any earthly master might say, "Ego dominus tuus," and perhaps for that reason Scripture never gives so limited a self-identification to God. By these discrepancies, Dante equivocally develops Amore's appearance of divinity.

The same Biblical coloring and the same cultivation of ambiguity continue in Chapter 12. In Chapter 3 Dante recast the poetic god of love in Biblical imagery; that is, he literalized Amore's divinity. In Chapter 12 he does the same for the angelic Amors of the *Roman de la rose* and its numerous literary and artistic progeny. Guillaume had described a grown-up Love who looked like "an angel come straight from heaven"—a resemblance that Dante pushes toward an identity.[7] In the midst of sleep he seemed to see sitting at his side "a young man clothed in whitest garments" (12.3). This figure, again identified as Amore only in the verses, is freed of the *Roman*'s retinue of personifications and recalls the angel in the sepulchre (Mark 16:5) or even more the angel who appears to the centurion Cornelius in the ninth hour, the same hour as Dante's vision (Acts 10:30).[8] Here too Amore half echoes Biblical phrases, and his notorious obscure words—"Ego tanquam centrum circuli . . ."—are a commonplace image for God in whose eternity all time is equally present. But, as in Chapter 3, Amore's claim to deity is qualified even as it is asserted. His obscure words, with their claim to the divine attribute of foreknowledge, come in reply to Dante's question, "Perchè piange tu?" (Why are you crying?) and seem to make sense only as a veiled prophecy of Beatrice's death.[9] More than one critic has concluded from Amore's "true prophecy of an event which comes true after seven years, namely Beatrice's death, [that] he cannot be 'an accident in a substance,' a mere personification of the fact that Dante is in love."[10] But "death, as the Psalmist saith, is certain to all"; Amore's foreknowledge is the one sort that mere mortals can have to a certainty. As Dante reminds himself in Chapter 23, "One must necessarily accept that the most gracious Beatrice will someday die." It is a particularly appropriate sort of foreknowledge here in Chapter 12 where the loss of Beatrice's greeting provides a natural occasion for remembering her death. This angelic Amore admits that he holds power over Dante only through Beatrice and later in the chapter identifies himself with the harmony of the ballad he counsels Dante to write. The question of Amore's divinity, clearly raised in the visions of chapters 3 and 12 with their Scriptural recasting of traditional poetic motifs, remains unresolved. It is resolved, we shall find, only in the broadest form, the widest intention of the work itself.

Similar equivocations and ambiguities keep unresolved the second traditional question: "Is Love a personification?" The troubadour Amors could merge indistinguishably with the lady, as we saw, yet resided within the lover's heart or mind. In the troubadours, this ambiguity had little thematic significance; it was merely a symptom of their use of Amors in the lyric fashion as an unincarnated personification. One might expect to find it precluded by the *Vita Nuova*'s more substantial Amore, but in several chapters Dante turns this ambiguity, too, to his own purposes. Amore is not always a substantial "character" in the *Vita Nuova,* and some hints at his assimilation to both Beatrice and Dante closely follow troubadour precedents. At the first sight of Beatrice, for example, Dante's vital spirit utters the fateful words, "Ecce deus fortior me . . . ," for a moment as though Beatrice herself were the god destined to rule over it (2.4). Similarly, in chapters 19 and 21 Love resides in Beatrice's face, and in Chapter 11 in Dante's. Love and the gentle heart, we learn in 20, are one thing.

In other places, however, the seeming substantiality of Amore puts the troubadour conventions under stress. Chapter 8 concerns the death of a young woman whom Dante had once seen in the company of Beatrice. Amore does not appear in the prose at all, but he appears, incarnated and, Dante tells us, in his true form, in the first sonnet:

Audite quanto Amore le fece orranza,
ch'io 'l vidi lamentare *in forma vera*. . . .

(9–10, emphasis added)

(Hear how great an honor Love paid her: in his true form I saw him there lamenting.)

Amore's actions in the sonnet parallel Dante's in the prose, suggesting that Amore is merely an externalization of Dante's own emotions, but the prose explains, somewhat obliquely, that Amore "in forma vera" is Beatrice.[11]

Other chapters make the assimilation of Amore to both Beatrice and Dante more explicit. Chapter 9 relates the third major apparition of Amore to Dante in the *Vita Nuova*, one which occurs, not in Dante's sleep like the two *visioni*, but in his waking imagination:

Cavalcando l'altr'ier per un cammino,
pensoso de l'andar che mi sgradia,
trovai Amore in mezzo de la via
in abito leggier di peregrino.
Ne la sembianza mi parea meschino,
come avesse perduto segnoria;
e sospirando *pensoso* venia. . . .

(1–7, emphasis added)

(Riding along a road the other day, and brooding over my journey which I disliked, I found Love in my path, meanly dressed like a pilgrim. In his looks he seemed downcast as though he had lost authority; and he came along pensive and sighing. . . .)

(trans. Foster and Boyde, 1:37)

Both Amore and Dante are travelers, both are *pensoso* and downcast, both sigh; the pensiveness and the sighs are redoubled after Amore merges himself into Dante, now "molto pensoso" and troubled by "molti sospiri." Finally, the manner of Amore's disappearance makes explicit his function here as an image, if not quite a mirror image, of Dante's internal state:

. . . disparve questa mia imaginazione tutta subitamente per la grandissima parte che mi parve che Amore mi desse de sè. (9.7)

(This phantasm of mine suddenly disappeared through the great part of himself which it seemed he gave to me.)

In Chapter 24, on the other hand, Amore appears again in Dante's imagination. He comes from the direction in which Beatrice lives and tells Dante, among other things, that "he who wished to consider subtly would call Beatrice Amore because of the great similarity she has to me" (24.5). But even such a bald assertion does not lay the ambiguities to rest, for this Amore who speaks to Dante is also merely his heart speaking with the tongue of Love ("queste parole, che lo cuore mi disse con la lingua d'Amore," 24.3). Even Chapter 25, which says unequivocally that Amore is not a substance, but an accident in a substance, does not say whether it is an accident in Beatrice or Dante.

These ambiguities are no doubt exaggerated by isolation from their contexts in the *Vita Nuova*, but they are, nevertheless, the sort of difficulties that lead critics to suggest that "Dante's rather confusing treatment of Amore" is the result of "a somewhat ungainly compromise" between poetic convention and individual genius or that Amore is merely a "rhetorical expedient."[12] My survey of these ambiguities suggests, however, that Dante chose rather to exaggerate than conceal the ungainliness of his compromise. Dante's Amore, too, is marked by conspicuous contradictions, and, as in Alain de Lille and the *Roman de la rose,* they serve to remind the reader long before Chapter 25 that Amore is only a figure of speech. But this is not their principal function. To make sense of Amore requires, as in the other works, more than an inventory of his features. It requires a view of the work as a whole.

Amore appears four times in the *Vita Nuova* in what we can call the epic fashion, and, although it would be silly to call the *Vita Nuova* an epic, in Chapter 25 Dante does establish a line of succession from Virgil and Ovid to himself and his contemporaries, and in a narrow, perhaps a metaphorical, sense, the term *epic* can be illuminating. The political and historical preoccupations of epic are internalized, heroism and warfare entirely absent, but at the very center of interest stands the epic, and theological, concern with divine intervention in human affairs. But to inquire further, we need the contrast of a true epic intervention, the most convenient probably being the first book of the *Aeneid.*

Virgil presents from the outset the Olympian antagonisms which have buffeted the Trojan survivors. We see Juno vowing further revenge and Venus pleading before the throne of Jove. Later we see Venus, still mistrustful, revolving new schemes, new counsels,

> . . . ut faciem mutatus et ora Cupido
> pro dulci Ascanio veniat, donisque furentem
> incendat reginam atque ossibus implicet ignem.
>
> (l.658–60)

(. . . how Cupid, changed in face and form, may come in the stead of sweet Ascanius, and by his gifts kindle the queen to madness and send the flame into her very marrow.)

(trans. Fairclough)

The poet knows all the details of the divine impersonation; no part of the story is clearer or more concrete. Yet Venus's strategem is easily translated out of the epic mode into the lyric one, turned from history into simile: Ascanius was not lulled asleep, but came to Dido's feast where, for the effect on Dido, he might as well have been Cupid himself. The son's unscarred youth made the father irresistible to a childless widow.[13] The celestial machinery tells us the proximate cause of Dido's passion, but more importantly, it tells us that her passion, like every event in Virgilian history, transcends itself in the divinely ordained destiny of Rome.

Dante presents the *Vita Nuova* as a transcription from the book of his memory. It is a fragment of an autobiography, the history of his devotion to Beatrice, but at the same time an anthology of juvenilia with a commentary by a somewhat older poet. It could hardly be called an epic, even metaphorically, except for the strand which runs through its diverse materials and holds them together—the gradual revelation to Dante and to the reader of Beatrice's miraculous nature. The book of memory, the record of subjective experience, is meaningful to Dante, not for its own sake in the fashion of troubadours or sonneteers, but in the way it was to St. Augustine, for the traces it contains of God. Thus seeming coincidences—occurrences of the number nine, the nickname of Cavalcanti's Giovanna—become intimations of Beatrice's divine mission—intimations, that is, of divine intervention in Dante's life. "Thus the history of our loves," wrote Santayana, "is the record of our divine conversations, of our intercourse with heaven."[14]

Like the divinity of Amore, Beatrice's miraculous nature can be seen as a literalization of a poetic commonplace. In Guinizelli and his followers, the idea of the *donna angelicata* was more than a conceit. It implied a theory of love in which a lover, by purifying his desire of all sensuality, might through love of the lady's immortal soul ascend to her Creator. She was angelic because her soul originated in heaven, the light of which could still be glimpsed in her physical beauty. Although not merely a conceit, neither was the *donna angelicata* really an angel; her angelic nature remained a figure of speech. If her existence represented a mediation between the divine and the human, it was a mediation with no specific end; it was not a divine intervention. In the *Vita Nuova*, however, Dante discovers that Beatrice is literally angelic. At least the fiction of the *Vita Nuova*, as Singleton has said of the *Commedia*, is that it is not a fiction, that Beatrice's angelic nature is not figurative.[15] Like Christ, to whom she is compared in Chapter 24 by the analogy of Giovanna to John the Baptist, Beatrice represents a direct divine intervention with a specific end—to redeem Dante. As in the course of the *Vita Nuova* Dante comes to recognize her miraculous nature, he recognizes also how his passion for Beatrice, like Dido's for Aeneas, transcends itself in the design through which Providence works out the destiny of men and of empires.

If Dante, in asserting that Beatrice was a miracle, claims something like the epic poet's sway over the gods, he employs something more like their technique in his use of Amore. Amore is, in fact, the chief piece of Dantean machinery in the *Vita Nuova*. As in the troubadours, he provides a way of talking about the force of love, so strong as to seem external, but he also serves much the same purpose as Cupid does in *Aeneid* 1, illustrating with his ambiguous divinity the harmony of this overwhelming force with the divine purpose. It is worth noting how different this usage is from that of a cosmological "epic" like the *De planctu Naturae.* There, we remember, Cupid came to signify the place of well-ordered human love in the divine plan, rather than divine intervention in the operation of the cosmos. In the *Vita Nuova*, however, Amore is defined by no relationships with Nature, Venus, or Hymen and tells us nothing about the place of human love in the divine plan for the simple reason that Dante's experience, though exemplary, is not typical. His lady is not like other women; she is a miracle. Amore does not signify human love, well-ordered or not, but rather Dante's own love for Beatrice. The *primary* impulse of the *Vita Nuova* is not moralistic or didactic. Rather, like Virgil's, it is historical. To borrow Dr. Johnson's characterization of *Paradise Lost,* the *Vita Nuova* "contains the history of a miracle."[16]

The historical impulse of the *Vita Nuova* may itself be a fiction; a modern reader is in no position to tell. Its claim to historical veracity, however, is explicit and requires a few sentences of comment, since it determines the status of Amore. Chapter 1, presenting the work as a transcription from the book of Dante's memory, puts forward Dante's draft on the reader's credence. It has a function precisely opposite to the prologue scenes in poems like the *Roman de la rose*, in which the narrator falls into a deep sleep. The dream vision acknowledges its oblique relation to truth, while the book of memory trope, though it does not rule out error, rules out invention entirely. If Providence, and not Dante, is seen as the author of the events recorded in the *Vita Nuova*, then Dante must play faithful scribe, guaranteeing no interpolation of fiction. This guarantee is confirmed in Chapter 2 where Dante cuts short the account of his childhood experiences in fear that he may appear to be speaking fictitiously ("parlare fablioso"). The claim to historical veracity does not rest only upon a few explicit assertions. It is implicit in the prosimetrum form where the prose exists, not to continue a narrative, as in Boethius and his medieval imitators like Alain de Lille, but as in troubadour *razos* to disclose the meaning of the verses, divesting them of deceptive colors of rhetoric and unfolding the true experience which lies behind them.[17] Dante seems to aim beyond Alain's effort to stabilize his mythopoeia in order to convey true doctrine, since the form of the *Vita Nuova* appears to guarantee not merely veracity, but veracity finally unobscured even by figurative expression.

Precisely this claim to historical veracity, however, distinguishes the *Vita Nuova* from classical epics and raises the problem of the admissibility of invention, which in a later century would vex poets and theorists pursuing the coy muse of Christian epic. In the *Vita Nuova*, the problem is most apparent in the way Dante distinguishes Amore from epic machinery like that of *Aeneid* 1, even while using him to similar ends. As we have seen, Virgil gives his machinery the same status as other events of his narrative, but Dante, determined to avoid the appearance of fiction, allows Amore to appear as a "character" only in dreams and visions.[18] The way Dante describes these appearances underlines their lower status in the narrative: "In my room I *seemed* to see . . ."; "Love *seemed* to say to me. . . ."[19] Dante thus gains the resonance of epic machinery without abandoning the role of faithful scribe, for while it is not credible that Amore, fully incarnated in the true epic fashion, sat at Dante's bedside or spoke with him on the road from Florence, it is completely credible that Dante dreamed or imagined that he did.

We are perhaps close enough now for a direct approach to Chapter 25, the landmark and goal of this winding itinerary. At the close of Chapter 12, Dante anticipates a difficulty that the ballad of that chapter may present and reassures the reader that he will clarify the matter later with reference to a still more doubtful passage. The *dubitazione* which prompts Chapter 25, then, is not a new one. Why does Dante postpone its resolution? Why does he keep the riddle of Amore's status unresolved, demythologizing him in Chapter 25 and not before? A satisfactory answer to these questions will go a long way toward answering those critics who see the chapter as a final symptom of Dante's embarrassment with an outworn poetic figure and, because they see that embarrassment as external to the work, judge Chapter 25 to be a flaw, digression, or excursus.[20]

Chapter 24 contains the *imaginazione* where Amore suggests that "he who wished to consider subtly would call Beatrice Amore because of the great similarity she has to me," and, as Singleton notes, this proves to be his farewell speech. He does not appear again incarnated as a "character." "No longer," says Singleton, "will the sign of the power of a passion be other than the object and agent of that passion."[21] Chapter 25, in this view, merely confirms Amore's exit from the history of Dante's devotion, at the same time disposing of a stock topic of poetic debate, the substantiality of love.[22]

If putting a full stop to Amore's role is its function, however, Chapter 25 employs means out of proportion to its ends. It begins with an explicit reference to Chapter 24. Someone may have doubts about the sonnet in which Love is spoken of as a man capable of locomotion, speech, and laughter. But since the prose insists that Amore appeared and spoke only in Dante's imagination, these doubts should hardly have been urgent. Dante might easily have reminded his objector that in dreams and visions things may appear as substances which in reality are only accidents. If he wished to parade his learning, he could have discussed the dream-vision convention, cited Macrobius, echoed the opening of the *Roman de la rose*. But instead he puts forward a different line of defense. The precedent of Ovid justifies his usage. Any figure of speech permitted to the ancient poets ought to be permitted to moderns who write of love. But this assertion of poetic *licenza* presents several difficulties. First, Dante has described Amore in the prose for which he claims no license (the Biblical echoes that accompany the lord of fearful aspect in Chapter 3 are all in the prose). Second, and more important, Dante's assertion of poetic license justifies the *Vita Nuova*'s Amore at the expense of its claim to historical veracity. Of course the transparent, "lyric" uses of Amore are figures of speech, but so are the "epic" ones. Amore's biblical colors are the poet's invention, no longer revelations of providential design that he has merely witnessed. In Chapter 25, Dante concedes that he has been speaking fictitiously all along. No wonder it has been said to throw "away the baby with the bath-water" (Hardie, p. 41).

This radical demythologization is necessary, not to confirm Amore's departure from the scene, though it does that too, but to prepare for his re-entrance in a different and now ominous form in chapters 35–39, the episode of the *donna gentile*. More than a year after Beatrice's death, Dante notices a lady who seems to take pity on his grief. At first, reminding him of Beatrice, she increases his devotion, but soon he begins to speculate: "She has appeared, perhaps by the will of Amore so that my life may find peace" (35.1). The idea is repeated again in Chapter 38 and in its sonnet. Coming after Chapter 25, however, "the will of Amore" can only be a delusion, a delusion we have met before. If Amore is an accidental passion in Dante's corporeal substance and rules "through the power which [Dante's] imagaination gave to him" (2.7), then Dante is tempted here to make a god of his own desire, to mistake a rhetorical figure having meaning only in reference to the power and providentiality of his love for Beatrice, for a divinity having, as divinities must, his own *virtù*. This is precisely the abuse of poetry that the nobleman attempts in Andreas's dialogue and that Nature reproves in the *De planctu*. Although a transparent personification here, Amore cannot represent merely Dante's attraction to the *donna gentile*, but implies a moral judgment that this new love is genuine judged by the standards of his love for Beatrice. By those standards, to be genuine it must be divinely sanctioned. Chapter 25, in demythologizing Amore, exposes in advance the dangers of the rhetorical figure with its implicit rationalization for inconstancy. The embarrassment with Amore which critics sense in Chapter 25 is not extraneous. It is focused and given point by the later episode of the *donna gentile*. In fact, it is less embarrassment with an outworn poetic figure than the poet's anxious awareness of the duplicities of poetry, an awareness that will find richer expression when Francesca, telling how poetry can prove a pandar, echoes the *Vita Nuova* and particularly the word *amor* (*Inf.* 5.100–6, 137).

Dante's traditional quandary in the *donna gentile* episode is developed in equally traditional terms. Like Lancelot faced with the cart, he experiences internal warfare between reason and desire (38.5). In this debate Amore, whose association with reason had been one indication of Beatrice's miraculous nature, becomes a tool of the "avversario de la ragione" (39.1). In the tempting thought of his sanction for a new love, Amore himself reverts to the old alliances of *folle amore*.

Unlike Lancelot or the dreamer of the *Roman*, however, Dante is rescued from temptation by a more powerful force than reason. In the ninth hour an apparition of Beatrice in glory recalls him to his former devotion, at the same time restoring Amore to his former association with Beatrice. The sonnet of 39 says that Amore circles Dante's eyes with the crowns of martyrs and faints within his heart from great pain. The sonnet of 41 relates the progress of a sigh, impelled by Amore's weeping, upward beyond the widest of the circling spheres to Beatrice. This Amore is transparently an accident in a substance and lacks the beguiling substantiality he had in his earlier appearances in Dante's dreams and visions. Nevertheless, mention of Amore in lines designed to show that Dante's "evil desire" and "vain temptation" were destroyed reaffirms Amore's association with Beatrice and denies the tempting idea that he might have willed Dante's attraction to the *donna gentile*. The episode as a whole teaches Dante that Amore is a poetic fiction (and love an emotion) whose proper meaning is always, for him, linked to Beatrice. It exemplifies for the reader, forewarned by Chapter 25, the danger that poetic *licenza,* when it figures desires as divinities, may contribute to *licenza* of other forms. When Dante opens *Paradiso* 8,

> Solea creder lo mondo in suo periclo
> che la bella Ciprigna il folle amore
> raggiasse, volta nel terzo epiciclo;
> . . . .
> e dicean ch'el [Cupido] sedette in grembo a Dido.

(The world once believed, to its peril, that the fair Cyprian, wheeling in the third epicycle, rayed forth mad love . . . and told that Cupid lay in Dido's bosom.)

(trans. Sinclair)

the peril he means is that of mistaking self-indulgence for obedience to divine compulsion. He is applying a lesson earlier reiterated by Virgil in answer to Dante's doubt "that if love is offered to us from without and if the soul moves with no other feet, it has no merit whether it goes straight or crooked" (*Purg.* 18.43–45).

If Chapter 25 functions primarily to forewarn the reader against this peril before Dante meets it in the *donna gentile*'s gaze, it has also the effect that Singleton notices of confirming Amore's exit as a character from the *Vita Nuova.* Singleton associates Amore's disappearance with the general ascent of the *Vita Nuova* through three stages of love and three corresponding poetic subject matters. Amore signifies "troubadour love" for Singleton, and "the disappearance of the God of Love . . . is all in the way of recantation of troubadour love which the *Vita Nuova* makes."[23] Amore's alliance with reason, however, argues against identifying him with troubadour "fin'amors," and if Dante wished to recant an earlier, troubadour stage of his love and distinguish it from his later devotion, why would he mention Amore in the last poems of the *Vita Nuova*? Yet Singleton surely sets out on the right track. In the *Vita*

Nuova we do leave old positions for new, and the God of love seems to be the sign of an old position. But what, more precisely, we may ask, is the old position?

It is first of all a poetic position, making Amore less the sign of an old stage in Dante's love than an old sign of Dante's love. The *Vita Nuova* ends with the poetic future, with an expression of poetic aspiration:

> . . . Apparve a me una mirabile visione, ne la quale io vidi cose che mi fecero proporre di non dire più di questa benedetta infino a tanto che io potesse più degnamente trattare di lei. E di venire a ciò io studio quanto posso, sì com'ella sae veracemente. Sì che, se piacere sarà di colui a cui tutte le cose vivono, che la mia vita duri per alquanti anni, io spero di dicer di lei quello che mai non fue detto d'alcuna. (42.1–2)

> (A wondrous vision appeared to me in which I saw things which made me resolve not to say anything further about this blessed one until I was able to write more worthily of her. And to arrive at that end I study as much as I can, as she truly knows. Thus, if it shall please Him by whom all things live that my life last a few years, I hope to write of her that which has never been written of another.)

If this hope to pursue things unattempted yet in praise of a woman presages the *Commedia,* it can help to explain why Amore must be set aside as an old sign. The *Vita Nuova* begins with the *maravigliosa visione* of Beatrice in Amore's arms and ends with the *mirabile visione* of Beatrice in glory. Both elaborate and literalize conventional metaphors: the *dio d'amore* and the *donna angelicata.* The first of these leads to a poetic *cul-de-sac,* for Amore can never be more than a metaphorical divinity, an oblique reflection of providential activity, and he can, as Dante learns in the *donna gentile* episode, be considerably less. The closer Amore is made to resemble literal, that is Biblical, divinity, the more deceptive he becomes, the more like an idol. The metaphor of the *donna angelicata,* on the contrary, is not a dead end. The very process of elaborating it turns the poet toward God, and, combined with literalization of another metaphor, the *itinerarium mentis in deum,* it supplies a root element of the *Commedia.* Chapter 25 can thus be seen as a point of choice between what Dante will later call the allegory of the poets and the allegory of the theologians. Amore may conceal a true meaning under his fictive surface, but, like all poetic fables, literally he is only a beautiful lie. Beatrice, however, is (or is presented as) historically true both in the *Vita Nuova* and the *Commedia.* What she means in Dante's life can be read, therefore, as Scripture is read, according to the allegory of the theologians.

New poetry must not repeat the old, but it need not repudiate it. Chapter 25 invites us to consider Amore as a part of the vernacular tradition of love poetry that Dante, at the end of the *Vita Nuova,* aspires to go beyond. But Dante's new poetry will transcend by succession. The older poets have prepared his way, just as in Chapter 24 Cavalcanti's Giovanna goes before Beatrice, preparing the way like John the Baptist for the greater successor.

Amore is a part of the poetic past Dante hoped to transcend, but also a sign of a past stage in his love for Beatrice. Here again, the new succeeds rather than repudiates the old. Among the first words of Amore to Dante are "Vide cor tuum" (3.6), and Amore is always at least partially a reflexive image. He signifies emotion, not merely experienced, but contemplated. To be a liegeman of Love is thus to be partially in love with love itself, and indeed the ambiguities we noticed at the outset serve to make this point. Beatrice must share her power with the emotion her power creates. Hence it is uncertain whether Beatrice or Amore is the "deus fortior me," and Amore resides with Beatrice (19, 21), yet whispers in Dante's heart (24). If this is divided emotion, nothing in the *Vita Nuova* suggests that its parts conflict. Amore himself indicates its resolution in his "farewell speech": Beatrice "has the name of Love so much does she resemble me" (24.9, 5). Amore disappears as Dante's devotion to Beatrice matures and becomes less self-regarding and as his poetry makes a corresponding change from its first subject matter, his own emotional state, to his *nova matera*, "words that praise my lady" (18.6, 17).

It is tempting to call this change in Dante's love natural; at any rate, it is a mistake to theologize it as a recantation of troubadour love and an embrace of Christian *caritas*. In the sonnet of 41, it is Amore who gives Dante's pilgrim spirit the "intelligenza nova" that impels it to seek Beatrice in heaven. Recantation implies discontinuity, but Dante's usage of Amore insists upon the continuity of his love for Beatrice. Amore, as Shaw wrote in 1929, "is no other than Dante's own holy love for Beatrice."[24] If the emphasis falls at first on "Dante's own" and later on "holy love for Beatrice," the shift is more a clarification than a conversion. When, like Virgil in the *Purgatorio*, Amore resigns to Beatrice, he affirms himself as a means while repudiating himself as an end, as a divinity. Stabilized as a hierarchy of significances, poetic theology is no longer an ironic dream mimicking the delusions of men in love; it has become a way to truth.

Perhaps because of its unwieldy and unclassical form, perhaps because of its complexity and idiosyncrasy, the *Vita Nuova* was never as well-thumbed in the Renaissance as the work that comes next in the long poetic career of the god of love. Petrarch's *Trionfi* was, in fact, "the most triumphant poem of the early Renaissance." Well over a hundred manuscripts survive from the period between Petrarch's death in 1374 and the first edition a century later (1470). Before 1500, nine editions of the *Trionfi* alone, and sixteen together with the *Canzoniere*, had appeared.[25] The sixteenth century multiplied the number of annotated editions, the most popular of which went through twenty-seven editions between 1525 and 1585. The poem's vogue was not limited to Italy—in France alone there were four competing translations—nor was it limited to literature. In the visual arts and in spectacles, pageants, and tournaments, themes descended from the *Trionfi* appear by the thousands.[26]

The six *Trionfi*—of Love, Chastity, Death, Fame, Time, and Eternity—are, like the *Vita Nuova*, a stylized history of the poet's love. Because Petrarch, unlike Dante, saw his experience as both exemplary and typical, the *Trionfi* also constitute a meditation on the stages of human life, as has been the standard reading of the poem since the Renaissance.[27] In other ways, too, the *Trionfi* may seem more medieval than either the *Vita Nuova* or Petrarch's other works. They are a dream vision, or rather a series of visions within a single dream, and they may, in reading, seem the static allegory that they usually became in the visual arts. Their catalogues have been judged medieval in their exhaustiveness and disproportion to literary function.[28] They contain little of the psychological and dramatic tension often seen as a Renaissance symptom in Petrarch's other works, and little glorification of human art. Their poetic theology is once again a delusive dream. Despite these appearances, the *Trionfi* are far from being a throwback. Less subjective than Dante perhaps in style, they are much more subjective in ideology. Petrarch's dream visions give no access, as Dante's had, to objective (that is, transcendent) truth; they reveal only the way of the world. He imagines rather than witnesses the Triumph of Eternity and, where Dante met Beatrice in the earthly paradise, Petrarch can only wonder "what it will be to meet [Laura] again in heaven?"[29] It is a secular heaven, however, for, though drawing often on the Old Testament, he excludes all reference to Christ or even to the New Testament.

Most conspicuous among Renaissance themes in the *Trionfi*, however, is a radical concern for the spirit and integrity of the human individual. The six triumphs alternate between forces that crush human spirit and individuality and forces that restore or exalt them. This pattern in turn works a shift in the significance of the god of love. No longer a specious but handy justification for inconstancy or license, he becomes a far more malevolent figure, subduing diverse individual wills to the same low servitude, where before he had liberated them from the restraints of sexual morality.

The alternation between forces that crush and forces that exalt individual identity divides the *Trionfi* into three pairs and reflects not merely the dialectical pattern of the series, but also the manner of their composition. The *Triumphus Cupidinis* and *Triumphus Pudicitiae* date from the early 1340s and were designed as "an independent poem . . . before Petrarch had any thought of writing the later Triumphs." The death of Laura prompted the *Triumphus Mortis* and *Triumphus Famae*, which followed in the early 1350s. The last pair, the *Triumphus Temporis* and *Triumphus Aeternatis*, may date from 1374, the last year of Petrarch's life. The circumstances of composition require us, then, to look at the first pair from two points of view: first, "as a two-fold poem, complete in itself" and then more briefly as the first movement of the larger sequence.[30] The god of love whose meaning we pursue is here, as elsewhere, not to be abstracted from his function in the poem.

Like the *Roman de la rose*, the *Trionfi* is a dream vision, but the relation between dream and dreamer differs radically from the *Roman*. The *Roman* opens with a defense of its significance:

> Que songes est senefiance
> Des biens as genz e des enuiz;
> Car li plusor songent de nuiz
> Maintes choses covertement
> Que l'en voit puis apertement.
>
> (16–20)

(A dream signifies the good and evil that come to men, for most men at night dream many things in a hidden way which may afterward be seen openly.)

Petrarch may have had this claim in mind when, sending a copy of the *Roman* to Guido Gonzaga, he remarked that its author ". . . dreams as he relates his dreams: / Awake he seems no different from asleep."[31] The *Roman*, he seems to have judged, simply never "came true." At any rate, his own dream vision does not come true because it is already true. Like the *Rime sparse* and the *Secretum*, it is retrospective. Hence, in the opening lines of the *Triumphus Cupidinis*, spring does not stir desire, but memory:

> Al tempo che rinova i mie' sospiri
> per la dolce memoria de quel giorno
> che fu principio a sì lunghi martiri. . . .
>
> (TC 1.1–3)

(The season had come which renews my sighs for the sweet memory of that day which was the beginning of such long suffering.)

In structure, though not in substance, the *Trionfi* is as much a book of memory as the *Vita Nuova*, and it makes a similar, though less consistent, distinction between the present tense of the writing and the past of the dream, a distinction which corresponds to that between poet and glossator in the *Vita Nuova* or between pilgrim and poet in the *Commedia*. On the other hand, Petrarch's dreamer, caught up as an actor in his dream, might seem closer to the dreamer of the *Roman de la rose* than to Dante's glossator, except that, like Dante and unlike the medieval dreamers, he is capable of recognition. Though still dreaming at the end of the *Trionfi*, within his dream he repeatedly awakes from illusion to a reality that he comes eventually to recognize as equally illusory. He does not "dream as he relates his dreams," as he complained of the *Roman*; he is all too awake. The chief illusion exposed in the first two triumphs is Love's divinity, but more than this illusion troubles the poet's conscience. His bad conscience has two sources: what he did (subject himself to love) and what he is doing (writing the poem). Both sources of bad conscience involve Cupid and the familiar question of his divinity and are so intertwined in other ways that differentiation may finally be arbitrary. It will be convenient, nevertheless, to treat them separately: first, the guilt produced by the action reenacted in the dream; then, the anxieties produced by giving the dream literary expression.

As Petrarch, having wandered out before dawn, is overcome by sleep, memory of his present pain and its origin fades, and his dream reenacts his experience of love beginning at a time before his subjugation to Cupid (*TC* 1.52–69). Nevertheless, his dream begins with Cupid:

> Vidi un vittorioso e sommo duce,
> pur com'un di color che'n Campidoglio
> triumfal carro a gran gloria conduce.
> ....
> Quattro destrier vie piú che neve bianchi;
> sovr'un carro di foco un garzon crudo
> con arco in man e con saette a' fianchi;
> nulla temea, però non maglia o scudo,
> ma su gli omeri avea sol due grand'ali
> di color mille, tutto l'altro ignudo.
>
> (1. 13–15, 22–27)

(I saw a victorious and supreme leader exactly like those whom triumphal chariots carried to great glory on the Capitol. . . . I saw four horses whiter than snow and on a chariot of fire a cruel boy with bow in hand and arrows at his side. He feared nothing and therefore had no mail or shield, but only two great wings of a thousand colors on his shoulders; everything else was naked.)

Around the chariot are innumerable captives, one of whom approaches Petrarch to serve as guide and identify Love's captives as they pass. There follows a procession of emperors, generals, heroes, gods, and eventually patriarchs and knights, until, in the third *capitolo*, Petrarch himself is captured. Why does the dream begin with Cupid if Petrarch does not join his triumph until much later? Undoubtedly because the poet's *lunghi martiri*, forgotten by the dreamer, continues to determine the content of his dream. But within the dream, the order also makes clear that Petrarch knew *about* Love before he knew Love by experience.

As Petrarch explores the dream world opened to him at the beginning of the *Triumphus Cupidinis*, his chief desire is, in fact, to know more *about* Love and his captives. No desire but the desire to learn prompts him to inspect Cupid's triumphal chariot, and, since he renounced love in his youth, he believes his curiosity to be scholarly and disinterested. What can seem a tedious catalogue of figures from Greco-Roman history and legend represents for the dreamer a wish fulfillment of his desire for knowledge, nowhere more clearly than in the second *capitolo*, where he questions Massinissa and Sophonisba, the tragic

lovers of Book 5 of his *Africa,* begun a few years earlier and never finished.
What is tedious about this roll call of famous lovers is that their variety serves
chiefly to confirm their likeness. They are all *exempla* of a single adage, so
obvious that Petrarch leaves it unstated: "Omnia vincit Amor." This is a
dangerous idea, as we learned from Alain's *Natura,* because it denies human
free will and consequent moral responsibility. If Love conquers all, then the
only sensible conclusion is Virgil's: "let us submit to Love" (*Ecl.* 10.69).

After his capture, Petrarch consoles himself with just this logic:

> Quando ad un giogo et in un tempo quivi
> domita l'alterezza de gli dèi,
> e de gli uomini vidi al mondo divi,
> *i' presi essempio de' lor stati rei,*
> facendo mio profetto l'altrui male
> in consolar i casi e i dolor mei;
> ché s'io veggio d'un arco e d'uno strale
> Febo percosso e 'l giovene d'Abido,
> l'un *detto deo,* l'altro uom puro mortale,
> e veggio ad un lacciuol Giunone e Dido,
> . . . .
> non mi debb'io doler s'altri mi vinse. . . .
>
> (*TP* 1–10, 13; emphasis added)

(When I saw there the pride of gods and of near-divine men subdued at the
same time and under the same yoke, *I took example from their sorry state,*
making from others' ills my own gain in consoling my fated sorrows. For, if I
see Apollo and the youth of Abydos [Leander] struck with the same bow and
the same arrows, the one *called a god* and the other just a mortal man, and
see Juno and Dido caught in the same snare, I should not grieve if I am also
overcome.)

He finds consolation in knowing that he has illustrious company under Love's
yoke, but he has taken "example from their sorry state" in another sense. He
has followed their example, submitting to Love because he has learned that
Love conquers all. Petrarch's complacent consolation does not differ much
from a passage in St. Augustine's *Confessions,* a book he kept always at hand.[32]
In the first book, reviewing his youthful pursuit of the wrong kinds of knowledge and renouncing his love of literature, Augustine alludes to the scene in the
Eununchus in which Terence

brought a lewd young man upon the stage, propounding Jupiter to himself as
an example for his adultery and eyeing a certain picture on the wall in which
is realistically painted the story of Jupiter's raining a golden shower into
Danae's lap. . . . See how that young man provoked himself to lust as if he
had celestial authority for it: "But what do I imitate?" he says; "even that god

who with mighty thunder shakes the very arches of heaven. May I not then, frail flesh and blood, do as much?"[33]

Petrarch's consolation has not edged over into alibi, and he carefully claims no "celestial authority" (Apollo is only "detto deo"), but he does abuse his knowledge, like Terence's young man and like the young St. Augustine, in masking self-indulgence as compulsion.

In the *Triumphus Pudicitiae*, as Laura and the other chaste ladies prove that Love does not conquer all, he acknowledges his mistake:

> Ma vertú, che da' buon non si scompagna,
> mostrò a quel punto ben come a gran torto
> chi abandona lei d'altrui si lagna.
>
> (*TP* 46–48)

(But virtue, which never abandons the good, showed clearly then how much to blame is he who, abandoning virtue, complains of others [i.e. of anyone but himself: fate, the gods, etc.])

He goes on to repeat what Nature had said in the *De planctu Naturae* and Reason in the *Roman de la rose*—that Cupid's blow is painful and deadly only to those who await it (". . . colpo, a chi l'attende, agro e funesto," *TP* 54), but this lesson comes too late. He has not merely awaited Cupid's blow, but in his curiosity courted it, and the anaphora at the end of *capitolo* 3, "Or so . . ." (Now I know . . .), emphasizes the ironic conversion of his "love of knowledge" into knowledge of love. The connection between "l'amor del saper" (3.8) and "sapere dell'amor" is not merely ironic. That the connection is finally moral is the major source of Petrarch's bad conscience for his subjection to love and a major theme of the first two *Trionfi*.

Petrarch's bad conscience as a poet in the *Triumphus Cupidinis* is more subtle, but can easily be summarized. If in his dream Petrarch acts like Terence's young man, in recounting his dream he acts like Terence himself. He demonstrates how to use the adage "Omnia vincit Amor" to excuse self-indulgence and, as Terence did not, provides vivid examples to verify the adage. The first *trionfo* marks a bad renaissance; it revives the sort of lascivious fable against which the early Fathers fulminated, and Petrarch subtly concedes as much at the end of *capitolo* 1:

> Ché non uomini pur, ma dèi gran parte
> empion del bosco e de gli ombrosi mirti:
> vedi Venere bella, e con lei Marte
> cinto di ferro i pie', le braccia e 'l collo,
> e Plutone e Proserpina in disparte;
> vedi Iunon gelosa, e' l biondo Apollo,

> che solea disprezzar l'etate e l'arco
> che gli diede in Tesaglia poi tal crollo.
> Che debb'io dire? In un passo men varco:
> tutti son qui in pregion *gli dèi di Varro*,
> e di lacciuoli innumerabil carco
> *vèn catenato Giove innanzi al carro.*
>
> (1. 149–60; emphasis added)

(Not only men, but gods fill a great part of the shadows of the myrtle grove. See lovely Venus and with her Mars, his feet, arms and neck bound with irons; Pluto and Proserpina are further off. See jealous Juno and fair Apollo, who once scorned the age and the bow that afterwards gave him such a fall in Thessaly. What should I say? To finish briefly, all Varro's gods are here in prison, and, burdened with innumerable bonds, Jove goes chained before the chariot.)

Varro, however, repudiated myths of the gods' adulteries as poetic fictions, as Petrarch knew from Augustine's discussion in *The City of God*.[34] The phrase "Varro's gods," therefore, acknowledges that the gods are fictional, but acknowledges it at the cost of implicating Petrarch in Augustine's attack on pagan poets who corrupt their readers with just those fictions. The last line of the passage above compounds this ambiguous effect by echoing a second Father, Lactantius, who provides the most specific ancient source for the *Triumphus Cupidinis:*

> . . . A certain poet wrote of the triumph of Cupid [triumphum Cupidinis]: in which book he not only represented Cupid as the most powerful of the gods, but also as their conqueror. For, having enumerated the loves of each, by which they had come into the power and dominion of Cupid, he sets in array a procession in which Jupiter, with the other gods, is led in chains before the triumphal chariot [in qua Jupiter cum caeteris diis ante currum triumphantis ducitur catenatus].[35]

Lactantius, describing this lost pagan poem, also describes Petrarch's. The passage comes from a chapter of the first book of the *Divinae Institutiones,* "De falsa religione," in which Lactantius argues, like Augustine, that poets ascribed men's faults to the gods. As Petrarch wrote later, "Who unless he were mad would worship adulterous or lying gods? . . . Besides, who can doubt that sins that rob men of their humanity itself similarly but much more surely take away divinity from such gods?"[36]

Petrarch's bad conscience is not only indicated by these subtle allusions, but is built into the structure of the poem. The *Triumphus Cupidinis,* unlike the other *Trionfi,* is a pageant with two presenters. The unnamed guide interprets the pageant to Petrarch the dreamer, and Petrarch the poet interprets it (with the intermediary guide and dreamer) to the reader. The dreamer is thus analogous to the reader, and the guide to the poet, and it is, in fact, the guide who reflects most clearly Petrarch's anxious sense of the duplicities of his poem.

From the beginning, the guide seems to warn Petrarch against love:

> Questi è colui che 'l mondo chiama Amore;
> amaro, come vedi, e vedrai meglio
> quando fia tuo, com'è nostro signore;
> giovencel mansueto, e fiero veglio;
> . . . .
> Ei naque d'ozio e di lascivia umana,
> nudrito di penser dolci soavi,
> fatto signore e dio da gente vana.
>
> (1. 76–79, 82–84)

(This is he whom the world calls Love: bitter, as you see and will see better when he is your lord as he is ours—in his youth gentle and fierce in old age. . . . He was born from idleness and human lust, nursed by sweet and pleasant thoughts, and a vain folk made him their lord and god.)

The first critic of the *Trionfi*, Bernardo da Pietro Lapini da Montalcino, annotated these lines with a quotation from Seneca's *Hippolytus:* "Base and servile lust feigned love to be a god and, in order to be less restrained, has given passion the title of an unreal divinity."[37] The quotation is apt, for, in the guide's account, Love's genealogy and variable age suggest that he is merely a personification of each man's desire, and, like Seneca, the guide emphasizes how these individual errors combine to make a corrupt orthodoxy. The guide himself is one of Love's captives, however, and he does not mean to warn Petrarch off, but to draw him in. He gratifies the dreamer's desire for knowledge, knowing that the truth *about* Cupid will not prevent him from joining the vain folk who make love their god. His cynicism is fully justified; the motto for the dreamer's experience could be "I did not then understand him" (Io no' l'intesi allor, 1. 61.). Despite what he knows *about* Cupid, the dreamer believes that Venus, not idleness, is his mother (TC 4.96) and laments:

> Dura legge d'Amor! ma, ben che obliqua,
> servar convensi, però ch'ella aggiunge
> di cielo in terra, universale, antiqua.
>
> (3.148–50)

(Hard is the law of Love! but, though unjust, it is expedient to obey, for it prevails from heaven to earth, universal and ancient.)

Like the humanist, the guide tends to equate "universale" with "antiqua," but his duplicity does not become apparent until the dreamer's capture. Then, though he has been called "friend" and even "brother," the guide makes of another's ill his own gain, exactly as the dreamer will soon do in consoling himself with the loves of the gods:

> L'amico mio più preso mi si fece,
> e con un riso, per piú doglia darme,
> dissemi entro l'orecchia:—Omai ti lece
> per te stesso parlar con chi ti piace,
> ché tutti siam macchiati d'una pece.
>
> (3.95–99)

(My friend came nearer to me and, with a laugh to give me greater pain, whispered in my ear: "Now you are free to speak for yourself with whomever you wish, for all of us are stained with the same pitch.")

The dreamer goes on to say, "I was one of those to whom another's good is more displeasing than his own ill" (Io era un di color cui più dispiace / de l'altrui ben che del suo mal, 3.100–1), referring to Laura, but explaining the guide's behavior at the same time.

As presenters of the same pageant, the guide and the poet are analogous, and their behavior runs parallel in several specific details. The poet adds to the guide's emphasis on lovers' sorrows and warns the reader even more forcefully against the unreal divinity who "is made a god by slow, dull, and foolish minds" (è fatto deo / da tardi ingegni, rintuzzati e sciocchi, 4.89–90). Moreover, his initial description, hesitating between the medieval mature Amore and the babyish classical Cupid, corresponds to the guide's mention of Cupid's variable age. The poet first sees

> . . . un vittorioso e sommo duce,
> pur com'un di color che'n Campidoglio
> triumphal carro a gran gloria conduce.
>
> (1.13–15)

(. . . a victorious and supreme leader exactly like those whom triumphal chariots carried to great glory on the Capitol.)

Editors often provide a note identifying this figure, for neither the words "vittorioso e sommo duce" nor the historical simile lead one to expect a winged, naked "garzon" seven lines later.

The poet knows from experience how futile these warnings are. No contempt heaped upon his own mistake can salve his bad conscience, for it merely adds to the parallels between his actions and the guide's. He cannot retell his dream of Cupid's triumph without leading his readers astray in the same way as he has been led, and by implication he too would find satisfaction in the ills of every reader whom his poem helped to enthrall. The roles of the guide and poet do not run entirely parallel, however. Having led the dreamer to his fall, the guide disappears from the poem, except for a line at the end of the *Triumphus Pudicitiae*. His contemptuous whisper, "Now you are free to speak with whomever you wish," is his farewell speech. In this the poet and guide diverge, for Petrarch does not disappear, leaving the reader stained with the same pitch, but looks ahead to Laura's victory over Cupid. He answers his seductive *Triumphus Cupidinis* with an uplifting *Triumphus Pudicitiae*. But this is to skip over one further source of poetic bad conscience in the first *trionfo*.

When Love's folk console themselves with the adage "Omnia vincit Amor," they make Love a god by attributing to him divine omnipotence. But the *Triumphus Cupidinis* makes Love a god in a second way that exacerbates the poet's guilty self-consciousness. We may remember that in Andreas's fifth dialogue, the would-be seducer makes Love a god by attributing to him power over the eternal state of souls, reporting that he witnessed a triumph of Love in which the captives were dead ladies. Petrarch does not have the same motive as Andreas's nobleman, but his dream inevitably does appear to make Love a god in the same way; it too is a vision of judgment. All of the famous lovers he names are dead, until, in *capitolo* 4, he meets the friends that he called Socrates and Laelius whom he makes clear are alive (76–79). By this point, however, this hedge against misinterpretation is no more effective than the warnings that Love is merely a personification. Petrarch himself has already misinterpreted his dream earlier when he entreats Massinissa and Sophonisba,

> Or dimmi, se colui in pace vi guide
> —e mostrai il duca lor—: che coppia è questa. . . .
>
> (2.25–26)

(Now tell me, so may he lead you in peace—and I pointed to their leader—who you two are.)

This last source of poetic bad conscience in the *Triumphus Cupidinis* is perhaps the most interesting, for it involves the poem's uncomfortable and obsessive relationship to the fifth canto of the *Inferno*, Dante's account of the circle of carnal sinners. The *terza rima* of all six *trionfi* is only the most obvious debt to Dante. Among Love's folk in the *Triumphus Cupidinis* is every figure that Dante names in *Inferno* 5, including Virgil, Beatrice, and Dante himself. Dante's shades, whirled like birds in the wind, become in Petrarch the lovers metamorphosed into birds at the end of *capitolo* 2. Petrarch's conversation with Massinissa and Sophonisba is a "conscious equivalent for Dante's Paolo and Francesca episode." Finally, the *Triumphus Cupidinis* contains at least ten verbal echoes of *Inferno* 5.[38]

If Terence, or Lactantius's unnamed poet, is the poet that Petrarch is in danger of becoming, Dante is the poet he refuses to be. The *Triumphus Cupidinis* is a revision of *Inferno* 5, declining to picture the ultimate sanctions of Christian ethics and relying instead upon knowledge of this world. But by refusing to describe the state of souls after death, while collecting and picturing examples from history and legend, Petrarch's poem creates a poetic limbo for lovers, ruled by a god who rewards and punishes his people indiscriminately. Augustus walks next to Nero in Cupid's triumph, Samson next to Holofernes, three examples of faithful love next to three notorious perverts. In refusing to be Dante, however, Petrarch does not wish to become Terence, and he acknowledges his anxiety by placing his own capture by Cupid immediately after he sees Paolo and Francesca, "the pair of Rimini who go together uttering sad laments" (la coppia d'Arimino che 'nseme / vanno facendo dolorosi pianti, 3.83–84). The lines echo Dante and so does the situation. If Laura had not resisted Petrarch, they would have followed the example of Paolo and Francesca, joining the triumph of Petrarch's Cupid, but perhaps also the circle of Dante's carnal sinners. But the spectre of Terence is here also. Paolo and Francesca fell through imitating in real life the literary actions of Lancelot and Guinevere, and Petrarch is writing a poem likely to prove as much a pandar to his readers as Paolo and Francesca's *Lancelot du lac* was to them.

Wilkins judges that "in view of Petrarch's failure to win love from Laura, it was inevitable that as a companion piece to his *Triumph of Love* he should write a Triumph celebrating resistance to love." But the inevitability is not merely autobiographical, but also moral. Even Petrarch, with the "negative capability" that permitted him to remain in the lifelong uncertainties, mysteries, doubts that the *Rime sparse* record, could not have accepted the moral consequences of the *Triumphus Cupidinis* without envisioning its corrective. Wilkins himself notes that the first two *trionfi* are the only ones joined by "interior linkages."[39]

The *Triumphus Pudicitiae* presents a battle between Cupid and Laura in which Laura's victory disproves the dangerous lesson of the *Triumphus Cupidinis* that Love conquers all and makes the first *trionfo* innocuous. Even the guide is redeemed, making a brief parenthetical reappearance at the end. More than this, Laura's victory gives Petrarch a consolation that his self-justifying pursuit of knowledge could not have arrived at—not a concession to his own desires in the guise of a force that crushes human integrity, but to an individual woman who maintains it. The active seeker after knowledge of the first *trionfo* becomes a passive spectator in the second, whom Laura rescues from the crowd of Love's victims and places with her among the elect of Chastity.

The battle between a god and a lady has seemed mismatched to many readers, who have used it to argue that Laura was not a woman, but an allegory. But the incongruity itself is significant. It demonstrates what the guide and poet of the *Triumphus Cupidinis* can only assert, that Cupid is merely a personification whom human beings make a god and can as easily unmake. Moreover, that Laura rather than some less specific embodiment of chastity triumphs over Cupid shows him to represent Petrarch's own desire, overcome or transformed, as was Dante's, by his own lady. Laura leads an army of both "all her bright Virtues" (76–77), such as Honor, Modesty, Prudence, and of ladies, previous incarnations of Chastity, like Lucrece, Penelope, and Judith. They too

> . . . queste gli strali,
> avean spezzato e la faretra a lato
> a quel protervo, e spennachiate l'ali.

(133–35)

(. . . had broken the arrows and the bow at the side of arrogant Love and had plucked his wings.)

Cupid is the image of each man's desires and also the collective image of all, and therefore none of these victories is ever final; they must be repeated in every age and for every man that makes his desires a god. At bottom, the conflict between Laura and Cupid figures the conflict, too painful to represent directly, between Laura and Petrarch, whose unbridled passion she wins to a kind of measure (see *TM* 2.90–3, 132). As in the *Vita Nuova*, the lady's character transforms love, but in the *Trionfi* transformation emerges from conflict, not peaceful succession, because Cupid's divinity is always false. It does not reflect the designs of true divinity because Petrarch did not believe that Laura was a miracle or that his love was divinely ordained to assure his salvation.

The triumph of Chastity has only one captive, Cupid, and an army of victors, just as the triumph of Cupid has one victor and countless captives. Cupid is brought to a temple in Rome dedicated to "quenching flames of madness in the mind" and imprisoned finally in the temple of Chastity, "which kindles honest desires in gentle hearts" (*TP* 180–182). Cupid is neither killed, nor are his flames entirely extinguished, because chastity does not destroy love, but controls it. The victory of chastity may free Petrarch from Love, but not from love of Laura. Indeed, it presents his fall to Cupid as a kind of *felix culpa*, a fall without which the ascent could not begin. The *Triumphus Pudicitiae* is then both a recantation of the *Triumphus Cupidinis* and a refinement that could not have occurred except through the *Triumphus Cupidinis*. In this paradoxical recantation and reaffirmation, the "two-fold poem, complete in itself" that Petrarch wrote before Laura's death, establishes the pattern that the four later *Trionfi* will follow.

After Laura's death, Petrarch saw that the design for his finished *Trionfi* could be transformed so that the *Triumphus Cupidinis* and *Triumphus Pudicitiae* would make the first movement of a larger poem. The four later *Trionfi* proceed by the same dialectical continuity as the first two. Death comes to Laura and to all men alike, but Fame "takes a man from the tomb and keeps him alive" (*TF* 1.9). Time obliterates even Fame, but all shall be remembered in eternity. After the *Triumphus Mortis*, the poem moves away from autobiography and becomes more meditative, or rather, as autobiography, it becomes less personal and more ideal, conforming to a version of the theme of the Ages of Man. In his youth, Petrarch rests his hope in Love, as a man in Fame, and in his old age in heaven. Each shift involves a recantation, sometimes a bitter one:

> Ma chi ben mira, col giudizio saldo,
> vedrá esser cosí. Ché no'l vid'io?
> di che contra me stresso or mi riscaldo.
>
> (TT 52–54)

(But he who considers well, with firm judgment, will see it to be so. Why did I not see it? For that I am now angry with myself.)

And yet, the underlying pattern of the Ages of Man asserts continuity despite recantation. By emphasizing the association of love with youth in the *Triumphus Cupidinis*, for example, the structure of the larger poem deemphasizes the moral conversion represented by the *Triumphus Pudicitiae*, just as the association of the *Roman de la rose* with youth blunts the moral edge of its satire. The final continuity will be in eternity, which destroys death and time, but perfects love and fame.

There are more explicit continuities, however. Petrarch sees among the adherents of Fame many whom he had seen bound by Cupid (*TF* 1.20–21). But the most striking continuity is the reinvocation of Laura and Amore in the *Triumphus Aeternatis*:

> E tra l'altre leggiadre e pellegrine,
> beatissima lei che Morte occise
> assai di qua dal natural confine!
> Parranno allor l'angeliche divise,
> e l'oneste parole, e i penser casti,
> che nel cor giovenil natura mise.
> . . . .
> E vedrassi ove, Amor, tu mi legasti.
>
> (TAe 85–90, 93)

(And among the other beauteous and rare ones, most blessed will she be whom Death cut off so much before her time. Then will be manifest the angelic habits, the honest words, and the chaste thoughts that nature placed in her youthful heart. . . . And it shall be seen, Love, where you bound me.)

At the very end of the poem, Petrarch alludes to the scene and the emotion of the beginning:

> A riva un fiume che nasce in Gebenna,
> Amor mi die' per lei sí lunga guerra,
> che la memoria ancóra il cor accenna.
> . . . .
> Se fu beato chi la vide in terra,
> or che fia dunque a rivederla in cielo?
>
> (TAe 139–41, 144–45)

(On the bank of a stream that rises in Monginevra, through her Love gave me so long a war that the memory still beckons the heart. If he was blest who saw her on earth, what will it be then to see her again in heaven?)

Unlike Dante, Petrarch still waits to see his lady again, and in that regard his poem is open-ended. Still, the final reinvocation of the beginning gives the *Trionfi* a sense of formal closure that points toward its major theme. It is not merely a collection of "scattered rhymes," like the *Rime sparse,* or an inconclusive debate, like the *Secretum.* In those works, Petrarch was never able to convince himself either that he did or did not have to renounce Laura and Amore to escape damnation. The *Trionfi* is his *Commedia,* though it is not a revelation, but an earthbound dream, a dream from which he does not awake because "this mortal life, which so pleases, is only a dream" from which he will awake in eternity (*TC* 4.65–66). Amore returns at the end of the *Trionfi* for the same reason and in the same unincarnated fashion as he reappears at the end of the *Vita Nuova.* Both Dante and Petrarch strive to affirm their experience of love, though in Petrarch the striving is more evident than the achievement. Every fall is therefore fortunate, and every renunciation encompassed within the final continuity.

4
Renaissance Poetry

WHEN Dante and Petrarch wrote, poetry itself held hardly more than a precarious place in the range of endeavor sanctioned by medieval culture. Influential clerics repeated patristic charges that it repeated lies and thereby diverted readers from the truths of religion. Rationalists of a more secular stripe would soon charge that it had no practical use. Both complaints center on the fictiveness of poetry, the crux of which remains poetic theology, poetry's most heterodox and dangerous fiction. Against this background, the *Vita Nuova* and the *Trionfi* appear not only as poems, but as vindications of poetry. By incorporating earlier ironic uses of the god of love within a larger continuity, they control his deceptive ambiguity and give one kind of answer to the detractors of their art. The example of Dante and Petrarch, together with the great trecento defenses of poetry and the more general ideological shift they represent, did not so much silence the detractors as deprive them of general assent for almost two hundred years. In this new atmosphere, poets can claim vatic authority without irony, and the emphasis in Cupid's poetic theology shifts from the old ironies or iconoclasm to a new mythopoeia. Unchallenged confidence in the truths of fiction made for an ambivalent renaissance, however; it quickly became devitalizing.

Cupid proliferates in Renaissance poetry in ways that would be inordinate and unilluminating to pursue in detail. Still, the general shape of his career in Renaissance poetry ought to be suggested before we look more closely at the mythographers and Neoplatonists who sustained and deepened the animating tension between god and personification and before we turn to Edmund Spenser, the last major poet to make Cupid's theology a sustaining fiction and the one whose works comprehend nearly all the phases of Cupid's career and bring it to culmination.

An external history of Cupid in Renaissance poetry and art would have much to report. From Plato and various *platonisti* he gets new parents, Porus and Penia, a brother Anteros, and a child Voluptas. His wife, Psyche, though known to the Middle Ages, was seldom mentioned until her story enjoyed a fifteenth and sixteenth century vogue. From closer imitation of antique models and ecphrases, Cupid grows younger, becoming again the classical winged infant. But from the rediscovered *Greek Anthology* and *Anacreontea* Cupid gains most of all: a huge new repertoire of epithets and exploits, as well as a manner that freed moderns to invent many more of both. Some idea of this proliferation can be had from Mario Praz's summary of an emblem book of 1613 entitled *Het Ambacht van Cupido* (The Occupations of Cupid), in which

> Love is seen in the capacity of a tennis-player, a cooper, a painter, a joiner, a tailor, a sailor, a geometrician, a scholar; he sits at the spinning-wheel like Hercules for Omphale, plays at dice . . . , whips the top, runs after the hoop, plays at blind-man's-buff, puts on a helmet and girds himself with a sword, rides on the handle of a broom, turns somersaults, makes soap-bubbles, threshes the corn . . . , sows seed . . . , tortures the lover on the rack and burns him at the stake.[1]

Hundreds of emblems like these were copied and reinvented and modified through the sixteenth and seventeenth centuries, and most of them depict an incident, commonplace, or conceit borrowed from classical or modern poets. The mode itself, joining *pictura* with *poesis* as it does, works against iconoclastic exposure of Cupid as only an image, a product of human art or illusion. Among those hundreds of emblems, therefore, only Alciati's "In Statuam Amoris," which I discussed in Chapter 1, debunks Cupid's ontological status, and it was imitated far less than most of Alciati's emblems.

Most Renaissance poetry similarly accepts Cupid as a fictive god without the medieval and early Renaissance worry about the status and dangers of this fiction. This development appears clearly in late medieval love allegories, most of which have the family likeness of their common descent from the *Roman de la rose*. With few exceptions these works neglect the sharp dialectics of the *Roman* in favor of elaborate and static descriptions of landscapes, gardens, or architecture, as their titles often imply: *Le Paradis d'Amours, L'Hospital d'Amours, Le Parlement d'Amours, Die Minneburg, The Court of Love*.[2] Colonna's *Hypnerotomachia Poliphili* represents the extreme of this tendency, as of others; it was printed with profuse and influential illustrations, diagrams, and hieroglyphics to supplement its literary obscurities.

Though they regularly call Love a god, few of these allegories develop his fictional divinity or exploit its ambiguities. Marot's *Le Temple de Cupido*, one of the latest of this form and old-fashioned when it was written, is representative. The poet's springtime quest for True Love leads him to Cupid's temple where the liturgy is as poetic as the god:

> Ovidius, maistre Alain Charretier,
> Petrarque, aussi le *Rommant de la Rose,*
> Sont les messelz, breviaire et psaultier,
> Qu'en ce sainct temple on lit, en rime et prose.[3]

(Ovid, master Alain Chartier, Petrarch, and also the *Roman de la rose* are the missals, breviary, and psalter read in that holy temple, in rhyme and prose.)

The poet finds *Amour venerique* and *Amour legiere* in the nave of the temple, but in the choir he finds *Ferme Amour,* the object of his fictional quest, together with the King and Queen of France, objects of a more practical quest for patronage also conducted in this poem. The poem ends by unfolding a pun— the choir (cueur) of the temple is only the heart (cueur)—and so Cupid becomes once again an accident in a substance. But the desire for witty compliment rather than anxiety about the status of poetical gods has motivated his fall.

Lyrics and especially sonnets make a larger and later group of poems in which Cupid plies his trade, though they sometimes overlap with allegorical narratives, as in *La Retenue d'Amours* of Charles d'Orléans, where the court of love motif frames an autobiographical sequence of lyrics and helps to produce the work's unique late-medieval flavor. In most lyrics, however, as in emblems and allegories, Cupid's appearances are ornamental or anecdotal and do not challenge either the status of poetry as fiction or the poet's religious faith. This is not because he remains the unincarnated personification of the troubadour lyrics, for Cupid's role in lyric poetry shows a clear transformation in the Renaissance from the personified passion to the mythological divinity. In this development, as in so many others, the turning point was Petrarch, in whose *Rime sparse* Amore was closer to the troubadour Amors than to the god of the *Trionfi* or the *Vita Nuova.* Amore spoke in the *Rime sparse,* but always within the poet; he appeared as a "garzon con ali," but only in Laura's eyes (151). His power was absolute, but as Petrarch's *signore,* not his *dio,* and so, hailed before the court of reason at the end of the sequence, Amore could claim to have served the True God in inspiring Petrarch's love and poetry:

> da volar sopra 'l ciel li avea ali
> per le cose mortali,
> che son scala al Fattor, chi ben l'estima.[4]

(I gave him wings to fly above the heavens through mortal things, which are a ladder to the Creator, if one judges them rightly.)

Reason reserved her judgment; lacking the taint of paganism, Amore was harder to renounce than in the *Trionfi.* Petrarch saw his experience in terms of several myths, but despite specific precedent in Ovid, he did not develop Amore's role in even the chief of them, the metamorphosis of Daphne. In the *Rime sparse* Amore was so transparent a way of figuring Petrarch's experience of love that he seemed inseparable from the experience itself and therefore wanted neither elaborating nor demythologizing.

Out of Petrarch's subtle use of mythology, his imitators elaborated on Alexandrianism even before the original Alexandrianism became a direct influence with the publication of the *Greek Anthology* in 1494 and the *Anacreontea* in 1554.[5] In poems by exuberant *petrarchisti* like Chariteo, Tebaldo, and Serafino Aquilano, in civic pageantry, Neolatin epigrams, and in the voluminous works of the Pléiade, Cupid reenacts his old mythological exploits or improvises new ones complimenting the lady's beauty or expressing the poet's grief. No longer a riddle, the god of love becomes petrified in these poems as a stock device, now saved from cliché by clever fabling rather than by its opposite, guilty recognition of the dangers of fable.

Sonnet 63 of Ronsard's *Continuation des Amours* makes a good example of how antique myths may combine with newly invented ones for purposes of witty compliment:

> Amour, voiant du ciel un pescheur sur la mer,
> Calla son aisle bas sur le bord du navire,
> Puis il dit au pescheur: je te pri que je tire
> Ton ret, qu'au fond de l'eau le plomb fait abymer.
> Un daulphin, qui savoit le feu qui vient d'aimer,
> Voiant Amour sur l'eau, à Tethis le va dire:
> Tethys, si quelque soing vous tient de vôtre empire,
> Secourés-le, ou bien tost il est prest d'enflammer.
> Tethys laissa de peur sa caverne profonde,
> Haussa le chef sur l'eau, & vit Amour sur l'onde
> Qui peschoit à l'escart: las, dit el', mon nepveu,
> Oustés-vous, ne bruslés mes ondes, je vous prie:
> N'aiés peur, dit Amour, car je n'ay plus de feu,
> Tout le feu que j'avois est aus yeus de Marie.[6]

(Love, seeing from above a fisherman at sea, bends his wings down to the side of the boat, then says to the fisherman, "Let me haul in your net, which the lead makes sound the bottom." A dolphin, who knows well the fire that comes from loving, sees Love on the sea and goes to say this to Thetis: "Thetis, if you care about your realm, protect it or it is quickly on fire." Thetis leaves her deep cavern in fear, lifts her head above the surface, and sees Love on the waves who is fishing on the sly. "Alas," she says, "my nephew, clear off and don't burn my waves, I beg you." "Don't worry," says Love, "for I have no more fire; all the fire I have is in the eyes of Marie.")

Hundreds of Alexandrian poems like this one stand at an opposite pole from the troubadour lyrics. Cupid is not at all a personification, but rather a deity in a mythological world into which the present of the poet and his mistress has been dissolved or sublimated. But such poems do not affirm themselves to be true; their world and its divinities are transparently fictional. Disinfected of belief, Cupid becomes what he could not be in Andreas Capellanus's fifth dialogue, in the *Vita Nuova* or *Trionfi*—an innocent ornament or plaything.

By no means all appearances of Cupid in lyric poetry after Petrarch have this Alexandrian isolation from belief and its consequences, however. In many poems, Cupid's divinity continues to figure the power of passion which seems an exterior force possessing the lover, while, as a personification, he continues to represent a double or shadow of the poet for purposes of self-analysis and self-expression. The Pléiade especially follow Neoplatonic doctrines—a subject of the next chapter—and find Cupid's divinity an appropriate metaphor for the force that moves the heavens and creates nature itself by binding the warring elements into harmony. Such affirmations of Cupid's divinity raise again the danger that men may invest their own desire with the name of divinity and then plead compulsion, but with only a few exceptions, these dangers, ignored by the major poets, were left to their opponents: pedants, literary reactionaries, and moralists. The author of an epistle who insisted that his intentions were strictly honorable might lamely explain his poem's lack of elegant ornament:

> Il ne fault point dépaindre ici les traicts
> De Cupidon en figure pourtraicts,
> Car tout cela n'est que fable & mensonge
> Des anciens l'Idolatrie & songe.[7]

(It's no good painting here Cupid's traits in a portrait, for all that is nothing but a fable and a lie of the ancients, an idolatry and a dream.)

And another enemy of fashionable mythologizing, perhaps remembering Seneca, could be even more severe: "l'Aveugle antiquité déifiant cette affection pallia son erreur insigne du voile de déité" (Blind antiquity by deifying this emotion hid its notorious error with the cloak of divinity).[8] Remy Belleau, an exception to the rule, made the same point, retracting his earlier Neoplatonic affirmations in an ode "Contra l'Amour":

> . . . car le charme inhumain
> Qui nous enchante, & la force indomtable
> Que dis avoir sur la nature aimable,
> Ne vient de toy [Amour] ny de ta fiere main:
> Il vient de nous, mais las! pour voiler mieux
> De nostre mal la trop folle entreprise,
> Nous voulons bien que ce Dieu favorise
> Nostre malheur d'un tiltre glorieux.[9]

(. . . for the inhuman spell which enchants us and the irresistible force that you say you have over the loving nature does not come from you nor from your cruel hand. It comes from us, but alas, to conceal better the most foolish undertakings of our sickness, we wish that god to favor our unhappiness with a glorious name.)

Such retractions can be conventional exercises, of course, but they could also be parts of longer sequences in which authors might work out, like Dante and

Petrarch, the ambiguities and dangers of Cupid's double nature while seeking the meanings of their experience of love. But in fact adventitiousness, more than conventionality, diminishes the interest of Cupid in the works of the Pléiade. Their sequences themselves seem mere *mélanges* in comparison with the autobiographical mode of the *Vita Nuova* and the *Rime sparse*. In Dante and Petrarch Amore's divinity could signify not merely the power of their love, but its providentiality. In the Pléiade, however, poetry no longer records the Augustinian introspective search for providential design, and therefore the divine origin of human love has withered to compliment or worse. Explaining to Marie, the mistress of his second sonnet sequence, why he loves her rather than Cassandre, the mistress of the first, Ronsard appeals to celestial authority:

> Si vous n'estes d'un lieu si noble que Cassandre
> Je ne scaurois qu'y faire, Amore m'a fait descendre
> Jusques à vous aymer, Amour qui n'a point d'yeus,
> Qui tous les jours transforme en cent sortes nouvelles,
> Aigle, Cigne, Toreau ce grand maistre des Dieux,
> Pour le rendre amoureux de noz femmes mortelles.[10]

(If you are not as noble as Cassandre, there's nothing I can do; Love has made me condescend to love you, Love who has no eyes, who is always transforming into a hundred new shapes—eagle, swan, bull—the great king of the gods, in order to make him amorous of mortal women.)

Though he imitates Petrarch of the *Triumphus Cupidinis* as well as the young man in Terence who justified his own infidelities by the example of Jupiter's, only the most severe moralist would condemn Ronsard's sonnet as an abuse of literature. But its privilege comes at the cost of isolation; it succeeds by dissolving a serious question into witty fiction. Much the same must be said of Ronsard's use of Amour as a muse. An arrow from Cupid's bow gave Ovid the matter for the *Amores*, and since then it has been hard to distinguish the inspiration of love from the inspiration of love poetry. For Petrarch, the displacement of love into poetry, the substitution of poetic laurels for Laura herself, is implied when Amore commands the poet to write. Ronsard's version is closer to Ovid; despite his mock humility, the playful poet obviously commands his gods, rather than vice versa:

> Amour abandonnant les vergers de Cytheres,
> D'Amathonte et d'Eryce, en la France passa:
> Et me monstrant son arc, comme Dieu, me tança,
> Que j'oubliois, ingrat, ses loix & ses mysteres.
> Il me frappa trois fois de ses ailes legeres:
> Un traict le plus aigu dans les yeux m'eslança.
> La playe vint au coeur, qui chaude me laissa
> Une ardeur de chanter les honneurs de Surgeres.

Chante (me dist Amour) sa grace & sa beauté,
Sa bouche, ses beaux yeux, sa douceur, sa bonté:
Je la garde pour toy le sujet de ta plume.
—Un sujet si divin ma Muse ne poursuit.—
Je te feray l'esprit meilleur que de coustume:
"L'homme ne peut faillir, quand un Dieu le conduit."[11]

(Leaving the orchards of Cythera, Amathus, and Eryx, Love passed into France and, showing me his bow as a god, he scolded me that I, an ingrate, had forgotten his laws and mysteries. He struck me three times with his light wings and shot the sharpest beam into my eyes. The wound went to the heart, which left me hot with ardor to sing the praises of Surgères. "Sing," Love told me, "her grace and her beauty, her mouth, her beautiful eyes, her sweetness and her goodness. I keep for you the subject of your pen."—A subject so divine my Muse cannot follow.—"I will bring you a better than usual spirit: a man cannot fail when a god guides him.")

A few pages can hardly do justice to the diversity among Renaissance lyric poets, but some conclusions about their use of Cupid will be found to hold in general. Lyric poetry after Petrarch shows a gradual but thorough effacement of Cupid's figural meaning as a deified personification with a vast compensatory growth in the number and range of his roles or activities as a member of a purely mythical pantheon. Use alone would have encouraged this change by a process analogous to the one that makes metaphors fade into ordinary, nonfigurative language, compensating their loss of connotation with a gain in versatility. But use also has its causes and conditions. The Alexandrian use of Cupid, and of mythology in general, shows how successful the defenders of poetry had been in winning for lyric poetry more than they claimed: a nearly autonomous realm within which the imagination could sport without the ambivalence that worried medieval and early Renaissance fabulists even when they were not telling stories about the gods. Isolated within these poems, the old ironic or guilty religion of Love becomes a *jeu d'esprit,* and Cupid a charming literary device—no longer a possible figure for the means of the poet's salvation or a potentially threatening example of the duplicity of poetry. Most of these poets would subscribe to the tone of Baïf's envoi:

Cupidon je te salue . . .
Puis qu'Eraton la sacrée
En mes chansons te recrée.[12]

(Cupid, I salute you since sacred Erato has recreated you in my songs.)

Lyric poems, then, use either Love the personified passion or Cupid the mythological divinity, but appear to lack the capacity to explore or dramatize the interrelations between the two. At most they record the cry of disillusionment or recognition.[13] In longer works, however, Renaissance poets do explore and dramatize those interrelations, but with a characteristic reversal of the medieval pattern. The religion of love becomes a positive expression of idealism, often Neoplatonic, and the recognition scene becomes a theophany, revealing a valid divinity to his scoffing enemies. Cupid's career thus comes round to the revelation ironically offered in Andreas Capellanus's fifth dialogue, but the reversal testifies as much to Renaissance confidence in poetic fictions as to confidence in erotic love.

By no means all longer Renaissance forms show this development. The epyllion, for example, was an Alexandrian form to begin with, and most of its Renaissance exemplars flaunt the same privilege as do the sonnets, the Alexandrian privilege of treating the gods as fictions. But a diverse group of longer poems do engage the tradition of poetic theology we have been surveying and reverse its usual pattern. Perhaps the most interesting of these forms is the epithalamion because of its specific responsibility to a historical event and usually to a patron. The form itself denies Alexandrian isolation by connecting its fictions to its nonfictional, historical occasion. This responsibility to an occasion may explain why most Renaissance epithalamia take their model from Catullus rather than from Statius, Claudian or their sixth-century imitators, since Catullus narrated the ceremonies of the wedding day, while Statius and Claudian sought to ennoble the occasion by discovering it to be made in heaven by a prior intervention of Venus and Cupid. Such tales risk demeaning the weddings they seek to celebrate, especially when a Christian sacrament is at the center of the historical occasion, and perhaps for that reason the most famous Renaissance example of this use of Cupid occurs in a poem that might be called a secular epithalamion: Poliziano's *Stanze per la giostra.* Writing a century after Petrarch, Poliziano borrows the machinery of Statius and Claudian to tell how Giuliano de Medici, inspired by love for Simonetta Cattaneo, won the Florentine tournament of 1475. All of Poliziano's poetry burgeons with allusions, but the deepest debt of the *Stanze* is to the first pair of *Trionfi*, which Poliziano seeks to revise, just as Petrarch had sought to revise the fifth canto of the *Inferno.* The *Stanze* begin with Giuliano, like many another proud youth, scorning Love in lines that weave together echoes of the *Triumphus Cupidinis.* Love is only a "vain frenzy that arises from indolent lust and sloth," a passion personified by blind error and flattery:

> Costui che 'l vulgo errante chiamo Amore
> è dolce insania a chi piú acuto scorge:
> sí bel titol d'Amore ha dato il mondo
> a una ceca peste, a un mal giocondo.[14]

(1.13)

(He whom the erring common folk call Love is, when more clearly perceived, a sweet madness: the world has given that beautiful name of Love to an unseen plague, to a gladsome evil.)

One lover so scorned prays that Giuliano may believe by experience, and
Cupid hears the prayer:

> Dunque non sono idio? dunque è già spento
> mie foco con che il mondo tutto accendo?
> Io pur fei Giove mughiar fra l'armento,
> io Febo drieto a Dafne gir piangendo,
> io trassi Pluto delle infernal segge:
> e che non ubidisce alla mia legge?
>
> Io fo cadere al tigre la sua rabbia,
> al leone il fer rughio, al drago il fischio;
> e quale è uom di sí secura labbia,
> che fuggir possa il mio tenace vischio?
> Or, ch'un superbo in sí vil pregio m'abbia
> che di non esser dio vegna a gran rischio?
>
> (1.23–24)

(Am I not then a god? is my fire with which I burn the entire world already
spent? Indeed, I made Jove bellow among the herd, I caused Phoebus to run
weeping after Daphne, I drew Pluto from his infernal seat: and what creature
does not obey my law? / I cause the tiger to lose its rage, the dragon its hiss,
the lion its savage roar; and what man, outwardly so secure, can escape my
tenacious lime? Is my godhead now jeopardized because one proud man
holds me in low esteem?)

To vindicate his godhead, Cupid converts Giuliano's passion for hunting to
passion for Simonetta by substituting her for an imaginary perfect doe as the
object of his chase. The hunter becomes the prey as Cupid, described with epic
concretion, fires his arrow from Simonetta's eyes. Recognition of Cupid's
power leaves Giuliano dumb, but the mocking narrator draws the moral:

> U' sono or, Julio, le sentenze gravi,
> la parole magnifiche e' precetti
> con che i miseri amanti molestavi?
> . . . .
> Ahi, come poco a sé creder uom degge!
> ch'a virtute e fortuna Amor pon legge.
>
> (1.58–59)

(Where now, [Giuliano], are your grave pronouncements, the magnificent
words and the precepts with which you used to offend miserable lovers? . . .
Alas, how little must man trust to himself! for Love imposes laws on virtue
and fortune.)

Giuliano's "grave pronouncements" and "magnificent words," which echoed
traditional exposures of Amore as a figure of speech, are here themselves

exposed as flattering and deceptive rhetoric. The dissociation between love as an experience and Love as a god, which in medieval works had expressed itself as irony or pseudo-debate, was dramatized by Dante and Petrarch as itself part of the poet's experience; it produced an anagnorisis. Giuliano experiences precisely the opposite recognition and must reaffirm the *association* of love as an experience with Love as a cosmological force, an association that, naively following the tradition, he had earlier denied. Poliziano's hero was not the first to experience this recognition, nor the last. Troilus preceded him in both Boccaccio and Chaucer; Chaucer himself met the god he had blasphemed, who required him to write the *Legend of Good Women* as penance; Prince Arthur is only the most prominent figure in *The Faerie Queene* to feel the power of the god he had scorned. And these are only a few examples of a widespread pattern. Reversal of the medieval recognition scene becomes the Renaissance norm.

Some of the implications and causes of this reversal will emerge from what follows the recognition scene in the *Stanze* and so will further evidence of the struggle Poliziano was conducting against the *Trionfi*. Subjugation of Giuliano establishes Cupid's power, but does not vindicate his godhead as other than the pagan divinity he had seemed to the dreamer of the first *Trionfo*, jealous of mortals' freedom and hostile to their achievements. To establish Cupid's godhead as a figure for positive, benevolent, and civilizing love, the *Stanze* leave the smitten Giuliano and follow Cupid to the realm of Venus where Poliziano fashions the real answer to Giuliano's (and Petrarch's) earlier heresy.

The *Triumphus Cupidinis* had also returned to Venus's realm, and, in keeping with his negative view, Petrarch had made it one of the enervating isles that became obligatory episodes in Renaissance epics, "banishing manly thoughts" and sinking heroes in "fleeting pleasures" and "sluggish idleness."[15] Poliziano, in contrast, makes his realm of Venus a genuine paradise and lavishes upon it all the resources of humanist art and optimism. To show Poliziano's thorough transvaluation of the earlier poetic theology summed up in the *Trionfi* it will suffice here to notice only the carvings on Venus's palace doors. The first of the pair of doors depicts the birth of Venus and undoubtedly influenced Botticelli's painting of the same subject. The second depicts the gods transformed "as love wills" (come Amor vuole), imitating Arachne's tapestry in the *Metamorphoses* and prefiguring Busyrane's in *The Faerie Queene*. Because of these *caelestia crimina*, the gods went chained before Cupid's chariot in the *Trionfi*, but we have seen how Petrarch alluded to the ancient tradition that saw these myths as lies of the poets and thereby indicated the illusory nature of his own poetic dream. For the same reason Petrarch had "errors, dreams, and vain imaginings" around Cupid's triumphal arch, and on his doors "false opinions" (errori, e sogni, et imagini smorte / eran d'intorno a l'arco triumphale, / e false opinioni in su le porte, *TC* 4.139–41). Poliziano affirms exactly what Petrarch denied. The loves of the gods are no longer crimes that poets attribute to the gods to excuse men's lust, but fables expressing the downward moment in the circuit of love that sustains the universe. And Venus's doors are no deceptive artifice, but the supreme work of Vulcan himself, the "divin fabbro":

> né 'l vero stesso ha piú del ver che questo;
> e quanto l'arte intra sé non comprende,
> la mente imaginando chiaro intende.
>
> (1.119)

(Truth itself has not more truth than this; whatever the art in itself does not contain, the mind, imagining, clearly understands.)

The confidence in artistic or poetic truth which these lines declare has already been reflected in Poliziano's use of Cupid. It too reverses the earlier tradition that, from Alain de Lille to Petrarch, had exposed the potential for abuse or delusion in poetic art by debunking Cupid.

Confidence in artistic and poetic truth is, of course, a characteristic Renaissance development, related to others like veneration of antiquity and a view of the poet and artist as *vates*, diviner and teacher of hidden truths. These developments might have been enough in themselves to account for Poliziano's reversal of the earlier poetic theology, but there is another change equally important—a more radically optimistic view of human love than Petrarch could affirm, perhaps more optimistic than Poliziano himself could sustain. This view finds its fullest expression in Ficino's recreation of Plato's *Symposium,* the first of the *trattati d'amore* that will be discussed in the following chapter. Poliziano was a member of Ficino's Platonic Academy, and details in the *Stanze* are sometimes glossed from Ficino, but in general the *Stanze* present love less as Neoplatonic rapture than as a civilizing force, an inspiration to secular and courtly achievement. In this change too, Poliziano is reversing Petrarch.

After the long and elegant description of Venus's isle and architecture, Poliziano's Cupid reports his victory over Giuliano:

> Ma 'l bel Julio ch'a noi stato è ribello,
> e sol di Delia ha sequito el trionfo,
> or drieto all'orme del suo buon fratello
> *vien catenato innanzi al mio trionfo.*
>
> (2.10; emphasis added)

(But handsome [Giuliano], who has been a rebel unto us, and followed only Delia's triumph, now, following his good brother's steps, comes chained in the forefront of my triumph.)

Though echoing Petrarch, who had written "ven catenato Giove innanzi al carro," this triumph differs radically from Petrarch's. It does not represent a crushing victory of erotic passion over all human individuality and endeavor, but rather leads to a second triumph, Giuliano's triumph in the tournament which is the occasion of the poem. Inspired by love, Giuliano's triumph is also Cupid's:

> né mosterrò già mai pietate ad ello
> finché ne porterà *nuovo trionfo:*
> ch'i' gli ho nel cor diritta una saetta
> dagli occhi della bella Simonetta.
>
> (2.10; emphasis added)

(I will not show any pity to him until he carries off a new triumph for us: for I have shot an arrow into his heart from the eyes of the fair Simonetta.)

In Petrarch, the triumph of Chastity followed and redeemed the triumph of Cupid, but Poliziano reverses the order and relationship. In the second book, Giuliano dreams a version of the *Triumphus Pudicitiae* (28–29); his lady, clad in Minerva's armor, has tied Cupid to a tree, plucked his wings, and broken his bow. But this is only a dream, a "false" vision of Cupid sent as prologue to a vision of Glory descending with Poetry and History to inspire Giuliano in the tournament and strip his lady of her armor. At this point in Poliziano's mythologization of history, however, events turned decisively toward the Petrarchan pattern he was trying to transform; Simonetta died. Where Petrarch made Laura after her death a type of chastity, Poliziano resurrects Simonetta "in forma di Fortuna" (2.34), the public and active force controlling Giuliano's destiny. Giuliano sees her "govern his life, and make them both eternal through fame" (2.34). Petrarch's *Triumphus Mortis* and *Triumphus Famae* have been compressed into two stanzas, and Cupid, inspiring both the hero and the poet, has become something more than love for a woman, but also something more secular than the love Dante found to be the source and agent of his salvation. When shortly after Simonetta's death, Giuliano was assassinated, Poliziano left the *Stanze* unfinished.

Like the epithalamia of Statius and Claudian, and like the Alexandrian sonnets discussed above, the *Stanze per la giostra* work by the Virgilian strategy of ennobling present events by revealing their mythological and divine causes. But Poliziano wants to exhort and reveal as much as to flatter. Unlike the sonnets, the *Stanze* use their mythology to interpret the world and men's achievements in it in a fashion at least poetically theological. The death of the hero with his promise left unfulfilled emptied and perhaps exposed the public, secular, and active premises of the poem. Rather than retract, writing his own version of the triumphs of Time and Eternity and necessarily demythologizing Cupid as Dante and Petrarch had done, Poliziano let the rest be silence.

Tasso's *Aminta* can end this far-from-exhaustive survey of the range of Renaissance poems in which Cupid plays a prominent role because it incorporates or alludes to almost his whole repertory. It includes one Alexandrian anecdote, "Cupid and the Bee," and is framed in its prologue and epilogue by another, the first idyll of Moschus, "Amor Fugitivus," which Poliziano had earlier put into Latin.[16] Tasso's Cupid is egalitarian and has fled to the pastoral world because his mother, in accord with the literary strategy represented by Stratius, Claudian, and Poliziano, restricts his activities to princes and nobles. Cupid does not appear on stage in *Aminta* except in the prologue, but he is present nonetheless, as he himself explains:

> In questo luogo a punto io farò il colpo,
> Ma veder non potrallo occhio mortale.
> Queste selve oggi ragionar d'Amore
> Udranno in nuova guisa; e ben parrassi
> Che la mia deità sia qui presente
> In sé medesma e non ne' suoi ministri.

(In this place I shall suddenly strike my blow, but mortal eyes will not be able to see it. These woods today will hear love disputes in a new guise; it will appear clearly that my godhead exists, which here is present in itself and not in its agents.)

The old distinction between the passion and the god dissolves into the mystery of Cupid's transcendence and immanence. The prologue presents itself as a theophany, introducing the audience but not the characters to the transcendent deity whose existence and power the rational and wordly among the shepherds will continually call in doubt. The plot at first sharpens this doubt by piling up obstacles to Aminta's desire for Silvia, but her conversion justifies the pious who, despite the complications of the plot and without the Prologue's theophany, believed all along in Cupid's immanence and benevolence. This piety finds its fullest spokesman in the hermit who in the final choric act answers those who had condemned love as merely a passion deified by the credulous and deluded:

> Veramente la legge con che Amore
> Il suo imperio governa eternamente
> *Non è dura né obliqua;* e l'opre sue,
> Piene di provvidenza e di misterio,
> Altri a torto condanna. Oh, con quant'arte
> E per che ignote strade egli conduce
> L'uomo ad esser beato, a fra le gioie
> De 'l suo amoroso paradiso il pone . . . .

> (5.1; emphasis added)

(Truly the laws by which Love eternally rules his empire are not hard or unjust; and his works, full of providence and mystery, are wrongly condemned. Oh, with how much skill and by what unseen ways he leads man to be happy and places him among the joys of his amorous paradise.)

Perhaps chief among those whom the hermit refutes, though he is not in the dramatis personae, is Petrarch, who had concluded: "Dura legge d'Amore! ma, ben che obliqua, / servar conviensi" (*TC* 3.148–9).

Aminta depicts a pastoral world, of course, but in sufficient length and coherence to present a providence like Poliziano's that is not merely witticism of flattery. Its erotic cosmos is a facet or mirror of our own world, a wider theater in which we too play our parts without certain knowledge of a transcendent prologue or epilogue. Tasso wrote *Aminta* in 1572 or 1573 when he was 28 years old, but even then, before Counter-Reformation doubts and guilt darkened his imagination, he was hardly teaching Neo-pagan worship of Cupid. *Aminta* does teach, however; its pastoral religion of love figures an openness to experience, a humility before the beneficent and humanizing power of love.

The preceding examples should show that when Renaissance poets do not escape altogether into an Alexandrian world apart, they tend to reverse the medieval pattern in which Cupid is first mistaken for a deity, then exposed as a deceptive trope, and sometimes reaffirmed, his deceptiveness now controlled, as a figure for the providentiality of human love. Since the medieval pattern includes a reversal, it should not be surprising that, when it is itself reversed, the result comes near to the starting point, the original fictive divinity, now free of the ironies of its medieval contexts. The false deity of Andreas Capellanus's fifth dialogue becomes the god revealed in the Prologue of Tasso's *Aminta* and affirmed in its action; both work to save ladies from hardness of heart, though there is a moral gulf between them. The god of love of the *Roman de la rose* leaves his enclosed garden and delusive dream to act in the history transfigured in Poliziano's *Stanze*. And not just in the *Stanze*. Florentine rites of spring in Poliziano's time included a procession of youths garlanded and in costume drawing a chariot in which rode the god of the festivities—Cupid.[17]

The reasons for this reversal have already been mentioned. For the most part they are the broad shifts in ideology and style that distinguish the Renaissance from the Middle Ages. The defense of fiction, the prestige of antiquity, and a general if not pervading secularism are obviously interrelated and join to make Renaissance poets less troubled by figurative divinity, less disposed to figure erotic obsession as idolatry or paganism, and less likely to accept moral responsibility for readers who misunderstand or abuse their fictions. At the same time, Florentine Neoplatonism provides a transcendental, yet secular and purportedly antique, affirmation of erotic passion. It should come as no surprise that this optimistic phase of Cupid's career, confident of both human art and love, should be the phase that coincides with the great mythological works in Renaissance visual art.

These developments are familiar to stuents of Renaissance poetry, and examples of their effects on Cupid's career might be multiplied far beyond the poems already discussed. It will be less repetitive to pursue the Renaissance transformations of Cupid in two related kinds of prose work that flourished in the sixteenth century, the mythological encyclopedia and the Neoplatonic *trattato d'amore*. It will also be more illuminating because these forms do not simply adopt a poetic mythology, but rather engage directly the problems and possibilities of creating or sustaining one.

5
Renaissance Mythographers and Neoplatonists

IN the Renaissance, mythography catches up with medieval poetry, focusing as medieval mythography had not on the divinity of Cupid and the other gods. It asks what it means to make Cupid a god, as well as what he may mean as a rhetorical figure. Yet Renaissance mythographers lag behind the most daring poetry because they must engage the problems of poetic theology more immediately than poets, who may evade this task, though at peril to their poetic longevity. A mythographer's explicit task is to recreate his figures from the *disjecta membra* of classical fables and then to reveal their meaning. His entry on Cupid will tend, therefore, to fall into a pattern like that of the most complex and profound *poetic* uses of Cupid, in which a deluded perception or belief about the god of love is followed by recognition of the less apparent truth. Poets could learn more than information from Renaissance mythographers.

Boccaccio is the first great Renaissance mythographer, and his *Genealogia deorum gentilium,* written between 1350 and 1370 and first printed in 1472, went largely without competition, except from older and less ambitious compendia, until the middle of the sixteenth century. Beginning in 1548, three major treatments of the ancient gods appeared in Italy and were quickly reprinted and distributed throughout Europe. These were Lilio Gregorio Giraldi's *De deis gentium varia et multiplex historia . . .* (1548), Vincenzo Cartari's *Le imagine colla sposizione degli dei degli antichi* (1556), and Natale Conti's *Mythologiae sive Explicationis fabularum libri decem* (1568).[1] The essential development between Boccaccio and the later mythographers began toward the end of the fifteenth century with Marsilio Ficino's commentary on the *Symposium* (written 1474–75, first published 1484) and culminated at the beginning of the sixteenth in a remarkable profusion of commentaries, dialogues, and treatises passing under the name *trattati d'amore.* The most influential of these are Pietro Bembo, *Gli Asolani* (1505), Mario Equicola, *Libro di natura d'amore*

(1525), Baldassare Castiglione, *Il Cortegiano* (1528), and Leone Ebreo, *Dialoghi d'amore* (1535).[2] All of the *trattati* have threads of mythographical inquiry woven into their fabric, and the later mythographers adapt ideas from the *trattatisti.* Cupid, along with Venus, is probably the most important meeting place of these two strains of Renaissance thought.

For both the mythographers and the Neoplatonists, the chief question about Cupid is the same one traced in the preceding chapters: is Love a god or a passion of the mind? In the Neoplatonists, the question is resolved by the doctrine of emanations and the *scala amoris*. In the mythographers, it is often closely allied to another question: is there one Cupid (the god) or are Cupids as many and varied as the human desires they personify? Cupid's ambiguity is in no way lessened in the Renaissance, but it comes to be seen less as a dangerous potential for abuse and self-deception than as a reflection of the sacredness of love and of the dignity of man.

Boccaccio is a convenient place to begin this account, for as a mythographer he is like Janus, "simul ante retroque prospiciens."[3] Most of his interpretations of Cupid look backward toward medieval mythographical conventions, but his account of the Cupid and Psyche story and the general conception of his project look forward to Renaissance developments. The medieval aspects are easy to summarize. While medieval poets and commentators, as we have seen, put Cupid's divinity to complex figurative uses, medieval mythographers were much more cautious.[4] Boccaccio, too, endeavors to explain away Cupid's divinity. His discussions of Cupid are scattered through five different books, each, according to the scheme of the *Genealogia*, treating the descendants of a different "primary" god.

Euhemerism—the ancient doctrine that the gods were great men deified by the worship of grateful contemporaries—accounts for one of Boccaccio's Cupids: he was a boy beautiful enough to be called another Cupid.[5] For the most part, however, Boccaccio explains Cupid as a personification, that is by a figurative euhemerism that makes him a reflection of human experience rather than its cause. In Book 1 he says: "The ancient belief held love to be a passion of the mind, and whatever we desire is love. But since our desires tend to diverse ends, it must be that love is not the same for all of them" (1.15). Aristotle, among other ancients, divided love into three types—honorable, delightful and useful—but, Boccaccio continues, certainly Cupid is not on that account divine. Indeed, human abuse determines his genealogy: because of "his usefulness to degenerate spirits," Cicero called him the son Erebus and Night—"that is, of a blind mind and obstinate heart" (1.15). Identification of Cupid as a personification here tends to the conclusion that there must be multiple Cupids and to an emphasis on abuse.

Boccaccio's major treatment of Cupid (9.4) is also the most medieval. He is again a personification, but here represents only sexual passion. The entire discussion revolves around the problem of his divinity and its abuse. Boccaccio begins by quoting from Seneca a description of Cupid's tyranny over the other gods. We may remember that Alain de Lille and Petrarch, following a long tradition, repudiated these myths because they appear to affirm Love's omnipotence, thus lending celestial authority to human self-indulgence. Here Boccaccio gives them a moral-astrological interpretation. Cupid is said to be the son of Venus and Mars because a man born in the conjunction of those planets will become "a voluptuous fornicator and practicer of all sexual abuses." Jove is human reason whom sexual passion forces to leave Olympus and take bestial form. This interpretation deprives Cupid of his divinity, but nevertheless denies human free will, and Boccaccio therefore frames it in qualification: "He whom we call Cupid is therefore a passion of the mind, excited by external things, introduced by the corporeal senses, and approved by the internal will, to which the celestial bodies may contribute an aptitude."

The stars may incline, but men must consent. Later Boccaccio criticizes the very genealogy he reports: "Passion is not produced by Mars and Venus, but . . . men so inclined are moved to submit to passion following a bodily disposition; if this does not exist, passion is not produced. Therefore, to assert broadly, Cupid is born of Mars and Venus for only a slight and highly remote reason."

This genealogy of Cupid, then is false, as well as the omnipotence suggested by the myths of the gods' involuntary loves. Both are abuses of fiction, as Boccaccio makes clear by quoting the same tag from Seneca that Bernardo Lapini applied to the *Triumphus Cupidinis:* "Certainly miserable mortals, driven by passion to excuse their imbecility, have invented this most powerful pest of a god, whom Seneca the tragedian detested, saying in the *Hippolytus:* "Base and servile lust feigned love to be a god and, in order to be less restrained, has given passion the title of an unreal divinity."

Boccaccio's account goes on to interpret Cupid's attributes, for the most part recapitulating medieval conventions, which themselves go back to Roman poets and commentators.[6] Cupid is a boy because boys are subject to irrational passions and because passion makes men childish. His wings signify the flightiness of love; his arrows the sudden captivity of the foolish; his torch the ardor of lovers. His blindfold signifies that lovers are led by passion, not reason, and do not know where they are going, and his griffon feet, picked up from Francesco Barbarino, reflect love's tenaciousness. This account of Cupid's attributes is introduced by the statement: "But now it is time to put aside fictions and see what is hidden beneath them. They invent this boy in order to sketch the age and manners of those who suffer this passion." These are obviously not the same inventors as those miserable mortals who gave to passion the title of an unreal divinity. These inventors, in fact, seem to be poets who, by holding a mirror up to nature, present a cautionary image. But this image proves duplicitous. Merely by attributing literal divinity, "degenerate spirits" can change it from a cautionary image to an exemplary one, from satire to justification. For Boccaccio, as for Andreas Capellanus, "unreal divinity" is falsehood rather than fiction. This Cupid is the opposite of a Silenus Alcibiadis, that ugly statue which contained little images of the gods and could therefore become an image of how, in an allegorical figure, a kernel of divine truth may be contained within a husk of fiction.[7] This Cupid wears his divinity on his sleeve, but conceals no mystery, only a mundane admonition.

Another of Boccaccio's Cupids discloses a positive, though still mundane, significance:

> Everyone thinks that Love was the son of Jupiter and Venus, which I will believe of the planets, but not of people. For both planets are similar in substance, warm and humid, and both are benevolent also and gleam with equal light. So from these love arises, and he is feigned to be the power by which we live together and join in friendship—as we know since love and friendship arise from agreement of dispositions and morals among mortals. . . . Of concupiscible love enough has been said above. (11.5)

This is not an astrological interpretation, since the planets do not incline men to love, but merely symbolize factors that do: benevolence, equality, virtue. This love is to be contrasted with concupiscible love, yet it remains a moral, rather than a physical or metaphysical power. Though it shares the responsibility for human society with Boethian cosmic love, "the holy bond of things," this love remains thoroughly earthly.[8]

Only once does Boccaccio find a more than earthly significance beneath Cupid's exterior. His discussion of the Psyche myth, as Osgood notes (p. xviii), is one of his rare anagogical interpretations. After her many trials, Psyche "attains again the supreme good of divine joy and contemplation, and is joined to him [Cupid] forever, and, leaving mortal things behind, is brought into eternal glory. From this love is born Pleasure which is eternal joy and gladness" (5.22).

Boccaccio's interpretation tacitly affirms Cupid's divinity since he becomes a figure for God himself. When, for example, he comes to Psyche only by night, forbidding her to look upon him, he is warning her to be lowly wise, not to inquire into the secrets of "eternity, the origins of things, and omnipotence, which are known to him alone." This is a far cry from Fulgentius's interpretation of Cupid as *cupiditas* and Psyche's torments as just punishments for yielding to carnal desire (*Myth.* 3.6). Boccaccio's view, with its affirmation of Cupid as a true Silenus concealing divine truth, looks forward to more inclusive affirmations in the High Renaissance. More than that, Boccaccio's discussion marks something of a renaissance of the legend of Cupid and Psyche itself. After Fulgentius, the story had died for most of the Middle Ages, although the first Vatican mythographer offered a précis without interpretation. After Boccaccio, "it became a great fecundating myth that was never lost again."[9]

Although the general conception of the *Genealogia* is often said to look backward to the medieval encyclopedists,[10] in several ways it also contains the germ of Renaissance developments. Boccaccio is the first mythographer since late antiquity to view his material as a system rather than as a collection of tales and to take it seriously as the relics of an ancient religion at least intermittently parallel to Christianity. The latter impulse, though not consistently carried through in the body of the *Genealogia*, tends to affirm the divinity of the gods. A century later it comes to fruition in various programs for reconciling paganism and Christianity in a "theologia poetica" and affects Cupid perhaps more than any other god.[11]

Boccaccio's treatment of mythology as relics of pagan religion is closely linked to the defense of poetry which occupies the final two books of the *Genealogia* and lies behind the whole project. His fundamental argument—that mythology is poetry and conceals a kernel of truth within a husk of fiction—is hardly new, but marginal differences prove to have radical effects. In the Middle Ages, doctrinal interpretation of mythology was an act of will—of imposition, to borrow Rosemond Tuve's term—and apparently needed no justification beyond faith that "all that is written is written for our doctrine" (Rom. 15:4).[12] Renaissance interpreters, however, want to avoid the appearance of imposition. Needing therefore to explain how Christian truth found its way into the husk of ancient mythology, they revive speculations of late pagan and early Christian writers. Myths are disguised or confused derivatives of Hebraic truths, contain inklings of true divinity such as human reason could reach without revelation, or were mysteriously inspired by the Holy Ghost.[13] These explanations and their variants all imply that, for the Renaissance, divine truth no longer resides in the faith of the interpreter, but in the myths themselves. Mythology thus acquires some of the prestige of Scripture.

Boccaccio's interests are not primarily theological. He maintains that the pagan poets are theologians chiefly to defend them from charges that they are tellers of empty tales, liars, seducers to all kinds of vice. Their theology turns out to be largely figurative, Varro's "physical theology," comprising moral and natural truths figured in tales of deities and demigods (see 14.8). Nevertheless there are times when their myths figure true divinity and they can rightly be called "sacred theologians" (sacri theologi, 15.8):

> Poets do say in their works that there are many gods, when there is but One. But they should not therefore be charged with falsehood, since they neither believe nor assert it as a fact, but only as a myth or fiction. . . . The multitude of other gods [other than Jupiter] they looked upon not as gods, but as members or functions of the Divinity. . . . But to these functions they gave a name in conformity with Deity because of their veneration for the particular function in each instance. (14.13; Osgood 65)

The gods could figure not merely the functions of Deity, but also his agents—angels and devils (11.1)—and could thus represent specific divine intervention in human affairs.[14] Cupid's conversion to an angel, hinted rhetorically in the *Vita Nuova* and literally accomplished in Ficino, is justified at least implicitly by Boccaccio's defense of poetry.

An attack on the abuse of poetry follows almost immediately from a defense of poetry as cousin to Scripture, for if poetry can be used to figure divine truth, then it can be abused to misrepresent unreal divinities as real ones. Abuse of poetry, for Boccaccio, is typically abuse of figurative divinity; crimes of kings or heroes are tolerable, but crimes of gods, and especially their adulteries, call forth his condemnation: "But those seductive performances of the gods presented chiefly by comic poets, in whatever way, I neither praise nor commend, but detest, and I hold such writers to be as execrable as the scenes themselves. . . . The fault for such corruption lies in the licentious mind of the artist" (14.14,6; Osgood 70, 38). Boccaccio's defense of poetry thus has a paradoxical effect upon all the gods and especially upon Cupid, the author of these seductive performances. It implicitly affirms that his divinity may figure "real" divinity or his functions and agents, but it also comdemns the abuse of "unreal" divinity that its affirmation has made more dangerous.

A mythographer who offers such a defense of his subject is obligated to distinguish uses from abuses, and Boccaccio does distinguish them through the genealogies that also order his book. Here too, like Janus, he looks forward and backward. He follows late pagan rationalists who also multiplied Jupiters, Venuses, and Cupids to preserve the respectability of the gods from their discrepant scriptures and their own misbehaviors. But his deepest impulse is to provide for future use of the "poetical gods."[15] He hopes that genealogy will become a kind of grammar, the inflections of a mythological language which the Middle Ages allowed to sink into unintelligibility. This impulse to provide for future poets, as it applies to Cupid, can be seen in his discussion of Ovid's invocation of Venus as "geminorum mater amorum" (mother of the twin loves): "But what do Ovid's twin Cupids intend? I believe Love to be one, but to change character and acquire a new name and father as he permits himself to be drawn into diverse passions" (3.22).

Here Boccaccio revises his opinion "that since our desires tend to diverse ends, it must be that love is not the same for all of them," and, more importantly, declines to endorse the medieval distinction between two Cupids, "alter bonus et pudicus . . . alter impudicus et malus," which was often linked to Ovid's phrase.[16] Instead, he suggests how genealogy might be used to distinguish "diverse passions" within the unity of love. The suggestion looks forward to poetic use of mythology rather than backward to classical mythology, however, because several Cupids in the *Genealogia* have changed both parents.[17] The future Boccaccio looked forward to was, for the most part, to ignore his genealogies of Cupid, but would codify and elaborate his wavering affirmation of Cupid's divinity and unimplemented decision in favor of Cupid's ambiguous singleness.[18]

Cupid regained his divinity at a stroke, we might say, on 7 November 1474 when the Florentine Platonic Academy observed the anniversary of Plato's birth and death by reenacting the banquet reported in the *Symposium*. Such, at least, is the purported origin of Ficino's *Commentarium in Convivium Platonis de amore*, which "marks a turning point in the history of love speculation" and if not a turning point, at least a sudden acceleration in the evolution of the god of love.[19] Before Ficino, Cupid was now a god, now a personification, but never, except by delusion or abuse, both at the same time. In Ficino, Cupid's equivocal double nature becomes daemonic, simultaneously divine and human, and becomes in addition his most important attribute.

Ficino and his followers greatly expand the theory that ancient myths contain veiled mysteries of true divinity, but this theory of a *prisca theologia* is no longer, as in Petrarch, Salutati, and Boccaccio, merely a rejoinder to pious enemies of poetry. Cupid's divinity, too, is no longer a potentially dangerous side effect of a defense of poetry, but a consequence and expression of a novel philosophical system that comprises a theology, cosmology, psychology, and ethics, all centered on the idea of love.[20] The system is most easily approached through its cosmology, which, following Plotinus's version of Plato, represents the universe emanating from "the One" or God in a hierarchy of four grades of being: *mens, anima, natura,* and *materia.* The "perpetual knot and binder" of this universe is love, because it is the motive force of both the downward emanation and the upward return: "There is one continuous attraction, beginning with God, going to the world and ending at last in God, an attraction which returns to the same place whence it began as though in a kind of circle."[21] Love is always "desire of beauty" or, more precisely, "desire for the fruition of beauty" (1.4; see also 2.9). In whatever grade of the hierarchy it appears, Beauty is incorporeal—"the radiance of the Divine Goddess"—and so the ultimate object of love is God (2.3; see 5.3–4,). When Ficino sent a copy of the *Commentary* together with his treatise *De Christiana religione* to a friend, his witticism in the accompanying letter was entirely just: "I send you my *Amor* as I promised; but I also send my *Religio* so that you will recognize that my love is religious and my religion amatory."[22]

Ficino presents these doctrines, none too consecutively, in speeches by his reenactors expounding the speeches of the original *Symposium.* His originality should not be overestimated. His idea of love draws elements from Plato, Plotinus, Aristotle, Cicero, St. Paul, St. Augustine, the *stilnovisti,* and Petrarch.[23] The Middle Ages knew a simpler version of his cosmology, visible for example in the *De planctu Naturae,* through Chalcidius's translation of the *Timaeus.* Even the doctrine of the ladder of love, which sanctified human love as a preliminary form of divine love, was medieval. But the synthesis Ficino made was new, as was the fact that its major vehicle was the mythology of Cupid and Venus. Plato's dinner guests, obligated to speak in praise of love, had presented and interpreted mythological themes, and Ficino's *Commentary,* therefore, consists in large part of mythographical interpretation.

The hierarchical cosmology is the basis of Ficino's mythography. Like Alain de Lille's simpler version, it allows the gods their circumscribed divinity, but it also serves Ficino in the same way that genealogy had served Boccaccio, permitting him to account for discrepancies among myths by distinguishing multiple gods of the same name. There is a Saturn, Jupiter, and Venus in each grade of the hierarchy, for example (2.7). Pausanias, the second speaker of the *Symposium*, had made a start on this type of explanation by distinguishing a celestial and an earthly Venus, each having different parents and accompanied by a different Cupid. Invoking his cosmology, Ficino explains that the celestial Venus is said to have been born without a mother because *mater* signifies *materia.* She is the immaterial beauty of the *mens angelica*, the realm of essences next below God. The second Venus is the "power of generation" (vis generandi) in the next lower grade, the *anima mundi.* Her Cupid is the desire that inspires her to translate the sparks of divine beauty into the bodies of the third grade of the hierarchy, *natura.* She is born from the principles of the *mens angelica* that the poets call Jupiter and Dione. The contradictory myths of the birth of Venus, then, no longer threaten the prestige of mythology, but conceal the nature of the cosmos that, in the Neoplatonic reading, mythology presupposes.

This multiplication of entities may seem obscurantist, but it allows Ficino not only to explain discrepancies that Boccaccio had been able only to acknowledge, but also to resolve them. As in Plato's parable of the cave, the entities in each grade of Ficino's hierarchy are shadows or simulacra of those in the superior grade, both representing and obscuring the higher realities (2.3; 5.4). Properly speaking, then, Venus and Cupid are "duplex" (twofold) rather than double, for the first Venus and Cupid contain the second as potentials within themselves (2.7). The second pair are images of the first. The great merit of the Neoplatonic cosmology when applied to mythology is that it both multiplies and reassembles the gods, rationalizing their unity in multiplicity. There is not, for example, one Cupid who is older than the other gods and another who is younger, but one god, whose status is allusively assured by his being "the beginning and the end, the first and last of the gods" (principium . . . et finis, deorum primus atque novissimus, 5.10).

These duplex Venuses and Cupids represent metaphysical processes entirely divorced from human experience, but, because the order of the universe repeats itself in the human soul, they have their shadows also in man (see 2.7; 6.7–8). The ancient doctrine of the correspondence between macrocosm and microcosm brings Ficino's theology and cosmology down to earth where they become a psychology and an ethics, but do not lose their mythological features. Like the universe, the soul contains two Venuses accompanied by two Cupids: "When the beauty of the human body first meets our eyes, the mind, which is the first Venus in us, worships and adores the human beauty as an image of the divine beauty. . . . But the power of generation in us, which is the second Venus, desires to create another form like this. Therefore there is a Love in each case: in the former, it is the desire of contemplating Beauty; and in the latter, the desire of propagating it" (2.7).

Physical beauty should be a road by which we ascend to the higher beauty

(6.9), and therefore both loves are honorable and praiseworthy, for each is concerned with the divine image" (2.7). "Desire for physical union," on the other hand, is "bestial love," not love at all because it is not desire of beauty (1.4; 2.9). It is "madness" (insania), and to it "the sacred name of Love is given falsely" (falso sacratissimum nomen amoris tribuitur, 7.3).

The most important effect of Renaissance Neoplatonism on Cupid, then, is to shift the twin Cupids of the medieval mythographers upward so that no longer is one pair good and chaste and the other unchaste and evil. Both of Ficino's Cupids are divine; the second is a simulacrum of the first, and to both "the sacred name of Love" is given truly.[24]

The correspondence of macrocosm and microcosm has another, more subtle effect on Cupid; it links Cupid the god to Cupid the personification. As a shadow or image of divine love, human love is no longer merely an "accident in a substance," but also a "prior and essential being in the intellectual world, and thence is extended to the corporeal."[25] This extension becomes, in the sixth speech of the *Commentary*, an identity. Cupid is a daemon, half divine and half human (6.2–3). Ficino's enthusiasm for concord here leads him to neglect the dialectics of the original *Symposium*, in which Socrates proclaims Love a daemon in order to criticize rather than to fulfill the earlier speeches. For Ficino, following the ancient syncretist Dionysius the pseudo-Areopagite, Plato's daemons are our angels (6.3). The line of evolution that begins with Isidore of Seville's interpretation of Cupid as a *daemon fornicationis* and continues through the ironically angelic Amors of the *Roman de la rose* and the insidiously Biblical Amore of the *Vita Nuova* reaches its apogee in Ficino. Cupid has become a true Silenus, uniting in one figure the human effect with its divine cause. A clever transposition clinches the point. While in Plato Alcibiades had compared Socrates to a Silenus, the ugly exterior concealing a godlike interior (hence the name *Silenus Alcibiadis*), Ficino compares Socrates to Cupid (7.2; see *Symp.* 215b–217a). Both true lovers and personified love conceal divinity within themselves.

Ficino's reconciliation of the god of love with the passion he inspires puts an end to the tension that animated many of Cupid's appearances in the Middle Ages. While medieval poets dramatized the abuse of Cupid's unreal divinity, Ficino urges men to participate in his real divinity, to deify their own desires by ascending from desire for physical beauty to contemplation of God. Men may still descend the ladder of love and color their descent with "the sacred name of Love," but Cupid's real divinity makes these abuses, which had been inherent in his old ambivalence, mere contingencies. Ficino is vigorously orthodox in his approval of sex only for generation, dwells at length on the opposite of "Socratic love," and expels the profane from his "heavenly feast." But all these prohibitions do not touch upon Cupid. The divine potential figured in Cupid interests Ficino, not the dangers of abuse, and so he confidently develops the transvaluations that follow from Cupid's divinity. *Voluptas,* the daughter of Cupid and the consummation of love, becomes divine joy; *furor amoris* becomes the irrationality of holy rapture, transcending rather than rejecting reason. Ficino gives a generally positive reinterpretation to the odd collection of attributes that Eros has in Plato, and writers after Ficino regularly will reverse the ancient moralizations of Cupid's attributes to accord with his divinity. Pico della Mirandola, for example, maintains that love was blind "because he is above the intellect."[26] The mythographers Cartari and Conti will give divine significations for his other attributes as if they were commonplaces.

Ficino affirms, then, what Boccaccio had only hinted—both Cupid's divinity and his unity in multiplicity. What is more, his *Commentary*, by neglecting the discontinuities of the original, mirrors in its form the doctrine it asserts. Alain de Lille, Dante, and Petrarch, we may remember, proceeded from confusion to clarity by excluding misconceptions or abuses of Cupid's fictional divinity. Their final affirmations of Cupid followed recognition that he is merely a figure of speech. Ficino's *Commentary*, in contrast, proceeds by accretion of meaning, unfolding Cupid's unitary divinity into the multiplicities of his emanations and effects. The first three speeches deal with Love as he is in himself, but the later speeches are increasingly concerned with Love as he affects men. At the same time the hierarchy of being appears more and more in the aspect of a ladder. The *Commentary*, then, descends from the divine to the human, but at the close begins the return whose means it has explored. The last chapter, "How Thanks are to be Given to the Holy Spirit Which Has Illuminated and Inspired Us for this Discussion," gives thanks to the Love that was discussed: "The cause and teacher of this most fortunate discovery was the very same Love who has been discovered. . . . With the result that, aroused by love of finding Love, so to speak, we have sought and found Love, so that we must be thankful to Him equally for the question and its answer" (7.17). The form of the *Commentary* itself and the wordplay of its conclusion reveal the self-reverting circuit of love which lies at the center of Ficino's system and which restored both divinity and singleness to Cupid.[27]

With one exception, the writers of the *trattati d'amore* who followed Ficino and Pico were popularizers. Their works, all in the vernacular, "show little originality of thought," but for that very reason helped to fix as literary conventions ideas that philosophical scrutiny might have exploded. In matters of detail and emphasis, they differ among themselves and with Ficino—even Pico invented a third Venus—but for the most part they faithfully reproduce Ficino's central ideas.[28] Love is the desire for beauty, a definition which, as in Ficino, excludes sexual appetite. The cosmos remains a hierarchy of emanations created and preserved by love and, at the same time, a ladder upon which men can ascend from love of physical beauty to contemplation of God. Moreover, the form of several *trattati* mirrors this ascent, though here they modify Ficino, who had seen in the *Symposium* a more complex circular pattern. Because none of the *trattatisti* was bound to a text as Ficino was, their borrowed ideas often slip free from the mythological vehicle through which

Ficino had expounded them. With few variations, however, his realignment of the mythology of Cupid and Venus held, always ready to rejoin the doctrines which had provoked and justified it.

The *trattati* we have to consider were not published in the order of their composition, and this fact may justify treating them in an artificial order. Since Bembo's *Gli Asolani* and Castiglione's *Cortegiano* are linked by more than the common figure of Pietro Bembo, it will be convenient to keep them together and to begin with Mario Equicola's *Libro di natura d'amore* and Leone Ebreo's *Dialoghi d'amore.*

Equicola began his chaotic work in 1494, aiming apparently to collect everything ever written about love. His eclecticism is easily ridiculed, but it led him to recognize a historical tradition similar, except for its inclusiveness, to the one we have been surveying. Book 5, for example, contains a chapter entitled "How the Latin and Greek Poets, Provençal minstrels, French rhymers, Tuscan story tellers, and Spanish troubadours have praised their loves . . ." (253v). In the first book, he reviews the moderns more particularly, among whom are Guittone d'Arezzo, Cavalcanti, Dante, Petrarch, Barbarino, the "Romant de la Rose," Boccaccio, Ficino, Giovanni Pico della Mirandola, and Bembo.

Equicola's own ideas are barely recognizable amid his hundreds of references, but in a sense his inclusiveness, his refusal to make distinctions, is his deepest argument. He cites, for example, Dionysius, Jerome, and Augustine on the Bible's failure to discriminate consistently among its words for love (80r–82r). In a chapter entitled "Divisione d'amore," he offers several categorizations, but asserts: "Whether we understand love to be divine or angelic or intellectual or animal or natural, we do not believe it to be other than one force" (104r). For Equicola, the fundamental unity of his subject seems to justify the baffling multiplicity that he records with "wearisome and empty precision."[29] Cupid gains a similarly amorphous unity from Equicola's catalogue of his various genealogies; he too is a single impulse about which men have had diverse notions (93v–96r). As in Ficino, his unity includes both the god and the passion of the mind, for, by a genealogical mystery, "he was born . . . before the elements were divided from the confusion of Chaos; born before us, reborn with us, and continually renewing himself with us through being the child of the senses and taking from them his first being" (93v).

Equicola's diffuse Neoplatonism saves his idea of love and his Cupid from the moral ambiguity which his eclecticism might otherwise have produced. He goes beyond even Ficino in defining love "simply as the desire for the Good," but more precisely as "that desire by which we are drawn to produce and give birth in beauty" (56v–57r). His affirmations of Cupid's divinity on the whole outweigh the denials he repeats from his authorities. In the "Laude de Amore" which prefaces Book 3, for example, Cupid's "somma potenza" gives to books eternal life and to their authors eternal fame, in addition to its more conventional benefits: moving the wheels of the "mundana machina," holding the elements in concord, perpetually regenerating the Creation and so forth (120r–

120v). Despite its shapelessness and inelegant style, the *Libro di natura d'-amore* enjoyed a wide diffusion. Equicola added little to the Neoplatonic transvaluation of Cupid except the weight of his reading, but that in itself helped to give it a currency and accessibility lacking in Ficino and Pico.

Leone Ebreo's *Dialoghi d'amore,* written in 1502 but not published until 1535, is an anomaly among the *trattati.* Popular without being popularizing, it is an original and critical restatement of Neoplatonic doctrines, as befits dialogues between an ardent Philo and a skeptical Sophia. Leone is far less complacent than the other *trattatisti,* and his *Dialoghi* mirror neither the descent of divine love to human nor the return ascent. He is also more of a mythographer, giving Philo ingenious interpretations which reassert the old moral distinctions between multiple Cupids, yet also affirm their divinity. This theodicy of Cupid is closer, in spirit though not in detail, to the third book of *The Faerie Queene* than are any of the other *trattati.*

Leone repeats the Neoplatonic doctrine that the cosmos is a hierarchy of emanations animated and unified by the self-reverting circuit of love.[30] Human love ought to be desire for the incorporeal divine beauty, traces of which still survive in the body: "Love . . . for inferior [corporeal] beauty is fitting and good only when its purpose is to extract from it the spiritual beauty which is truly lovable, and when love is mainly directed towards this spiritual beauty, and the corporeal only receives the second share, and this for the sake of the spiritual" (397).

Men who desire the body for its own sake, on the other hand, imitate Narcissus in mistaking the image for the reality. Both impulses are species of desire, but only the first merits the name love; the second is mere appetite (429). The distinction parallels Ficino's between human and bestial love, but Leone's mythological vehicle does not, for he reinstates the medieval distinction between a good and evil god of love. Moreover, in order to name his two gods he breaks with both Ficino and the medieval consensus by differentiating between Amor and Cupid. Amor, for Leone, represents virtuous and divine love whose "end is the contemplation of the beauty and omnipotence of Jupiter"; Cupid represents "voluptuous and wanton love and the lust of the body."[31]

Traditionally, as we have seen, distinction between a good and an evil god of love leads to identification of the second as a personification deified by rhetorical abuse, as in the passage from Seneca used by Boccaccio and Bernardo Lapini: "Base and servile lust feigned love to be a god and, in order to be less restrained, has given passion the title of an unreal divinity." Leone breaks with this tradition too, ignoring completely the issue of abuse and maintaining Ficino's unification of gods and personifications. Both Cupid and Amor are psychological accidents in men, but also "prior and essential being[s] in the intellectual world," Platonic ideas to which it was natural that the ancients attributed divinity.[32] Cupid is a god, Leone maintains, because each vice as well as each virtue has "for divine principle an immaterial Idea": "Among the Platonic Ideas there are principles of good and virtue and others that are principles of evil and vices, because the Universe needs both for its preservation. And in the light of that need every evil is a good" (119). A god, or at least a divine principle, then causes base and servile lust in humans, making the issue of abuse negligible. Leone's determinism, to which astrology also contributes, overturns the usual logic that had governed the mythology of love and gives even to voluptuous and wanton love the title of a real divinity.

This odd blend of Platonism and determinism may seem to offer, in Nesca Robb's words, "a somewhat unstable basis for practical morality," but, as Leone employs it, it leads to a morality considerably more practical than Ficino's.[33] Jewish tradition did not emphasize free will as a condition of moral responsibility, and Leone, a Jew expelled from Spain, made his determinism the basis for a commonsensical justification of human love and its integral portion of physical desire. Although he outlines the Ficinian ascent, the cosmos appears for the most part as a static hierarchy rather than as a ladder. Most men, he implies through Philo, the dominant speaker in the dialogue, must be content to do God's bidding in this world, not hoping to rise above it.[34]

Philo himself is not a Platonic lover, although he believes that true love, like Ciceronian *amicitia*, is born of reason (57). He argues that virtuous human love entails desiring the body for the sake of the soul, and not, as in Ficino, ceasing to desire the body. Indeed, Leone praises physical desire, not merely for the traditional reason that it causes the species to increase and multiply, but also because "physical union increases and perfects the spiritual love" (55). Sophia has objected that gratification turns physical desire to disgust, but Philo replies, "nay, it makes possible a closer and more binding union, which comprises the actual conversion of each lover into the other, or rather the fusion of both into one. . . . Thus the love endures in greater unity and perfection; and the lover remains continually desirous of enjoying the beloved in union; which is the true definition of love" (54).

Philo's true definition affirming loyal human love clearly contemplates Judaeo-Christian marriage rather than Neoplatonic ascent, which, indeed, requires both transcendence of physical desire and disloyal striving for superior beauty. Although a species of love may be the child of desire, Philo goes on to say, desire is also the child of true love. In its true definition, that is, human love includes desire. Had this definition controlled his mythology, Philo would have found it harder to draw the distinction between Cupid and Amor. He implicitly concedes as much at the end of the *Dialoghi*. Attempting to explain why his virtuous love causes him such suffering, he returns to the usual explanation for the evil in love—human imperfection thwarts the ends of divine benevolence: "Although love brings affliction, torment, distress and grief in its train, and many other troubles which it would be tedious to describe to you, these are not its true end, but rather that sweet delight which is the very contrary of these things" (462).

Later *trattatisti* such as Varchi, Speroni, Betussi, and Tullia d'Aragona take up Leone's affirmation of human love as against Neoplatonic asceticism, but seldom his distinction between Cupid and Amor. The tradition accepts, almost without question, the principle that a god may not be the cause of evil. Spenser, who may have known Leone and who, except in the second pair of the *Fowre Hymnes,* shares his idealization of loyal human love, accepts this principle too, but not without questions formulated, like Leone's, through the vehicle of mythology.[35]

With Pietro Bembo's *Gli Asolani,* published in 1505, the *trattato d'amore* becomes a literary form and rejoins the literary tradition. For Ficino, who coined the phrase, "platonic love" meant virtuous love between male friends, akin to Cicero's *amicitia,* and it retained that meaning in Pico and in Ficino's disciple Francesco Cattani da Diacceto.[36] It was Bembo, writing shortly before Leone, who transformed "platonic love" into an idealization of love between the sexes and at the same time linked it to the literary tradition with borrowings from the *stilnovisti* and especially Petrarch's *Trionfi. Gli Asolani* is a work of literature by virtue of more than literary reminiscences, however. Set in the paradisiacal and fully evoked garden of the palace of Asolo, its dialogues substitute idealized courtly conversation for Ficino's thinly masked commentary and Leone's philosophical dialectic. Finally, Bembo did not merely rehearse Ficino's doctrines with variations, but dramatized them.

Gli Asolani records a *tenzone* consisting of three speeches with interwoven dialogue. Perottino, the unsuccessful lover, argues that love is "always evil and never can be good."[37] Gismondo, an "amorous and pleasant bachelor," counters with a redefinition that includes a willingness to personify love. "Love [Amore] is a natural affection of our minds and therefore necessarily sober, reasonable, and good. So, whenever an emotion of ours is not sober, not only does it fail to be reasonable and good, but by the same token it cannot be [L]ove [Amors]" (100).

Lavinello, the third speaker, takes a middle ground. Love may be both good and evil depending upon its object: "Virtuous love [il buono amore] is a desire for beauty of mind no less than body, . . . [and if] we are led to beauty only by our eyes or ears or thoughts, all that lovers seek with their other senses, unless they seek it in order to nourish life, is evil and not virtuous love" (157–58). This affirmation of human love is further qualified in the speech of a hermit which Lavinello reports, just as Socrates had reported the speech of Diotima in the *Symposium.* The Hermit criticizes Lavinello's complacency; although his love is not mingled with bestial desire, neither does it prod him to ascend above mere human beauty: "For virtuous love is not merely desire of beauty, as you believe, but desire of true beauty, which is not of that human and mortal kind which fades, but is immortal and divine; and yet these beauties that you praise may lift us to it, provided we regard them in the proper way" (182).

Cupid plays an interesting, but minor role in this debate. Perottino and

Gismondo agree that Cupid is a personification to which men have attributed divinity, although they agree on little else and indeed put their common opinion to opposite uses. Lavinello suggests that this opinion is dangerous blasphemy, but does not explicitly extend his Neoplatonic resolution to mythology.

Perottino begins his speech by denying Love's divinity in words that echo Petrarch's guide in the *Triumphus Cupidinis* and mock Boccaccio's genealogies:

> Love is not the son of Venus . . . as we read in the fables of poets who, differing among themselves even in this very lie, make him the son of diverse goddesses, as if anyone could have various mothers. Neither is he begotten by Mars or Mercury or Vulcan or any other god, but rather is generated in our minds by those dark and base progenitors, overweening lust and sluggish idleness [da soverchia lascivia e da pigro ozio degli uomini], and is born almost the first offspring of wickedness and vice.

This knowledge does him, like Petrarch, little good. One of the ladies asks why the poets invented such fables since "whoever does evil is certainly not a god" (27). Perottino replies that, as the first teachers of conduct to uncivilized men, the poets deified love in order to show "under the name of *god* [nome d'Idio] what power this passion wielded over human minds" (28). Once men had made love a god, "they thought it fitting to give him a certain form, in order that he might be more completely known," and Perottino goes on to give a brief and conventional explanation of Cupid's attributes (39). He attributes no more *virtù* to Cupid in himself than did Aimeric de Peguilhan, Alain de Lille, Dante, or Petrarch, but argues that once a man concedes him power, Cupid becomes for that man an omnipotent deity (40). Literalizing poetic commonplaces like Dante in the *Vita Nuova* or Spenser in the Busyrane episode, Perottino mockingly presents Petrarchan conceits as miracles of the god: "One man lives in fire like a salamander; another, having lost all vital heat, grows as cold as ice; another melts like snow in the sunlight; a fourth, with no more sense or feeling than the rocks, stays mute and motionless. One lives without his heart, having given it to a lady who tears it in a thousand pieces every hour. . . . Does it not seem fitting . . . that the worker of these miracles should be called [God]?" (28, 36). Like the dreamer of the *Triumphus Cupidinis*, Perottino justifies revelling in the pains of love by pointing to a deity he knows to be fictitious.

Gismondo, the second speaker of the dialogue, retorts that all Love's miracles are merely "empty fables," inventions of lovers who, "no less than poets have a special license to feign things which are often far from any resemblance to the truth" (86). So too is the "imaginary portrait" of Perottino's imaginary god (90). Like Petrarch in the *Triumphus Pudicitiae*, Gismondo condemns the use of Cupid to mask self-indulgence as divine compulsion. A man enjoying freewill ought to confess his own responsibility rather than blame another. "But what am I saying?" he continues; Perottino intends precisely the opposite.

"The better to conceal his own falsehood and weakness, he complains of love, . . . laying every fault upon him" (74). The first two speakers of *Gli Asolani* thus follow the pattern of the first two *Trionfi*, although, with Petrarch's moral seriousness refined away, it is now a harmonious discord of courtly manners and personalities, though not yet the Alexandrian *préciosité* of the Pléiade.

Because Gismondo affirms love entirely on grounds of Nature, he has no interest in a *god* of love except to refute Perottino's arguments. He does not, for example, reverse Perottino's negative interpretation of Cupid's attributes. Yet among the social customs of sixteenth century Italy was a parlor game called "the Figure of Love"—"where it must be explained why Love is represented blind, young, naked, and armed with a bow . . . , and it is enjoined upon the company to give one reason which shall redound to the praise of Love and one to his blame, as Bembo did in the *Asolani*."[38] But no one in *Gli Asolani* gives an interpretation of Cupid's attributes that redounds to his praise. The parlor game may serve to exemplify how easily the mythological vehicle could rejoin even doctrine that, like Gismondo's, explicitly rejected mythology.

Lavinello, the third speaker, although rehearsing Ficino's doctrines, avoids Ficino's mythology almost entirely. The love he propounds, though in concord with true divinity, never becomes a god, except in one rejoinder to Gismondo, who had blasphemed Love by praising the "lower" senses of touch, taste, and smell: "And since Love is called a mighty god, I would encourage you to amend your error by doing the very opposite of Stesichorus in antiquity. . . . You should as much disparage these three senses as you contrived to praise them yesterday" (159).

Love's divinity here is, however, merely ornamental, and on the whole *Gli Asolani* reduces him to a personification more completely even than Boccaccio's *Genealogia*. In form, *Gli Asolani* clearly mirrors the Neoplatonic ascent from natural to divine love, but, unlike Ficino's *Commentary*, it reaches its final affirmation of love by repudiating the god of love. Bembo himself was given the opportunity to amend this fault, however, in the fourth book of Castiglione's *Cortegiano*, where, like Stesichorus, he recants, reuniting the god of love with the Neoplatonic justification of Love's deity.

Though in form *Gli Asolani* traces both the new ladder of love and the old progress through misconception and abuse to truth, it does not uphold the Hermit's doctrines unequivocally. Instead, it limits their application on grounds worth noticing, since Castiglione will make them the starting point for his discussion of love. The conversations of *Gli Asolani* take place on three successive days during the celebration of a royal wedding. Three ladies accompany Perottino, Gismondo, and Lavinello in the garden and join in their disputatious pastime. The idealized garden of Asolo itself derives from a long tradition of literary gardens, and, like most of these, it is a landscape of leisure, youth, and love. Age is as firmly, if not as explicitly, excluded from this garden as it was from the garden of Deduit in the *Roman de la rose*. Both the occasion and setting of Bembo's dialogues seem, therefore, to qualify the asceticism of the aged Hermit on his lonely mountain, and the Hermit himself associates, as Ficino did not, the Neoplatonic ladder with the old theme of youth and age. As in the *Roman de la rose*, natural love is almost inevitable and therefore appropriate in youth. In age one must repudiate transient earthly beauty, but the natural succession of man's life, as in the *Trionfi*, asserts continuity despite repudiation. The two sources of continuity come together when the Hermit alludes to his own youth before affirming that earthly beauty can conduct to divine beauty (181–2). Although *Gli Asolani* concludes on the mountaintop, it makes clear that one path there leads through the garden.

Midway through the fourth book of *Il Cortegiano*, the problem arises that, if the courtier's highest function is "with his worthinesse and credit" to "encline his prince to virtue," he must necessarily be old, for wisdom does not come in youth.[39] But how then can he be a lover? Pietro Bembo undertakes to answer this question, and his speech thus takes as its premise one of the conclusions of *Gli Asolani*, the non-Ficinian association of the ladder of love with the succession of youth and age. This famous speech, though in some ways irrelevant to the whole, is the reason that Castiglione's courtesy book, begun in 1508 and published in 1528, appears among the *trattati d'amore*.[40] Although conflating Ficino, Benivieni and Pico, and the real Bembo, Castiglione does without the details of Neoplatonic cosmology and omits its accompanying mythology entirely. His Amor, like Dante's, is not the son of Venus and has none of Cupid's attributes. Nevertheless, in *Il Cortegiano* Castiglione's Bembo restores to Amor the divinity that in *Gli Asolani* the real Bembo had denied to Cupid.

Bembo's speech both expounds and mounts "the stayres, by the which a man may ascend to true love" (307). As in Ficino, these "stayres" also connect love the emotion with love the god. Bembo begins with "a little discourse to declare what love is" (303). It is "a certain desire to enjoy beauty," namely the beauty of the human body which is itself "an influx of divine goodness" (Maier, ed., pp. 514–15; my translation). Love is therefore a single impulse with a divine object, but it may take various forms, since men perceive beauty through three faculties: sense, reason, and understanding. Sense predominates in youth and instills the false opinion that to possess the body is to enjoy beauty. Love is therefore not to be blamed for the torments of lovers; rather "the cause . . . of this wretchednesse in mens mindes is principally Sense." Indeed, people "wrapped in this sensuall love, which is a very rebel against reason, . . . make themselves unworthie to enjoy the favors and benefits which love bestoweth upon his true subjects" (305–6).

This routine figure of speech is Bembo's first personification of love, and it suggests, as does the whole argument, that the issue is not between true and false Love, but between Love's true and false subjects. Yet Castiglione does not share Leone's determinism. Love's false subjects may mature into true ones; sensual love can be a stage on the way to divine love. Since youths are naturally inclined to sense, the courtier, too, may love sensually while he is young. But when youth is past, he must change his ways and keep aloof from sensual desire "as from the lowest step of the stayres, by the which a man may ascend to true love" (312, 307).

Castiglione's Bembo is a reluctant speaker and must be pressed to expound the happiness of older lovers. In his explanation, the personified love who had earlier been exonerated from responsibility for sensual love becomes explicitly divine: "I will not refuse to reason upon this noble matter. And because I know my selfe unworthie to talke of the most holy mysteries of love, I beseech him to leade my thought and my tongue so, that I may shew this excellent Courtier how to love contrary to the wonted manner of the common ignorant sorte" (312).

The prayer is answered. As Bembo reviews the steps, derived from Benivieni and Pico, whereby a man can purify his desire of all earthly dross, he mounts them into the very "sacro furor amoroso" he describes. At the same time he rises from the third person indirect prayer quoted above to an ecstatic apostrophe to "Amor divinissimo":

> What tongue mortall is there then (O most holy love) that can sufficiently prayse thy worthines? Thou most beautifull, most good, most wise, art derived of the unitie of the heavenly beautie, goodnesse and wisedom, and therein dost thou abide. . . . Thou the most sweet bond of the world, a meane betwixt heavenly and earthly thinges, with a bountifull temper bendest the high vertues to the government of the lower, and turning backe the mindes of mortall men to their beginning, couplest them with it. Thou with agreement bringest the Elements in one, stirrest nature to bring forth, and that which ariseth and is borne for the succession of the life. . . . Therefore vouchsafe (Lorde) to harken to our prayers, pour thyselfe into our harts, and with the brightnesse of thy most holy fire lighten our darknesse. (321)

These are excerpts, much less than half, of Bembo's final praise and supplication, but even in translation they show clearly the liturgical echoes and rhetorical fervor with which Castiglione identifies Amor with God. Ficino's similar identification at the end of his *Commentary* may, in comparison, seem merely clever.

"From the doctrinal standpoint," it has been remarked, "Castiglione offered nothing that had not been said," but he, like all the *trattatisti,* offered it in a unique combination.[41] All of the *trattatisti* attempted a theodicy of love; by emphasizing sequence rather than hierarchy, Castiglione affirmed both the singleness and the divinity of love more convincingly even than Ficino. His "Amor divinissimo" is not Cupid, but later writers such as Natale Conti would find it easy to reunite them.

The main project of Renaissance mythography, at least as far as it influenced imaginative literature, was Boccaccio's—to reassemble the system of the ancient gods—but not all Renaissance mythographers shared this aim. In fact, of the three great sixteenth century Italian mythographers, only Conti, the last of them and the most influential, sought to restore the pantheon to order and integrity. Giraldi and Cartari, the two earlier mythographers, are worth considering here, however, because the contrast with Conti may suggest one reason for his greater influence.

Lilio Gregorio Giraldi was the earliest and most scholarly of the three, but the very scholarship that wins him modern esteem diminished the influence on imaginative literature of his *Historia de deis gentium* (1548). For each god, Giraldi catalogues names, epithets, images, and etymologies from various authorities and according to various local cults. Against this scholarly dismembering of the gods, he opposes no principle of reintegration such as Boccaccio's genealogy or Ficino's cosmology. His Cupid is unequivocally multiple: "I do not present one Cupid, but there are said to be many because loves of things are diverse: we love different things differently, and therefore Plato called Love a monster with many heads."[42] Plato's image affirms the unity of the monster despite the multiplicity of its heads, but Giraldi's learning effectively dissolves both the unity and the divinity of Love. As a genuine history of classical religion, Giraldi's volume helped neither to explain nor extend the poetic tradition of the god of love. Perhaps for that reason he proved less useful to poets and artists than to the later mythographers Cartari and Conti, both of whom plundered his lore.

Vincenzo Cartari's *Imagini degli dei degli antichi* (1556) was intended chiefly as a handbook for painters and sculptors, providing them, according to its publisher, "with ideas for a thousand beautiful inventions with which to adorn their statutes and paintings."[43] Unlike Giraldi, Cartari is a popularizer, writing, and even citing his ancient authorities, in the vernacular. But like Giraldi, he supplies no principle of re-integration to counter the multiplicity of *images* of the gods which are his main concern. He reproduces ideas that in some of the *trattati* had made Cupid both single and a god, but his Neoplatonism is unassimilated. It contributes to, but does not control, his discussion, from which Cupid therefore emerges either as a single god or as a multiple personification, much as he had been before Ficino.

Cartari begins with the single god:

Of all the affections of our spirit none is more common or more beautiful nor has greater power than that which is seen not only in us, but also in the eternal God (although in Him it is only pure substance and not emotion or passion), in the angels, and in all the ranks of the blessed, in each of the elements and in all things which are made out of them. . . . Because of these things, it is not surprising if the ancients regarded him among their gods, having not yet seen the light of truth, and that which they ought to have given to the Creator of all, they gave to his creatures, and as they did not know where virtue comes from, they worshipped many things as gods and set up their diverse statues and in various images depicted them, according as they operate in the human spirit. (256)

So far Cartari's account might be medieval, but Neoplatonic influence soon becomes apparent. He has searched

> the most authoritative writers, who considered Amore in diverse fashions and diverse modes because they saw how diverse were his powers. From whence it came to be said that there is not one Amore but many, and two principal ones were set down by Plato, just as he recognized two Venuses. From the one celestial Venus was born the celestial Cupid, that divine love which lifts the human spirit to the contemplation of God, of the separate spirits which we call angels, and of heavenly things. (256–57)

The multiplicity of Cupids results, then, from the same error as polytheism itself—judging divine things by their human effects—but Cartari does not go on to identify the earthly Cupid as a simulacrum of the celestial as Ficino had done. For Cartari, there are several Cupids, although only one divine Cupid, "entirely pure, spotless, and most true" (tutto puro, mondo, e sincerissimo). Reversal of the usual significances of his attributes follows from this affirmation. His youthful body represents uncorrupted perfection, his arrows the beams of heavenly beauty, his wings the power to lift our souls above the base earth. But to dilate upon divine love, Cartari says, is to wander from his subject, which, it becomes clear, is the imagery of earthly love (257). The ambiguity of Cupid's torch returns him to his subject. It signifies the radiance of divine love, but, as its light comes from destructive fire, it also signifies the mixed torment and delight of earthly love. Cartari's subject, then, is less the single divine cause than its multiple and troubling human effects, and most of his chapter, by treating earthly love, denies the affirmation of Cupid's divinity which has gone before.

In the Neoplatonists, the hierarchical relation between divine cause and human effect constituted a theodicy of love, but Cartari is not interested in theodicy. Despite his knowledge of Neoplatonic doctrine, he recognizes between love the god and love the passion only the old relation of abuse. He translates a denial of Cupid's divinity from Seneca and amplifies it with phrases that echo the *Triumphus Cupidinis:*

> The error of blind and miserable mortals, in order to hide their foolish and vain desire, feigned love to be a god. . . . Love is a vice of an unsound mind. . . . Idleness nourishes it and human lust. . . . But if anyone resists when blind desire consents to evil, . . . love immediately loses all its power.[44]

An exposition of the usual negative meanings of Cupid's attributes follows a few pages later, and Cartari finds no more intrinsic relation between the *in bono* and *in malo* interpretations of Cupid than did the much earlier Vatican mythographers. Where Ficino had shifted categories so that both Cupids were divine, Cartari reproduces the medieval distinction between a celestial Cupid, whom it is appropriate to call a god, and a personification of mere human desires, which men deify at their peril. Moreover, identification of the earthly Cupid as a personification quickly leads Cartari, as it had led Boccaccio, to assert Cupid's multiplicity:

> But if Cupid is no other than loving desire directed from us toward things, Love will not be one or two, but rather many, as those poets maintain who in their fables often express the powers of our souls (the diverse passions and their effects) and therefore say that there are many Loves . . . because we do not all love the same thing, nor in the same manner, but each man loves differently and often different things, which could not happen if there were only one Love. (260)

Among the poets who describe many Cupids, Cartari translates or paraphrases Propertius, Philostratus, Silius Italicus, and Apuleius.

Once having acknowledged the abuse that makes a false divinity of human desires and emphasized the multitude of those desires, Cartari can safely turn to various depictions of single Cupids, most of which are the personified passion of the moralistic tradition.[45] Pictures of Cupid conquering Pan or holding a key conceal doctrines of the "Platonici" that give him divine powers, "but Cupid does not therefore always have such powers that others do not often have more than he" (269). Cartari ends his chapter by translating Ausonius's poem on Cupid crucified, which, like the *Triumphus Pudicitiae*, celebrates the constraint of a powerless Cupid by a host of women. Nothing could be further from the ecstasy of divine love toward which several of the *trattati* ascend. While the *trattatisti*'s formal continuity reflected the continuity of the Neoplatonic universe, Cartari's fragmented account of Cupid reflects merely the multiplicity of his material, which is the pictorial traditions of Cupid. Within those images he looks for no unity of the being or idea imaged.

In contrast to Cartari and Giraldi, Natale Conti affirms both the unity and divinity of Cupid. He takes as his subjects the gods themselves, rather than their history or images, and treats them as poetic signs rather than as objects of antique worship or modern imitation. His book, published in 1568, is therefore appropriately entitled *Mythologiae sive explicationis fabularum libri decem.* Conti shows a predilection for Greek authorities, for which he provides Latin translations, yet his new authorities illuminate the old tradition. It would be misleading to claim too much for Conti; his account of Cupid does not represent a grand summation of the poetical uses of the god of love. Yet he does join, in an especially problematic way, the medieval concern for the abuse of Cupid's divinity with the Renaissance desire to affirm an irreducible truth within that dangerous fiction. Conti does not offer a theodicy of Cupid, as do the *trattatisti;* rather he offers a Cupid who himself embodies the problem of theodicy.

Conti begins by conceding that about Cupid's parents "there is no small doubt among the authors, since some believe that there is one Cupid and others that there are several."[46] While dutifully recording the several genealogies, he inclines to dismiss their importance, quotes Theocritus's noncommittal announcement that he was "born from whichever of the gods were his parents," and concludes that despite the various genealogies "everything said literally about Love is transferred to the one son of Venus" (tamen ad unum Veneris filium omnia propre quae de Amore dicta sunt, *transferuntur*, 404–5, my emphasis). The idea of transference is Conti's contribution to mythography. Here it allows him to convert Cupid's multiplicity into unity, acknowledging the malleability of these fables in a manner impossible for mythographers who treat myths as the scriptures of ancient religion. *Transfero* and *translatio* are the usual Latin terms for figurative or metaphorical substitution, and throughout Conti's account Cupid appears less as a god than as a poetic sign to which, among other attributes, men have ascribed divinity. His victories over the other gods, for example, are represented by an epigram in which he despoils them "of their attributes" (suis insignibus); they are the victories of one iconographical sign over others (407).

The long central section of Conti's chapter works out the logic governing Cupid's attributes, essentially the same logic that we have traced in the earlier works from Andreas to Boccaccio. After cataloguing Cupid's usual attributes, Conti turns to his original use and subsequent abuse:

> To speak briefly, these attributes, these powers, these spoils, these fierce companions, this hateful blindness, and this age least apt for prudence were given to Cupid by the ancient poets in order to express the insanity of men's lust so that nothing would seem more abhorrent to an honorable and well-disciplined man. Nevertheless, all of them are so converted *(conversa)* to men's pleasures that some even find sweetness to the spirit in recounting them. This seems to me very much like someone suffering from a serious illness whose very bad digestion turns medicines themselves to poisons. Cupid, then, was invented to deter men from depravity, but the mob of mortals worshipped him as a god, since they did not know that God is the author of all kindness, generosity, temperance, and all uprightness and humanity. (409)

Conti's discussion is clearer than Boccaccio's, but his logic is the same. The malleability of fables, their openness to figurative "conversion," proves dangerous. For men sick with lust, Cupid's unreal divinity converts him from medicine to poison.

Still following Boccaccio, Conti gives a litany of evils caused by "this god of the insane and frenzied," concluding: "Thus no man can rightly be held wise who praises Cupid" (410). But the abuse of Cupid, not Cupid himself, causes these evils, and Conti quickly revises his opinion: "Nevertheless, it is truer that Cupid is not evil, but is rather a pretext for evil action to vicious and reprobate men who are evil by their own inclination" (411). A few lines later the "god of the insane and furious" has become "the best of the gods," the name for the heroic ardor of Virgil's Euryalus and Nisus.

Up to this point Conti's account has followed the medieval pattern in which an affirmation of Cupid follows recognition that he is only a personification and a lengthy repudiation of the abuse that makes him a god. But for Conti this reduction of Cupid to a passion of the mind is only a preliminary. When Boccaccio wrote that it was "now time to put aside fictions and see what is hidden beneath them," he proceeded to expose Cupid as a personification. But the dialectic of abuse is not what is serious about Cupid for Conti, and only now does he move beneath Cupid's fictional surface: "Enough of the fables concerning Cupid; now let us investigate what serious matter is hidden beneath them" (412.)

What Conti finds hidden beneath Cupid's fables is extremely serious—"that ancient and onely power that formes and fashions all things out of Matter," as Bacon, developing Conti's interpretation, will later put it.[47] Beneath the fable that Cupid is the eldest of the gods is concealed the fundamental force of Empedoclean physics—the primal attraction that, binding the warring elements, fashioned the universe from chaos. A physical force might seem sub-human, but it is Conti's route to a general affirmation of Cupid's divinity. The elements can obey only a "principle more divine" (diviniore principio) than themselves, and this principle shortly becomes a "divine force" (vim divinam) and then, "to speak more accurately, a divine mind (Mentem divinam) which induces these same motions in nature itself" (412). Indeed, Conti says, this was Cupid's original meaning; only later was he "brought in, personified as it were, from the universal nature of things because of the unrestrained appetites of individuals" (412–13). In looking beneath the surface of the fables concerning Cupid, Conti uncovers an original and still operative divinity.

Reinterpretation of Cupid's attributes follows from and extends this affirmation of his divinity. His wings signify the swift flight of divine goodness more than the inconstancy of men's desires, his arrows "the miraculous swift-ness of the divine spirit" more than "the torments suffered by fools," his blindness the darkness of divine counsels more than the disgrace of men blind to their own dignity. For Conti, these contrary significances are not incompat-ible, but related through his process of *translatio:* "This god was feigned to be naked in order to explain the disgracefulness of lust, but transferred *(translatum)* to divine things it signifies the immense liberality and munificence of God" (413–14). *Translatio,* however, is also the very process by which wicked men translate an image of disgracefulness into a justification for it. In order once again to forestall this abuse, Conti denies that Cupid's divinity may be "transferred" to irrational human desires, which ought to be called madness or insanity rather than a god. The chapter ends with an even more forceful negation from the *Greek Anthology:* "Love is not a god, but the harmful disquiet of all men" (414).

Despite its final negation, Conti's chapter as a whole affirms Cupid's divinity. Unlike the other mythographers, he recognizes only one Cupid, a true Silenus whose divinity is hidden within an exterior anything but divine, signifying human madness and depravity. Conti's account, unlike Cartari's but like many of the *trattati*, ascends from sexual passion to divine love, though sexual passion is not excluded. The god and the personification are brought into a relation which endures despite repudiation of the abuse that transfers divinity to the personification. Conti's Silenus-Cupid thus exemplifies what Harry Berger has identified as a characteristic of the Renaissance imagination:

> Where medieval theories of art are always conjunctive—pleasure *plus* profit—or disjunctive—pleasure, ornament, vividness *here*, allegory, philosophy, theology, worship *there*—the enlightened Renaissance understanding . . . is *profit inside pleasure*.[48]

Conti's Cupid is problematical, however, for in him the outward pleasure is not innocent and the inward profit is infinite. Ficino had escaped (or evaded) this problem by realigning the two Cupids of the medieval tradition so that both were honorable and had then joined them through the doctrines of emanation and correspondence of macrocosm and microcosm. Like Leone, Conti rejects this sleight of hand, but, instead of affirming both good and evil *gods* of love, he fuses the god and the sinful passion into a single figure. Ficino or Pico might have seen this coincidence of opposites as itself a divine attribute, but for Conti it merely sharpens the problem of theodicy. A *god* of love cannot produce these effects, yet they are the outward and visible sign of his inward and invisible deity. Conti does not resolve this problem in the poetic theology of love; rather he presents a Cupid who incarnates it. Spenser, whose legend of chastity is also a theodicy of Cupid, will, like Conti, reject Neoplatonic evasions, yet affirm the singleness of Cupid.

6

Spenser's Minor Poems

BOCCACCIO nervously saw himself in the preface to the *Genealogia deorum* as a new Aesculapius, collecting the scattered fragments of the ancient gods and restoring them to life. Among the other mythographers and Neo-platonists, only Conti shared that aim, and he brought it closer to achievement than did Boccaccio by trying to imagine and reconstruct an antiquity in which the mythical gods made sense, in which poetic theology had an integrity and coherence that might make it more than poetic. Conti shared this project, as well as the general task of reading the tradition, with the poets and especially with Edmund Spenser, who in *The Faerie Queene* and much of his other poetry set the ancient gods to work in a world apart, an English antiquity with a coherent theology which is its own yet mirrors ours.

Spenser's poetic theology is predominantly a theology of Cupid. Though not what Beatrice was to Dante or Laura to Petrarch, Cupid is nevertheless to Spenser an archimage, one of the organizing ideas of his work, more sustained even than the image of himself as the poet-shepherd Colin Clout, which inaugurates and concludes his work and occupies a key position in the middle. Spenser's Cupid is never merely a mythological ornament, even when he seems most to be, as in *Muiopotmos*. Cupid's prominence testifies not only to Spenser's lifelong meditation on the nature and value of human love, but also to the growth and decay of his idea of poetic theology in its most ambitious sense—the idea that poetry can be a kind of scripture. Spenser made Cupid the deity of a poetic gospel that, unlike the ironic revelations of medieval poems, will not rival the Bible, but be its servant and guide. Poetic theology on this scale is an impossible project, as poets before and after Spenser also learned, but in attempting it Spenser engaged nearly all the phases of Cupid's career in post-classical poetry and brought it to culmination. He therefore claims and rewards closer attention than other poets in this study.

Spenser's use of Cupid in his minor poems from *The Shepheardes Calender* (1579) to *Fowre Hymnes* (1596) is most striking in its one-sidedness. To Plotinus's question, "What is Love, a god, a demon, or a passion of the mind?"

these poems answer, "A god or demon." Unlike Remy Belleau or Sidney, he never conceded that

> what we call *Cupid's* dart,
> An image is, which for our selves we carve;
> And, fooles, adore in temple of our hart.[1]

Like Ficino, Spenser treated Cupid as a supernatural power, thus ruling out the dialectic of abuse which had exercised medieval poets and Renaissance mythographers. Tension between Cupid as a god and Cupid as a demon (in the infernal rather than the Platonic sense) replaces the old ambivalence between the god and the personification. Spenser is close to Leone Ebreo here, except that Spenser never identifies two Cupids, one a god and the other a demon. For him there is only one Cupid, *either* a god or a demon. In the course of his minor works, Spenser resolved the tension between Cupid as god and Cupid as demon decisively in favor of the god and called attention to his decision in *Colin Clouts Come Home Againe* (1595). Colin, who had denied Cupid's divinity in the December eclogue, preaches Cupid's gospel in the later poem. Spenser's minor works thus move toward a theodicy of Cupid, a movement paralleled in *The Faerie Queene.*

Spenser wrote the *Shepheardes Calender,* as E. K. said, with "the sound of . . . auncient Poetes still ringing in his eares."[2] He saw himself neither as a mythographer nor as an anxious humanist but rather as a reborn antique poet, and he accepted from the beginning that the truest poetry is the most feigning. His imagination created a fictional world where, without the trappings of Neoplatonic cosmology, the distinction between gods and personifications has little meaning. When he is self-conscious about poetry—as he often is—he does not worry that the poetical gods may mark a renaissance of paganism. Within the imagined world of the *Shepheardes Calender,* he can adopt a pagan's skepticism about his fictional gods and especially about Cupid, "the Poets God of Love" (*March,* arg.), though this skepticism differs in kind from Alexandrian wit.

Colin Clout's plaintive disillusionment with love dominates the *Calender* and deepens as the months revolve.[3] One reflection of this disillusionment, though seldom noticed, is Colin's view of Cupid, which declines from highly rhetorical doubt in *January* to bitter denial in *December.* Colin's view dominates, but other views complicate the pattern.

The January eclogue introduces most of the major themes of the *Calender*— Colin's unfortunate love, its effect on his poetry, nature as a mirror of his plight—and Colin's first words introduce one version of the theology of the pastoral world:

> Ye Gods of love, that pitie lovers payne,
> (If any gods the paine of lovers pitie:)

> Looke from above, where you in joyes remaine,
> And bowe your eares unto my dolefull dittie.
> And *Pan* thou shepheards God, that once didst love,
> Pitie the paines, that thou thy selfe didst prove.

(13–18)

If the gods are distant, dwelling apart in their own joys, at least they do not joy in our woes. Colin's hope for their pity (and aid in obtaining Rosalind's) outweighs his showy doubt, "if any gods the paine of lovers pitie," and gives a significantly theological sense to his motto: "Anchora speme."

In *Aprill*, Hobbinol describes Colin as one whom "Love hath wounded with a deadly darte" (22), and in *June*, when Colin himself reappears, his theology has become Virgilian: Hobbinol may rest at ease in the paradise that Adam lost,

> But I unhappy man, whom cruell fate,
> And angry Gods pursue from coste to coste,
> Can nowhere fynd, to shroude my lucklesse pate.

(14–16)

Later lines identify Colin's "cruell fate" with the "ryper age" that has fettered him with "lincks of love" (34–36), identifying implicitly therefore the "angry Gods" with the "Gods of love" whose pity he implored in *January*. In Colin's view, the gods have left their joyful haunts above, but only to better pursue their victim. His hope for Rosalind's pity and the gods' favor has been disappointed, and his motto is now "Gia speme spenta."

When Colin reappears in *November*, his theology has changed again, its emphasis now Homeric, close to Achilles' tragic perception in *Iliad* 24: "Such is the way the gods spun life for unfortunate mortals, / that we live in unhappiness, but the gods themselves have no sorrows."[4] Like the Dido whom Colin laments, the gods are "enstalled" once again "in heavens hight"—"There lives shee with the blessed Gods in blisse, / . . . / And joyes enjoyes, that mortall men doe misse"—but they seem to have no concern with mortal men and, moreover, are not gods of love (177, 194–96).

In *December*, the month of the Nativity of Christ as E. K. notes in the general argument, Colin comes closer to the veiled Christianity which several other shepherds have expressed earlier:

> O soveraigne *Pan* thou God of shepheards all,
> Which of our tender Lambkins takest keepe:
> And when our flocks into mischaunce mought fall,
> Doest save from mischiefe the unwary sheepe:
> Als of their maisters hast no lesse regarde,
> Then of the flocks, which thou doest watch and ward.[5]

Also in *December*, Colin first recognizes his destroyer, a false god of shepherds:

The shepheards God (perdie God was he none)
My hurtlesse pleasaunce did me ill upbraide,
My freedome lorne, my life he lefte to mone.
Love they him called, that gave me checkmate,
But better mought they have behote him Hate.

(50–54)

Though echoing one of Boccaccio's demythologizations of Cupid in the *Genealogia deorum*, Colin here does not recognize Cupid as an image of his own desires.[6] Accepting a greater god, he also accepts a new definition of divinity, one which includes mercy and justice. He must, then, deny Cupid's divinity, but cannot deny his power and therefore leaves him as a malevolent and irresistible force, a demon.

Though not reduced to a psychological accident lacking independent existence or power, Colin's Cupid reveals himself only in his effects and is therefore in what we have called the lyric mode. Like the troubadours, Colin witnesses no theophanies, but infers the existence of Cupid from his experience of love. Unlike the troubadours, however, he questions whether the cause of his experience can be a god. Colin's Cupid is lyric, then, merely in mode and comes near to Natale Conti's, the divine cause similarly present but inaccessible within the experienced effects. Colin abandons the theodicy that Conti's Cupid incarnated, and his Cupid becomes an anti-Silenus ("perdie God was he none"), whose exterior conceals a demon rather than a divinity. Colin's lyric Cupid reflects his moment in time, after oracles have ceased and gods stopped appearing to men. The only epic Cupid of the *Shepheardes Calender* appropriately comes earlier in time, in March, the beginning of the natural year, and in an eclogue that, more than any other, "seemeth somewhat to resemble" a classical model.[7] To be more precise, the tale of Thomalin's surprising Cupid "within an Yvie todd" and exchanging bolts with him is mock-epic, a parody of the experience Colin describes in *December*. But, though "recreative," in E. K.'s classification, *March* shares with the "plaintive" eclogues the lesson that Love is an irresistible supernatural force. Though his story parallels the *Roman de la rose*, Thomalin's vision is no dream. Where the medieval tradition demythologized Cupid to expose abuse of the adage "Love conquers all," the March eclogue mythologizes the ill effects of denying the adage and especially its corollary, "Let us submit to love."[8]

E. K., the poem's original critic, agreed with this general interpretation, but presented two different accounts of Thomalin's fate. In the argument, he suggests that Thomalin represents "some secrete freend, who scorned Love and his knights so long, till at length him selfe was entangled, and unwares wounded with the dart of some beautifull regard, which is Cupides arrowe." If this is Thomalin's fate, he is in the good company of Spenser's Prince Arthur and Chaucer's Troilus, among countless others. But in his gloss E. K. offers another version of Thomalin's wound in the heel:

In the heele) is very Poetically spoken, and not without speciall judgment. . . . By wounding in the hele, is meant lustfull love. For from the heele (as say the best Phisitions) to the previe partes there passe certaine veines and slender synnewes . . . so that (as sayth Hipocrates) yf those veynes there be cut a sonder, the partie straighte becommeth cold and unfruiteful. Which reason our Poete wel weighing, maketh this shepheards boye of purpose to be wounded by Love in the heele.

In whichever sense we see Thomalin as a victim of Cupid, the gloss is at least truer than the argument to the mode of the poem.[9] Unlike Troilus or Arthur, Thomalin does not discover Cupid's power in a lady's beauty—no lady is present—and the arrow that revenges Thomalin's bird-bolts and "pumie stones" by wounding his heel cannot transparently figure "the dart of some beautifull regard." Moreover, the old counsel that depended upon regarding Cupid as a mirror image of a man's desires—"If you follow him, he will follow you; if you flee, he will flee"—is no longer effective.[10] When Thomalin turns to flee, Cupid shoots him in the heel. In the March eclogue, Spenser does not so much elaborate the conventional, lyrical allegory of enamorment as transform it into a comic-epic narrative.

Explaining his judgment that *The Rhime of the Ancient Mariner* had too much moral sentiment, Coleridge declared:

It ought to have had no more moral than the "Arabian Nights'" tale of the merchant, *because* one of the date shells had, it seems, put out the eye of the shells aside, and lo! a genie starts up, and says he *must* kill the aforesaid merchant, *because* one of the date shells had, it seems, put out the eye of the genie's son.[11]

The Cupid of the March eclogue is less arbitrary than Coleridge's genie—Thomalin does shoot first—but Spenser, more than Coleridge, avoids sentiments that either would hold the man morally responsible for his fate or justify the ways of the gods. Like Homer, Spenser depicts an archaic stage before religion and morals had grown together, before the gods had been moralized.[12] The *Calender* shows much of love's gall and little of its honey, however, and this emphasis may have led E. K. to distort its "generall dryft and purpose":

[The author's] unstayed yougth had long wandered in the common Labyrinth of Love, in which time . . . to warne (as he sayth) the young shepheards .s. [scilicet] his equalls and companions of his unfortunate folly, he compiled these xii. Aeglogues. . . .   (418)

Like the *Roman de la rose*, the *Trionfi*, *Gli Asolani*, or Bembo's discourse in *Il Cortegiano*, the *Calender* presents "the common Labyrinth of Love" less as a trap to be avoided than as an almost inevitable trial through which youth passes to be matured. Leo Spitzer's conclusion about *March* does better for the whole *Calender* than E. K.'s:

We find here no moral formulated, as with Bion ("keep away from Love!");
indeed, the only moral to be deduced would be: "Rejoice not in spring, be
not young!—for this is hybris, and nemesis must follow!"[13]

Only once does the *Shepheardes Calender* anticipate the theodicy of Cupid
that will be proclaimed when Spenser (and Colin Clout) return to the pastoral
world in *Colin Clouts Come Home Againe. October* presents a dialogue in
which Piers tries to encourage Cuddie, who laments the lack of a new Augustus
to make fit matter for new poets and, one feels more importantly, also the lack
of a new Maecenas to reward them. Finally Piers suggests that if the poet can
find no place on earth, he ought to make wings of his aspiring wit and fly back
to heaven. But Cuddie's discouragement overcomes even this possibility:

> Ah *Percy* it is all to weake and wanne,
> So high to sore, and make so large a flight:
> Her peeced pyneons bene not so in plight,
> For *Colin* fittes such famous flight to scanne:
> He, were he not with love so ill bedight,
> Would mount as high, and sing as soote as Swanne.
>
> (85–90)

This antagonism between Colin's love and his muse has prevailed since *January,* when Rosalind's scorn for his "rurall musick" made him break his pipe,[14]
but here Piers denies it:

> Ah fon, for love does teach him climbe so hie,
> And lyftes him up out of the loathsome myre:
> Such immortal mirrhor, as he doth admire,
> Would rayse ones mynd above the starry skie.
> And cause a caytive corage to aspire,
> For lofty love doth loath a lowly eye.
>
> (91–96)

Although Cuddie gets the last word, reasserting the prevailing view of Love—

> All otherwise the state of Poet stands,
> For lordly love is such a Tyranne fell:
> That where he rules, all power he doth expell—

Piers's argument is the stronger, adumbrating, in the words of the *Variorum*
editor, "the major Platonic ideas that are to be expanded into the complete
statements of the *Hymnes.*"[15] Piers's ambiguous address (is the "fon" Cuddie or
Colin?) and present tense hint that even now Love is leading Colin toward the
understanding of his experience that he will acknowledge in *Colin Clouts Come
Home Againe.* The figures of the *Shepheardes Calender* are still wandering in
love's labyrinth, however, and to them Cupid appears malevolent, both Minos

and Minotaur. As yet only Piers knows that, like the garden of youthful love, the labyrinth is a stage on a longer road and that on that road Cupid is certainly the guide and perhaps also the destination.

The archaic, unmoralized view of the gods that prevailed in the *Shepheardes Calender* appears once more in Spenser's work in *Muiopotmos: or The Fate of the Butterflie,* but here Cupid also serves as Spenser's comment on his poem. *Muiopotmos* was published in the *Complaints* volume of 1591. Defending the unity of this miscellany, Ponsonby noted that all its "smale Poems" were "complaints and meditations of the worlds vanitie, very grave and profitable." It has taken much unconvincing ingenuity, however, to make *Muiopotmos* grave.[16] Its profitable meditation on the world's vanity is embodied in a recreative myth which, like the March eclogue, presents a comic-epic version of divine causes whose effects are elsewhere (in the *Complaints* volume, in the *Shepheardes Calender*) presented tragically. Behind its recreative surface, however, the poem explores the paradoxes inherent in making myths about gods in order to teach the lesson that mortal happiness is fleeting. A similar self-consciousness appears explicitly in the Mutabilitie Cantos, but in *Muiopotmos* it appears only in three seemingly trivial mentions of Cupid.

Cupid is first mentioned at the end of a long and charming account of Clarion, the butterfly-hero, preparing for his day's adventure. The poet has been comparing Clarion's "furnitures" favorably with those of Achilles, Hercules, even Phoebus, but ends with a nervous doubt when he judges Clarion's wings more beautiful even than Cupid's. Such a comparison cannot be drawn "withouten perill," and the stanza ends with a plea for Cupid's forgiveness (97–104). At this point in the poem, the poet's peril and need for forgiveness hardly seem serious, but in fact the stanza masks tensions that become increasingly apparent later in the poem. Invidious comparisons of this sort between gods and men characterize all three of the tales that make up *Muiopotmos*—the central tale of Clarion's death and two inset tales of the metamorphoses of Astery and Arachne, which precede and in some sense cause the central action. The poet is conscious in this stanza that he is exemplifying conduct that will prove fatal to his characters.

The enmity of the spider Aragnoll is the direct cause of Clarion's fall, and its cause, in turn, is the metamorphosis of Arachne, Aragnoll's mother, who presumed to compete with Pallas at weaving. Spenser claims to repeat the tale "as in stories it is written found" (258), but the Chaucerian phrase calls attention to the ways that Spenser's version varies from its source in *Metamorphoses* 6. Unlike Ovid's envious goddess, Spenser's Pallas visits Arachne in order to yield her "due reward / For her prais-worthie workmanship" (267–68). Moreover, Pallas wins the contest outright, weaving into the leafy border of her tapestry an unOvidian butterfly so lifelike that Arachne withers into a spider from envy. Ever after spiders have hated butterflies as signs of their mother's defeat. Where in Ovid Pallas envied Arachne's success and transformed her into a spider to mitigate the severity of her punishment, Spenser transfers the envy to Arachne and makes the metamorphosis a self-inflicted punishment like that of Malbecco in the roughly contemporary Book 3 of *The Faerie Queene*. In another seemingly insignificant departure, Spenser's Arachne weaves into her picture of the Rape of Europa a detail that Ovid's Arachne, though depicting many more "caelestia crimina," neglected:

> Before the Bull she pictur'd winged Love,
> With his yong brother Sport, light fluttering
> Upon the waves, as each had been a Dove;
> The one his bowe and shafts, the other Spring
> A burning Teade about his head did move,
> As in their Syres new love both triumphing.
>
> (289–94)

The significance of Arachne's mythological ornament, like that of Pallas' ornamental butterfly, emerges only in the context of the linked tales.

The other inset tale, appearing earlier in the poem, reveals the cause of the butterfly's beauty and presents a counterexample to Pallas's just proceeding with Arachne, as well as another ornamental Cupid. Astery excelled all other nymphs at gathering flowers, and Venus, as prepared as Pallas to acknowledge mortal achievement, gave her just praise. But the envious nymphs then reported that Cupid had helped Astery. Venus, in irrational and "jealous feare" that Astery aspired to deification and might prove another Psyche, transformed her into a butterfly (129–34). Like her descendants, Astery bore her flowers "in her wings, for memorie / Of her pretended crime, though crime none were" (142–43). Unlike Arachne, then, Astery is the innocent victim of human slander and divine jealousy.

It is, of course, appropriate that Pallas should act justly and Venus jealously, but the significance of these opposed views of the gods lies less in a distinction between the goddesses than in the inconsistency itself.[17] The inconsistency is amplified in the central tale by the overdetermination of Clarion's fall. Is it caused by his own careless pride (377–84), by Aragnoll's malice, by "cruell fate" (235)? The alternatives finally make it impossible to be sure:

> The luckles *Clarion*, whether cruell Fate,
> Or wicked Fortune faultles him misled,
> Or some ungracious blast out of the gate
> Of *Aeoles* raine perforce him drove on hed,
> Was (O sad hap and howre unfortunate)
> With violent swift flight forth caried
> Into the cursed cobweb, which his foe
> Had framed for his finall overthroe.
>
> (417–24)

The gods in *Muiopotmos* do not envy human achievement, as did for example the gods of Sophocles or Herodotus, because that would be to counsel despair. Spenser's eye is on the practical instruction of his poem, what Chaucer called "sentence," and to this, as the inconsistencies go to show, the gods' justice or injustice is irrelevant. Though it uses the same analogy as the tragic aphorism from *King Lear*, *Muiopotmos* does not teach that "as flies to wanton boys are we to the gods," but merely that mortal glory and happiness are as frail as an insect's. Spenser counsels humility rather than despair, and his fictional gods (whom Clarion ignores) exist primarily as tokens of human limitation, as in the stanzas that come at the structural, as well as the thematic center of the poem:

> But what on earth can long abide in state?
> Or who can him assure of happie day;
> Sith morning faire may bring fowle evening late,
> And least mishap the most blisse alter may?
> For thousand perills lie in close awaite
> About us daylie, to worke our decay;
> That none, except a God, or God him guide,
> May them avoyde, or remedie provide.
>
> And whatso heavens in their secret doome
> Ordained have, how can fraile fleshly wight
> Forecast, but it must needs to issue come?
> The sea, the aire, the fire, the day, the night,
> And th'armies of their creatures all and some
> Do serve to them, and with importune might
> Warre against us the vassals of their will.
> Who then can save, what they dispose to spill?[18]

(217–32)

The paradox that the gods are tokens of human limitations yet are themselves created and controlled by the poet is inherent in any mythological fiction that teaches humility. At the end of Chaucer's *Knight's Tale*, for example, a version of this paradox produces an ironic reflection upon the human need for illusions. In *Muiopotmos*, the paradox reflects upon the poet himself, who counsels humility by being the opposite of humble and expresses itself in the three seemingly insignificant appearances of Cupid. The important similarity between the appearances of Cupid in the inset tales is that they are only appearances, mere fictions. The nymphs lied in reporting that Cupid had helped Astery, and Arachne wove him into her blasphemous tapestry, depicting a divine cause for the rape of Europa lacking in Ovid. Though demonstrating that men are helpless creatures of the gods, both inset tales thus paradoxically concede that the gods, or at least stories about them, are also creatures of men. In the context of the poem, this paradox is worrisome, for it aligns the poet with the slanderous nymphs and with presumptuous Arachne. Like the nymphs, the poet fabricates divine interventions, perhaps unjustly in order to disparage human achievements and potentials. Like Arachne, he presumes to hold sway over the gods and may also share Arachne's pride in the excellence of mortal art. The poet who meditates on the world's vanity will spin stories, moreover, closer to Arachne's picture of divine impingement than to Pallas's picture of divine justice and beneficence.

If we return now to the first appearance of Cupid in *Muiopotmos*, Spenser's self-consciousness will seem less offhand:

> Ne (may it be withouten perill spoken)
> The Archer God, the sonne of *Cytheree*,
> That joyes on wretched lovers to be wroken,
> And heaped spoyles of bleeding harts to see,
> Beares in his wings so manie a changefull token.
> Ah my liege Lord, forgive it unto mee,
> If ought against thine honour I have tolde;
> Yet sure those wings were fairer manifolde.
>
> (97–104)

The stanza, with its presumptuous comparison and its gesture of humility, encapsulates the paradox that teases the poet of *Muiopotmos*. The stanza is paradoxical in another sense as well; like Janus it looks two ways at once: backward to Colin's malignant demon in the *Shepheardes Calender*, forward to his divine liege Lord in *Colin Clouts Come Home Againe*. Most interestingly, however, the self-conscious realization in *Muiopotmos* that fictional gods are created to serve human ends corresponds to the full-scale dramatization of the theme in *The Faerie Queene*, Book 3—the Busyrane episode, published one year before.

Colin Clouts Come Home Againe, published in 1595 though its dedication is dated 1591, triumphantly resolves the paradox of *Muiopotmos* and also, explicitly looking back to the *Shepheardes Calender*, recants Colin's earlier disillusionment with love. Colin's life, therefore, reverses the sequence of earlier poems like the *Roman de la rose* and the *Trionfi* in which Cupid is the illusory god of youth whom men deny in their age. Neoplatonic ideas make their first detailed appearance in Spenser's work in *Colin Clouts Come Home Againe*, when toward the end of the poem Colin, like Castiglione's Bembo, is seized by a "celestiall rage of love" and becomes Cupid's oracle (823–25). Otherwise, Colin and his situation reverse the situation and ideas of *Il Cortegiano*. Colin's audience are shepherds and, where Bembo's speech answered a courtly *demande d'amour*, Colin's begins as an attack on the court. Explaining why he left Cynthia's court to come home to "this barrein soyle, / Where cold and care and penury do dwell" (656–57), Colin condemns Cynthia's courtiers, who, chief among their faults,

> do themselves for want of other worke,
> Vaine votaries of laesie love professe,
> Whose service high so basely they ensew,
> That *Cupid* selfe of them ashamed is,
> And mustring all his men in *Venus* vew,
> Denies them quite for servitors of his.
>
> (765–70)

To sharpen his complaint against the court, Colin here rejects the traditional association of Cupid with idleness, but his use of a story about Cupid to point a moral seems as yet little different from the mode of *Muiopotmos.*[19] Differences, however, soon become apparent:

> And is love then (said *Corylas*) once knowne
> In Court, and his sweet lore professed there?
> I weened sure he was our God alone:
> And only woond in fields and forests here.
>
> (771–74)

Corylas's question implicates Cupid in the poem's central contrast between court and country, and Colin's reply, developing the contrast, condemns courtiers who, like the Pléiade poets, carry the mode of *Muiopotmos* to extremes, reducing Cupid to a toy or instrument, powerless and even neuter:

> Not so (quoth he) love most aboundeth there.
> For all the walls and windows there are writ,
> All full of love, and love, and love, my deare,
> And all their talke and studie is of *it*.
> . . . .
> But they of love and of *his* sacred lere,
> (As it should be) all otherwise devise,
> Then we poore shepheards are accustomd here,
> And *him* do sue and serve all otherwise.
> For with lewd speeches and licentious deeds,
> His mightie mysteries they do prophane,
> And use his ydle name to other needs,
> But as a complement for courting vaine.
> So him they do not serve as they professe,
> But make him serve to them for sordid uses.
>
> (775–78, 783–92; emphasis added)

No doubt these courtiers make Cupid "serve to them" as did their ancestors in medieval poems, by masking their self-indulgence as heavenly compulsion, but now the nature of the abuse has changed. Andreas's nobleman, the dreamer of the *Roman de la rose*, Dante, and Petrarch all misrepresented or mistook Cupid (a poetic figure) for a literal divinity. But Cynthia's courtiers do the opposite; they blaspheme a real divinity by treating him as an architectural ornament, a figure of speech, an "ydle name." They too abuse fiction, but now, like Arachne in *Muiopotmos*, by making fictions—"leasing vaine" or "termes unworthie"—that abuse a real god (821–22). To say that in *Colin Clouts Come Home Againe* Cupid is a real god is not to question Spenser's orthodoxy, of course. It is rather to suggest that Cupid's divinity, which in *Muiopotmos* had been merely a localized trope, is here one of the central fictions of the poem— as, for example, was Beatrice's angelic nature in the *Vita Nuova*.[20] Indeed, Cupid's divinity is a central fiction in most of Spenser's poems in which he appears.

Any divinity except One must be either false or figurative no less than in earlier centuries, and Colin, turning from the courtiers to the shepherds, both concedes the fictiveness of Cupid's divinity and clarifies what it figures:

> But we poore shepheards, whether rightly so,
> Or through our rudenesse into errour led,
> Do *make religion* how we rashly go,
> To serve that God, that is so greatly dred.
>
> (795–97; emphasis added)

Where the courtiers make art from their love and love an art, the shepherds "make religion." The phrase is significant for it occurs once again in Spenser, when Artegall glimpses Britomart's face inside her sheared helmet:

> And he him himselfe long gazing thereupon,
> At last fell humbly downe upon his knee,
> And of his wonder made religion. . . .
>
> (*FQ*, 4.6.22)

The religion of love, ironical in the Middle Ages, now figures love's components of wonder, reverence, and faith. The irreligion of those who play with Cupid, like Cynthia's courtiers or Paridell or Busyrane, reflects their frivolity or complacency or will to power. Cupid's divinity, which had tempted men to evade responsibility by pleading compulsion, now enjoins and enforces responsibility.

Yet the shepherds' religion is fictive, made by them and ultimately by Spenser. How then does *Colin Clouts Come Home Againe* resolve the paradox of *Muiopotmos* that fictive divinities always exemplify the presumption they are invented to warn against? Except within the fiction of the poem the paradox is irresolvable, as Chaucer and Milton also knew. Within the poem it is triumphantly resolved by Spenser's self-presentation as Colin Clout. By the end of the poem, Colin has risen above the poets who are "makers" of verses and tales and whose "learned throng" he catalogues earlier (367–455). He is not a maker, inventing and disposing persons and plots like the fabulists of the March eclogue or *Muiopotmos*, but a seer, an Orphic poet-priest who can affirm

Cupid's divinity because he disclaims power over his poem. Its maker is the "high powre" that inspires him:

> Shepheard it seemes that some celestiall rage
> of love (quoth *Cuddy*) is breath'd into thy brest,
> That powreth forth these oracles so sage,
> Of that high powre, wherewith thou art possest.
> . . . .
> Well may it seeme by this thy deep insight,
> That of that God the Priest thou shouldest bee:
> So well thou wot'st the mysterie of his might,
> As if his godhead thou didst present see.
>
> Of loves perfection perfectly to speake,
> Or of his nature rightly to define.
> Indeed (said *Colin*) passeth reasons reach,
> And needs his priest t'expresse his powre divine.
>
> (823–26, 831–38)

In the October eclogue, Cuddy had denied Piers's belief that Love could teach Colin to mount up to heaven:

> All otherwise the state of Poet stands,
> For lordly love is such a Tyranne fell:
> That where he rules, all power he doth expell.
>
> (97–99)

Here, where Piers has been vindicated, Cuddy appropriately recognizes that if Love expels the power to make fictions, he replaces it with the power to reveal truths.

Colin reveals Cupid's "mightie mysteries" in two movements, separated by Cuddy's comment quoted above. The two movements are in some respects contradictory, and the second has therefore been explained as a "late insertion" or "afterthought."[21] In fact, the contradiction is an old one and, in its context, highly significant. Spenser will use it again in the *Hymne in Honour of Love*.

Colin first presents a mythological account of Cupid's birth:

> [Cupid] the greatest of the Gods we deeme,
> Borne without Syre or couples, of one kynd,
> For *Venus* selfe doth soly couples seeme,
> Both male and female, through commixture joynd,
> So pure and spotlesse *Cupid* forth she brought,
> And in the gardens of *Adonis* nurst:
> Where growing, he his owne perfection wrought,
> And shortly was of all the Gods the first.
>
> (799–806)

After Cuddy's comment follows another version, less mythological than cosmological:

> For long before the world he was y'bore
> And bred above in *Venus* bosome deare:
> For by his powre the world was made of yore,
> And all that therein wondrous doth appeare.
> For how should else things so far from attone
> And so great enemies as of them bee,
> Be ever drawne together into one,
> And taught in such accordance to agree?
> Through him the cold began to covet heat,
> And water fire; the light to mount on hie,
> And th'heavie downe to peize; the hungry t'eat
> And voydnesse to seeke full satietie.
> So being former foes, they wexed friends,
> And gan by little learne to love each other.
>
> (839–52)

Genesis presents two inconsistent versions of the Creation, and the parallel may be relevant, but more immediately Colin's two accounts draw on the commonplace distinction between an earthly Cupid, the youngest of the gods, and a heavenly Cupid, the first and eldest of all. In the first account, Cupid is obviously born later than Adonis, and his nursery, the gardens of Adonis, must be an earthly paradise, as it is in *The Faerie Queene,* because Jove later takes him *up* to heaven:

> Then got he bow and shafts of gold and lead,
> In which so fell and puissant he grew,
> That *Jove* himselfe his powre began to dread,
> And taking up to heaven, him godded new.
>
> (807–10)

Jove's diplomacy alone averts conflict with Cupid (and saves Colin from having to repeat the ancient lies about the gods depicted in Arachne's tapestry and Busyrane's house). This Cupid now wars exclusively on men:

> From thence he shootes his arrowes every where
> Into the world, at randon as he will,
> On us fraile men, his wretched vassals here,
> Like as himselfe us pleaseth, save or spill.
>
> (811–814)

In the second account, however, Cupid "was y'bore / And bred *above* in Venus bosome deare" long before his power made the world (my emphasis). This Cupid's power is not limited to earth, for Colin identifies his arrows with the rays of beauty "Against whose powre, nor God nor man can fynd / Defense, ne ward the daunger of the wound."[22]

Yet if details of Colin's speech hint that behind its inconsistent movements lies the distinction between earthly and celestial Cupids, other details and the speech as a whole suggest that the distinction is advanced chiefly to be subsumed. The distinction disappears where one would expect it to be clearest—in the effects of the two gods on men. In both accounts, men humbly pray to Cupid for grace, and he answers as he pleases. Colin distinguished between love and lust, but recognizes no distinction between Cupids and therefore, despite the mythographers, makes the Empedoclean, cosmogonic Cupid the son of Venus.[23] Spenser will carry this conflation of Cupid's genealogies a step further in the *Hymne in Honour of Love*, but here it is an instance of a general conflation that shows itself also in Cupid's appearance. The best student of Spenser's classical mythology, H. G. Lotspeich, distinguishes three "different aspects of Spenser's Cupid, though," he warns, "sharp divisions between them do not hold."[24] These are the full-grown feudal lord, the Alexandrian armed infant, and the cosmic force that holds the reins of the universe. Colin's speech combines these three aspects in less than a hundred lines and implies that sharp divisions between them do not hold because they are aspects of a unity. In the *Trionfi*, we may remember, the glaring inconsistency between two of these aspects—Cupid as a "vittorioso e sommo duce" and, seven lines later, as a winged, naked "garzon"—hints that he is merely a personification, an unreal divinity. But Colin's inconsistencies, far from casting doubt on Cupid's divinity or betraying Spenser's careless revision or habitual mingling of traditions, point toward the mystery, "which passeth reasons reach," of his single deity (837).

Colin's identification of the waspish Cupid with the Love that rules the heavens has many precedents. Empedocles asserted the same identification. Orpheus and Boethius wished that it were so, as did the sadly illusioned narrator of Chaucer's *Troilus and Criseyde*.[25] Dante experienced it at the end of the *Paradiso*. Ficino equivocally affirmed it, as we have seen, apportioning its aspects into the hierarchies of his cosmology. Sir John Davies would shortly use it for purposes of philosophical seduction in *Orchestra*.[26] But the closest to Spenser is Conti, who unified Cupid's contrarieties in a single Silenus-figure, concealing the Empedoclean divine force within an disreputable exterior signifying human passion. Colin Clout returns to the problem of theodicy posed by Conti's Silenus-Cupid, though he makes it somewhat easier, as did Ficino, by excluding "disloyal lust" from the province of Cupid. Still, the problem is essentially the same as in Conti: how can Cupid be "fell" and capricious ("randon"), inflicting needless suffering "on us fraile men, his wretched vassals here," and yet at the same time be "pure and spotlesse," "the greatest of the Gods," "Lord of all the world *by right*"?[27] How can the cause of men's suffering be a *god* of love? Colin does not address these questions directly in *Colin Clouts Come Home Againe;* rather he transcends them, attesting to the faith that Cupid is a god and that the pains of loyal human love are mysteriously benignant.

Several allusions to the *Shepheardes Calender* remind us that Colin once denied Cupid's divinity and encourage us to see his new faith as a recantation of that old apostasy, but the causes of his conversion are not obvious. Chief among the allusions to the *Calender*, for example, is the discussion of Rosalind at the end of the poem (introduced by pointed reference to Stesichorus, who lost his eyesight "till he recanted had his wicked rimes"), yet it rules out rather than offers a reason for Colin's conversion (923). His experience of love has remained a "long affliction" (944), and therefore to infer Cupid's nature from his unhappy experience, as he did in the *Calender*, would be again to conclude that Cupid is a demon rather than a god. On the other hand, Colin seems to have had no revelation to substitute for unhappy experience. Despite Cuddy's encomium—"So well thou wot'st the mysteries of his might, / As if his godhead thou didst present see" (833–34)—Colin does not claim to have seen Cupid or heard his voice from the whirlwind. He has arrived at humility like Job's without Job's theophany. Like most men, he must *make* his religion; his faith is not a sentiment, but a leap.

If the causes of Colin's conversion remain implicit, a process of elimination can make them somewhat clearer and also indicate some aspects of the poem's often disparaged unity.[28] Before his pilgrimage to Cynthia's court, Colin's state was nearly as sad as in the *Shepheardes Calender:*

> Nor of my love, nor of my losse (quoth he)
> I then did sing, as then occasion fell:
> For love had me forlorne, forlorne of me,
> That made me in that desart chose to dwell.[29]
>
> (88–91)

The song he did sing projects his own thwarted love onto the pastoral land-scape. His discontent at the beginning of the poem suggests that his conversion took place after he left the pastoral world, as does Cuddy's reaction to his praise of Cupid:

> But never wist I till this present day
> Albe of love I alwayes humbly deemed,
> That he was such an one, as thou doest say,
> And so religiously to be esteemed.
>
> (827–30)

At court, Colin witnessed the courtiers' profanation of love, of course, and his affirmation of Cupid's mighty mysteries comes partly in prophetic reaction. But more important is the vision of Cynthia herself, which he describes as a conversion:

> And since I saw that Angels blessed eie,
> Her worlds bright sun, her heavens fairest light,
> My mind full of my thoughts satietie,
> Doth feed on sweet contentment of that sight:
> Since that same day in nought I take delight,
> Ne feeling have in any earthly pleasure. . . .
>
> (40–45)

Colin asserts the divinity of beauty again at the end of the poem when he refuses to blame Rosalind for cruelty to him; the fault is rather his for presuming to love a "thing celestiall" (930). His defense of Rosalind shows him practicing the humility and patience in love that he had preached while describing Cupid, and it also completes the narrative of Colin's conversion, unifying the otherwise rambling poem. If a loosely Platonic deification of beauty lies behind Colin's affirmation of Cupid's divinity, it remains rather unemphasized. In the *Fowre Hymnes*, it will be argued explicitly.

The *Amoretti* and *Epithalamion*, published in 1595 and written, the title page tells us, "not long since," are thus roughly contemporary with *Colin Clouts Come Home Againe*, which was published in the same year and probably revised over the previous four.[30] Although they do not present Cupid as a god or develop the theodicy begun in *Colin Clouts Come Home Againe*, Spenser's sonnets and marriage song nevertheless bear out the contention that Cupid has for Spenser the integrity of figures like Colin Clout and that his minor poems therefore exhibit a consistent, if complex, pattern in the use of Cupid. Cupid is mentioned seven times in the *Amoretti*, aside from the puzzling anacreontics at the end, and once in the *Epithalamion*. The number of these references and, more importantly, their character show Spenser in his own courtship avoiding both the paradox that worried him in *Muiopotmos* and the abuses that Colin condemned in Cynthia's courtiers.

Brief comparison of a few of Spenser's sonnets with other poems will bring out most clearly the character of his use of Cupid in the *Amoretti*. Three sonnets (4, 19, 70) celebrate the coming of spring and bid the lady "therefore her selfe soone ready make, / to wayt on love amongst his lovely crew" (70). The association of love with spring is as old as poetry, and Spenser had used it in the March eclogue where Willye is eager for spring:

> Tho will we little Love awake,
> That nowe sleepeth in *Lethe* lake,
> And pray him leaden our daunce.
>
> (*March*, 22–24)

Similar imagery recurs in *Amoretti* 4, where the new year,

> calling forth out of sad Winters night,
> fresh love, that long hath slept in cheerlesse bower:

wils him awake, and soone about him dight
his wanton wings and darts of deadly power.
For lusty spring now in his timely howre,
is ready to come forth him to receive.

The difference between Lethe Lake and winter's cheerless bower, however, is
the difference between the epic or narrative fashion and the lyric. In the
Amoretti, Love is awakened and leads his subjects, but he remains a lyric
image, visible only in his effects. The lover can only pray for an epic intervention on his behalf such as Thomalin suffered in March or Colin prophesied in
Colin Clouts Come Home Againe:

> The merry Cuckow, messenger of Spring,
> His trompet shrill hath thrise already sounded:
> that warnes al lovers wayt upon their king,
> who now is coming forth with girland crouned.
> With noyse whereof the quyre of Byrds resounded
> their anthemes sweet devized of loves prayse,
> that all the woods theyr ecchoes back rebounded,
> as if they knew the meaning of their layes.
> But mongst them all, which did Loves honor rayse
> no word was heard of her that most it ought,
> but she his precept proudly disobayes,
> and doth his ydle message set at nought.
> Therefore O love, unlesse she turne to thee
> ere Cuckow end, let her a rebell be.
>
>   (19)

Amoretti 10 casts a similar complaint as an address to Love, drawing upon
Petrarch and Wyatt, but avoids even their modest references to Cupid's bow
and arrows:

> Unrighteous Lord of love, what law is this,
> That me thou makest thus tormented be:
> the whiles she lordeth in licentious blisse
> of her freewill, scorning both thee and me.
> See how the Tyrannesse doth joy to see
> the huge massacres which her eyes do make:
> and humbled harts brings captives unto thee,
> that thou of them mayst mightie vengeance take.
> But her proud hart doe thou a little shake
> and that high look, with which she doth comptroll
> all this worlds pride, bow to a baser make,
> and al her faults in thy black booke enroll.
> That I may laugh at her in equall sort,
> as she doth laugh at me and makes my pain her sport.[31]

Thomas Watson, whose *Hekatompathia* published in 1582 Spenser may have known, provides a full-scale mythological treatment of the same theme:

> *Cupid*, where is thy golden quiver nowe?
> Where is thy sturdy Bowe? and where the fire,
> Which made ere this the *Gods* themselves to bow?
> Shall she alone, which forceth my *Desire*,
>   Report or thinke thy Godhead is so small,
>   That she through pride can scape from being thrall?
> *Whilom* thou overcam'st the stately minde
> Of chast *Elisa queene* of *Carthage* land,
> And did'st constraine *Pasiphae* gainst her kind,
> and broughtest *Europa* faire to *Creta sande*,
>   Quite through the swelling Seas, to pleasure *Jove*,
>   Whose heav'nly heart was touch't with mortall love.
> Thus wert thou wont to shewe thy force and might,
> By conqu'ring those that were of highest race,
> Where now it seemes thou changest thy delight,
> Permitting still, to thy no small disgrace,
>   A virgin to despise thy selfe, and me,
>   Whose heart is hers, where ere my body be.[32]

Watson's quasi-sonnets are an extreme example of the mythological manner, but even Sidney provides a similar contrast with Spenser. The seventeenth sonnet of *Astrophil and Stella* involves Cupid, Venus, and Mars in a domestic wrangle and to these classical gods adds "grandame Nature" from the pantheon of philosophical epics like the *De planctu Naturae*:

> His mother deare *Cupid* offended late,
> Because that *Mars*, growne slacker in her love,
> With pricking shot he did not throughly move,
> To keepe the pace of their first loving state.
> The boy refusde for feare of *Marse's* hate,
> Who threatned stripes, if he his wrath did prove:
> But she in chafe him from her lap did shove,
> Brake bow, brake shafts, while *Cupid* weeping sate:
> Till that his grandame *Nature* pittying it,
> Of *Stella's* browes made him two better bowes,
> And in her eyes of arrowes infinit.
> O how for joy he leapes, o how he crowes,
> And straight therewith, like wags new got to play,
> Fals to shrewd turnes, and I was in his way.[33]

Sidney is the passive victim of this accidental intervention. "The active protagonists," as J. W. Lever says, "are Nature and the gods."[34] *Amoretti* 16 also has a "misintended dart," but its legion of *Cupidines* are so little divine that they can be thwarted by a mortal blink:

One day as I unwarily did gaze
on those fayre eyes my loves immortall light:
the whiles my stonisht hart stood in amaze,
through sweet illusion of her lookes delight.
I mote perceive how in her glauncing sight,
legions of loves with little wings did fly:
darting their deadly arrowes fyry bright,
at every rash beholder passing by.
One of those archers closely I did spy,
ayming his arrow at my very hart:
when suddenly with twincle of her eye,
the Damzell broke his misintended dart.
Had she not so doon, sure I had bene slayne,
yet as it was, I hardly scap't with paine.

Spenser's restraint in the use of mythology in the *Amoretti* was a gesture of conscious conservatism, for playful anecdotes like those of Watson and Sidney became a feature of the vernacular lyric only several generations after Petrarch in the poems of his imitators. Publication of the *Greek Anthology* and the *Anacreontea* further stimulated the fashion, which was diffused in emblem books, Neolatin epigrams, and, as we have seen, in the more *précieuses* works of the Pléiade. In the March eclogue, Spenser had been among the first to English this fashion, and he used it again, though transformed, for the runaway Cupid of *The Faerie Queene*, Book 3. But in his sonnet sequence he avoids the mythological manner almost completely. Heroes and demigods ornament a few sonnets, but Cupid is the only god mentioned, and even he is less the mythical Cupid than Love, the lyrical image. This conservatism helps to produce a tone that C. S. Lewis described as "devout, quiet, harmonious."[35] If Spenser does not make religion of Cupid in the *Amoretti*, neither does he repudiate the shepherds' religion of *Colin Clouts Come Home Againe*, profaning it by using Cupid's "ydle name . . . / But as a complement for courting vaine."[36]

Between the *Amoretti* and the *Epithalamion* there appear, however, four miscellaneous poems, all of them in the anacreontic fashion avoided in the sonnets. As well as being "out of keeping with the serious feeling of both the *Amoretti* and *Epithalamion*," their limited merits as poetry have made some readers suspect their authenticity.[37] If they are Spenser's and their placement not accidental, they serve as a pause or link between the *Amoretti* and *Epithalamion*, as Francesco Viglione long ago suggested.[38] But they also serve as a contrast that calls attention to the absence of such mythological anecdotes in the poems linked. They present a more general contrast as well. The first epigram compresses the lesson of *March* into six lines:

In youth before I waxed old,
The blynd boy Venus baby,
For want of cunning made me bold,

In bitter hyve to grope for honny.
But when he saw me stung and cry,
He tooke his wings and away did fly.

The fable of Cupid and the bee, the longest of the anacreontics, may imitate
Tasso, Ronsard, Baïf, and Watson.[39] The poem precisely reverses the analogy of
Muiopotmos. There men were mere insects as compared to the gods; here men
are to Cupid what he is to the bee. The fable itself with its "cruell" and
"wanton" Cupid, who suffers "neyther gods in sky, / nor men in earth to rest,"
recalls Arachne's tapestry. The anacreontics that intervene between Spenser's
most clearly autobiographical poems serve then at least partly to underline by
contrast the change in his use of Cupid since the *Shepheardes Calender* and
Muiopotmos.

A poet who makes Cupid a plaything, investing him with none of the mystery of love, may find it difficult to include him in the serious business of
marriage. He may even see Cupid as antithetical to marriage and exclude him,
as did Sidney in an epithalamion from the third eclogues of the Old *Arcadia:*

But thou foule *Cupid,* syre to lawlesse lust,
Be thou farre hence with thy empoyson'd darte,
Which though of glittring golde, shall heere take rust
Where simple love, which chastnesse doth imparte,
    Avoydes thy hurtfull arte.[40]

Spenser, however, who had earlier spoken of marriage as "Cupid's yoke,"
invites hundreds of Cupids to attend the consummation of his marriage in the
Epithalamion:

The whiles an hundred little winged loves,
Like diverse fethered doves,
Shall fly and flutter round about your bed,
And in the secret darke, that none reproves,
Their prety stealthes shal worke, and snares shal spread
To filch away sweet snatches of delight,
Conceald through covert night.
Ye sonnes of Venus, play your sports at will,
For greedy pleasure, carelesse of your toyes,
Thinks more upon her paradise of joyes,
Than what you do, albe it good or ill.
All night therefore attend your merry play,
For it will soone be day:
Now none doth hinder you, that say or sing,
Ne will the woods now answer, nor your Eccho ring.[41]

(357–71)

Milton hardly mentions Cupid at all and can therefore include him while
hailing the wedded love of Paradise:

> Here Love his golden shafts employs, here lights
> His constant lamp, and waves his purple wings,
> Reigns here and revels. . . .
>
> (*Par. Lost* 4.763–65)

Cupid's association with the innocent sexuality within marriage, a reflection of the original innocence, shows how consistently Spenser rejected the tradition that views Cupid as the "syre to lawlesse lust."

The hundred little Cupids of the *Epithalamion* are, as Thomas Greene suggests, the bridegroom-poet's solution to the problem of tactfully representing the consummation of his marriage. If they were no more than devices to divert attention from the bed, Greene's criticism would be entirely just: "An emotional vacuum is almost created at the point where conventionally emotions are highest."[42] But the Cupids also help to convey the sense of release that dominates this stanza and the ones preceding it. At first it is release from the bridegroom's conventional impatience, when the question beginning stanza sixteen—"Ah when will this long weary day have end?"—is answered in stanza seventeen: "Now day is doen, and night is nighing fast." In stanza eighteen, night also brings release from past pains:

> Now welcome night, thou night so long expected,
> That long daies labour doest at last defray,
> And all my cares, which cruell love collected,
> Hast sumd in one, and cancelled for aye:
> Spread thy broad wing over my love and me,
> That no man may us see. . . .
>
> (315–20)

With the Cupids of stanza twenty, Spenser finds release even from past delights, from the *Amoretti* themselves, which are recalled by way of a pun only to be benignly ignored.[43] Once invested with the mystery of love, Cupid now yields before the greater mysteries of generation, childbirth, and the "holy lawes of wedlock," to whose patron deities Spenser prays in the last stanzas of the poem. The *Epithalamion*'s hundred Cupids do imply an emotional vacuum, but a curiously affirmative one. Even while the poem celebrates release from the past, their presence affirms the past. They can be harmless diversions now, because Cupid was more than a plaything before.

The first of the *Fowre Hymnes*, published in 1596, returns to Colin Clout's theodicy of Cupid and parallels it closely enough for one scholar to suggest that passages of the hymn are "rewritings" of the earlier passages.[44] The *Hymne in Honour of Love* is quite different in tone, however, and presents several different issues. In *Colin Clouts Come Home Againe*, Cupid was the shepherds' god, his divinity circumscribed by the boundaries of the pastoral world. The *Hymne in Honour of Love* creates no imaginary world apart, and Cupid's divinity must be circumscribed in the later hymns. Even in their theodicies of Cupid, the two poems differ. Where Colin had been able prophetically to attest his faith in Cupid's providence, the poet of the hymn undertakes the harder task of justifying Cupid's ways to men and to himself. Against his arguments culled from an uncertain group of Neoplatonists and theologians, his own painful experience of love repeatedly asserts itself. Finally, the attempted theodicy appears to collapse in the second pair of hymns, where the poet claims to retract what he has said in the first.

Colin Clout began his praise of Cupid as a condemnation of court amours and only later had to prove that he could practice toward Rosalind what he preached about Cupid. The *Hymne in Honour of Love*, in contrast, begins in the midst of "sharpe sorrowes":

> Love, that long since hast to thy mighty powre,
> Perforce subdude my poore captived hart,
> And raging now therein with restlesse stowre,
> Doest tyrannize in everie weaker part;
> Faine would I seeke to ease my bitter smart,
> By any service I might do to thee,
> Or ought that else might to thee pleasing bee.
> And now t'asswage the force of this new flame,
> And make thee more propitious in my need,
> I meane to sing the praises of thy name,
> And thy victorious conquests to areed. . . .
>
> (16, 1–11)

Since the gods cannot be bribed, the poet does not quite offer his hymn in return for grace, but prays that Cupid will mitigate the sharp sorrows that have enfeebled his wits, so that he will be able to sing "the wondrous triumphs" of the god (15–20). He prays for the tranquility necessary for making verses, not for the "celestiall rage" that inspired Colin Clout, and later references to continued "smart" suggest that his prayer is unanswered. Unable to model himself on Orpheus, as had Colin, he models his poem on the literary hymns of Callimachus and his modern imitator Michele Marullo. As a maker rather than a *vates*, the poet of the hymn carries an imaginative burden that Cupid's "high powre" had carried for Colin.

The burden of proclaiming Cupid's omnipotence is light. In the six-stanza prologue, the poet declares his intentions:

> I meane to sing the praises of thy name,
> And thy victorious conquests to areed;
> By which thou madest many harts to bleed
> Of mighty Victors, with wyde wounds embrewed,
> And by thy cruell darts to thee subdewed.
>
> (10–14)

The hymn proper begins in the same vein:

> Great God of might, that reignest in the mynd,
> And all the bodie to thy hest doest frame,
> Victor of gods, subduer of mankynd,
> That doest the Lions and fell Tigers tame,
> Making their cruell rage they scornefull game,
> And in their roring taking great delight;
> Who can expresse the glorie of thy might?
>
> (43–49)

This god who reigns in the mind and, among the attributes of divinity, has only omnipotence is reminiscent of the personification mistaken for a deity in earlier works like the *De planctu Naturae* or the *Trionfi*. The poet who urges youths and nymphs to march amongst Cupid's conquered host might be thought specifically to honor Petrarch's god and in his form—the triumphal pageant. But, like Colin Clout and earlier Natale Conti, the poet immediately asserts the mysterious unity of the cruel boy-god with the cosmic force that created and rules the universe. The mystery, left implicit in *Colin Clouts Come Home Againe*, converges in Cupid's contradictory genealogies:

> Or who alive can perfectly declare,
> The wondrous cradle of thine infancie?
> When thy great mother *Venus* first thee bare,
> Begot of Plentie and of Penurie,
> Though elder then thine owne nativitie;
> And yet a chyld, renewing still thy yeares
> And yet the eldest of the heavenly Peares.[45]
>
> (50–56)

To explain, or at least to unfold, the mystery of Cupid's nativity, the poet first turns to the elder god, the Empedoclean primal force. Like Colin Clout, he signals his departure from mythographical tradition and from ordinary logic by making even "the eldest of the heavenly Peares" the son of Venus, and the cosmogony he goes on to report is substantially the same as Colin's, although both poetically and philosophically elaborated. The most significant elaboration—to be carried still further in the *Hymne in Honour of Beautie*—is a fuller exposition of the divine origin and human effect of beauty. All earthly beings exist and are moved to increase and multiply "through secret sparks of [Cupid's] infused fyre,"

> But man, that breathes a more immortall mynd,
> Not for lusts sake, but for eternitie,
> Seekes to enlarge his lasting progenie.
>
> For having yet in his deducted spright,
> Some sparks remaining of that heavenly fyre,

He is enlumind with that goodly light,
Unto like goodly semblant to aspyre:
Therefore in choice of love, he doth desyre
That seemes on earth most heavenly, to embrace,
That same is Beautie, borne of heavenly race.

For sure of all, that in this mortall frame
Contained is, nought more divine doth seeme,
Or that resembleth more th'immortall flame
Of heavenly light, then Beauties glorious beame.
What wonder then, if with such rage extreme
Fraile men, whose eyes seek heavenly things to see,
At sight thereof so much enravisht bee?

(97, 103–19)

Beauty in these lines is both a spur to generation and an object of contemplation, but Spenser is fusing—and not confusing, as Ellrodt suggests—functions that orthodox Neoplatonists held separate.[46] This fusion is, in fact, entailed by the fusion of the Alexandrian with the Empedoclean aspects of Cupid, as the next stanza, reverting to the Alexandrian younger god, makes clear:

Which well perceiving, that imperious boy,
Doth therwith tip his sharp empoisned darts;
Which glancing through the eyes with countenance coy,
Rest not, till they have pierst the trembling harts,
And kindled flame in all their inner parts,
Which sucks the blood, and drinketh up the lyfe
Of carefull wretches with consuming griefe.

(120–26)

This stanza also makes clear, however, that the divine origin of beauty and the fusion of the two Cupids do not constitute a theodicy for the poet of the hymn, as they had for Colin Clout. Recognition that Rosalind was a "thing celestiall . . . of divine regard and heavenly hew" (*Col.* 930, 932) led Colin to blame himself for his pains, justifying Rosalind and implicitly Cupid. But the same fusion and the same recognition only bring the poet of the hymn back to his starting point, to the "imperious boy" whose cruelty now seems more inexplicable because it seizes upon man's half-divine susceptibility to beauty. Three more stanzas detailing Cupid's tyranny further weight the imaginative burden until the poet comes to question the poem he is writing: "Why then do I this honor unto thee, / Thus to ennoble thy victorious name. . . ?" (148–49). Finally, remembrance of his own pain prompts him to question the identification of the two Cupids that he had assumed:

But if thou be indeede, as men thee call,
The worlds great Parent, the most kind preserver
Of living wights, the soveraine Lord of all,

> How falles it then, that with thy furious fervour,
> Thou doest afflict as well the not deserver,
> As him that doeth thy lovely heasts despize,
> And on thy subjects most doest tyrannize?
>
> (155–61)

The question is exactly that incarnated in Conti's Cupid: how can the apparent injustice and cruelty of love conceal, like a Silenus, an unseen divinity? Spenser's phrasing recalls, without echoing, Biblical doubts about the distribution of evils, and his answer is the same as the Psalmist's: "The Lord tests the righteous and the wicked" (Ps. 11:5):

> Yet herein eke thy glory seemeth more,
> By so hard handling those which best thee serve,
> That ere thou doest them unto grace restore,
> Thou mayest well trie if they will ever swerve,
> And mayest them make it better to deserve;
> And having got it, may it more esteeme.
> For things hard gotten, men more dearely deeme.
>
> (162–68)

Gall in love exists to make the honey sweeter and also to deter "baseborne mynds" who, wanting only immediate and unmingled gratification, "feele no love, but loose desyre" (173, 175). The pains that may seem to "make a lovers life a wretches hell" remain in sight till the end of the poem, but only to play their part in the affirmation that emerges finally in Christian trappings:

> By these, O Love, thou doest thy entrance make,
> Unto thy heaven, and doest the more endeere,
> Thy pleasures unto those which them partake,
> As after stormes when clouds begin to cleare,
> The Sunne more bright and glorious doth appeare;
> So thou thy folke, through paines of Purgatorie,
> Dost beare unto thy blisse, and heavens glorie.
>
> (273–79)

The poet of the hymn thus makes his religion, affirming his faith that that man is happy whom the god of love chastens. The future reward will redeem the present sorrow and then, concludes the poet,

> would I thinke these paines no paines at all,
> And all my woes to be but penance small.
>
> Then would I sing of thine immortall praise
> An heavenly Hymne, such as the Angels sing,
> And thy triumphant name then would I raise

Bove all the gods, thee only honoring,
My guide, my God, my victor, and my king;
Till then, dread Lord, vouchsafe to take of me
This simple song, thus fram'd in praise of thee.

(299–307)

These lines seem excessive, even in the occasionally perfervid hymn. They seem, in fact, to exemplify the problem acknowledged in *Amoretti* 72:

Oft when my spirit doth spread her bolder winges,
In mind to mount up to the purest sky:
it down is weighd with thoght of earthly things
and clogd with burden of mortality,
Where when that soverayne beauty it doth spy,
resembling heavens glory in her light:
drawne with sweet pleasures bayt, it back doth fly,
and unto heaven forgets her former flight.
There my fraile fancy fed with full delight,
doth bath in blisse and mantleth most at ease:
ne thinks of other heaven, but how it might
her harts desire with most contentment please.
Hart need not with none other happinesse,
but here on earth to have such hevens blisse.

The poet of the hymn tries to deny this failure of "earthly or naturall love" to lead to "heavenly and celestiall" love in lines that echo those of the sonnet:

For love is Lord of truth and loialtie,
Lifting himselfe out of the lowly dust,
On golden plumes up to the purest skie,
Above the reach of loathly sinfull lust,
Whose base affect through cowardly distrust
Of his weake wings, dare not to heaven fly,
But like a moldwarpe in the earth doth ly.

(176–82)

Since beauty is a divine spark and, as we learn in the *Hymne in Honour of Beautie*, not merely pleasing physical proportion, love has nothing whatever to do with lust, although it does not exclude physical satisfaction. Lust is necessarily disloyal, since it aims only at physical satisfaction, at the flesh, which is impermanent and therefore unreal, an "outward shew of things that only seeme" (*HB*, 91). But the distinction between love and lust in the second hymn does not resolve the failure of *Amoretti* 72, which describes an aborted flight, not of lust, but of love. The first two hymns present just such an aborted flight. Having insisted on the distinction between aspiring love and earthbound lust and set his foot upon the Platonic ladder, the poet seems to get no further. The lovers' paradise that ends the *Hymne in Honour of Love* is, like Blake's Beulah, a garden of earthly delights whose inhabitants in their "joyous happie rest" look for no further ascent (281). The *Hymne in Honour of Beautie* declines, after outlining a Neoplatonic contemplative progression, into a brittle blazon and cajolment of a mortal beauty. The first two hymns nowhere acknowledge this failure of natural love to lead to the true heaven, but in the *Fowre Hymnes* as a whole it is forcefully acknowledged. At the beginning of the *Hymne of Heavenly Love*, Spenser tells us that he has turned the tenor of his string from "that mad fit, which fooles call love" (9) and, in the dedication of the volume, offers the second pair of hymns "by way of retractation to reforme" the first pair. How seriously to take this "retractation" has been a topic of endless debate and would gladly be avoided here if it did not bear directly upon the theodicy of Cupid which is seemingly recanted in the last of Spenser's minor poems.

In the dedication, Spenser's reason for retracting the two hymns of his greener age is not that they are immoral in themselves, but "that the same too much pleased those of like age and disposition, which being too vehemently caried with that kind of affection, do rather sucke out poyson to their strong passion, then hony to their honest delight." Abuse does not require recantation, however. Spenser might have replied with Sidney, "But what, shall the abuse of a thing make the right use odious?" or, as he observes in the *Hymne in Honour of Beautie*, "Nothing so good, but that through guilty shame / May be corrupt, and wrested unto will."[47] The passage at the beginning of the *Hymne of Heavenly Love* where he echoes Chaucer's retractions reads more convincingly as a rhetorical offensive against his critics than as a chastisement of his muse. As many critics have noted, Spenser dedicates his hymns to the Countesses of Cumberland and Warwick "as to the most excellent and rare ornaments of all true love and beautie, both in the one and the other kinde."[48] The retraction, in other words, is rather ambiguous.

The fundamental issue for the continuity of the *Fowre Hymnes* is the continuity of the progression from "earthly or naturall love and beautie" to "heavenly and celestiall." The conventional image for this progression, the ladder loosely called Platonic, has confused the issue in at least two ways. It has made the continuity of the progression appear to depend upon identification of "rungs" or stages and therefore diverted attention to Spenser's possible sources. Secondly, the image of the ladder has radically oversimplified the nature of the progression, whose continuity is not that of a static hierarchy, one stage *above* another, but that of a sequence, one stage *after* another. The ladder itself is less important than the process of climbing it.

Climbing a ladder is a sequence of repeated actions; every step up transcends yet repeats previous steps. While climbing, you have no need to attend to rungs already passed, and, if you fear vertigo, you will not look down. If the ladder is Platonic, then its dimensions are moral, and you will have even more reason to scorn the base degrees by which you did ascend.[49] Indeed, to do otherwise is wicked, "for when the will abandons what is above itself, and turns to what is lower, it becomes evil—not because that is evil to which it turns, but because the turning itself is wicked" (*City of God*, 12.6). St. Augustine's is the static view, however. The careful climber does not fix his attention on his goal, but on the next step. Each step, therefore, requires him to turn from the rung just reached to the next higher. This process is the *raison d'être* of the Platonic ladder, on which the climber attends to the next step because his goal is inconceivable. The Platonic ascent was, of course, early grafted onto Christian thought, but, whether Neoplatonic or Christian, technical or vague, it is a sequence of repeated conversion, without which the upward movement would stall.[50]

If conversion is a part of the continuity of a Platonic progression, however, how could Spenser renounce his earlier hymns without continuing them, dramatically exemplifying their Platonic theory of love which he is trying to discredit? No amount of impatience or anger with the lower stages of the spirit can prevail against this paradox.[51] The only argument that can prevail is one that denies history, maintaining that it was not through, but despite, the first hymns that the poet came to write the second. This would be a hard argument for Spenser, whose sense of continuity is such that he can write:

> Like as a ship, that through the Ocean wyde
> Directs her course unto one certaine cost,
> Is met of many a counter winde and tyde,
> With which her winged speed is let and crost,
> And she her selfe in stormie surges tost;
> Yet making many a borde, and many a bay,
> Still winneth way, ne hath her compasse lost:
> Right so it fares with me in this long way,
> Whose course is often stayd, yet never is astray.
>
> (*FQ*, 6.12.1)

Moreover, by presenting the first hymns as products of "th' heat of youth" (*HHL*, 10), Spenser accommodates the hierarchy of his hymns to the succession of youth and age. This same appeal to sequence in Petrarch, Bembo, and Castiglione affirmed continuity despite their conversions or recantations. The final renunciation of the last hymn has perhaps a hint of discontinuity in the word "misled":

> Ah then my hungry soule, which long hast fed
> On idle fancies of thy foolish thought,
> And with false beauties flattring bait *misled*,
> Hast after vaine deceiptfull shadowes sought,
> Which all are fled, and now have left thee nought,
> But late repentance through thy follies prief;
> Ah ceasse to gaze on matter of thy grief.
>
> (288–94; emphasis added)

But repentance is not nought, and the passage as a whole accommodates to the Platonic movement. The closest the poet comes to asserting discontinuity—and therefore to a convincing retraction of the earthly hymns—is when, following the gospels, he inverts the Platonic progression in the *Hymne of Heavenly Love:*

> Him first to love, that us so dearly bought,
> And next, our brethren to his image wrought.[52]

Even this is not very close, for it lacks the emphasis of, to choose one example, Petrarch in the *Secretum:*

Francesco: Love of her [Laura] has without doubt led me to love God.
Augustine: But has reversed the order.
Francesco: In what sense?
Augustine: Because every creature should be loved out of love for the Creator, but you, however, caught by the charms of the creature, have not loved the Creator as you ought.[53]

While not insisting on the order, Spenser's lines not only admit, but enjoin human love. As in *Amoretti* 68, "Love is the lesson which the Lord us taught." Finally, the strongest statement of the Platonic theory is not in the first hymns, but in the fourth:

> Beginning then below, with th'easie vew
> Of this base world, subject to fleshly eye,
> From thence to mount aloft by order dew,
> To contemplation of th' immortall sky. . . .
>
> (22–25)

Later in the *Hymne of Heavenly Beautie* the image of the book of nature may seem more Christian because more medieval, but the fall of the natural world from revealing light to blinding darkness repeats the Platonic movement in miniature:

> The meanes therefore which unto us is lent,
> Him to behold, is on his workes to looke,
> Which he hath made in beauty excellent,
> And in the same, as in a brasen booke,
> To reade enregistred in every nooke
> His goodnesse, which his beautie doth declare,
> For all thats good is beautifull and faire.
>
> Thence gathering plumes of perfect speculation,
> To impe the wings of thy high flying mynd,

Mount up aloft through heavenly contemplation,
From this darke world, whose damps the soule do blynd. . . .

(127–37)

The world becomes dark only after one has mounted aloft.

If the argument of the heavenly hymns offers only an inconclusive recantation of the earthly ones, their imagery offers none at all. It is hard to see how the poet has turned the tenor of his string if the Love who lifts him to the heavens' height where he may sing his heavenly hymn is the same, at least in appearance, as the Love of the first hymn:

> For love is Lord of truth and loialtie,
> Lifting himselfe out of the lowly dust,
> On golden plumes up to the purest skie.
>
> (*HL*, 176–78)

> Love, lift me up upon thy golden wings,
> From this base world unto thy heavens hight,
> Where I may see those admirable things,
> Which there thou workest by thy soveraine might,
> Farre above feeble reach of earthly sight,
> That I thereof an heavenly Hymne may sing
> Unto the god of Love, high heavens king.
>
> (*HHL*, 1–7)

This likeness is a gesture toward continuity, Spenser's equivalent of the invocation of Amore at the end of the *Vita Nuova* and the *Trionfi*. It is only one of many such gestures. In his imagery the poet also faces a paradox, this one caused by centuries of commerce between the poetry of love and the poetry of devotion. This commerce is mutually profitable, as we have seen, except, perhaps, when a poet wishes to recant. If he has used the language of heaven, hell, and purgatory for profane love, how can he reclaim it for sacred love without suggesting the close relation between the two loves that he purports to repudiate? Elaborate parallelisms between the pairs of hymns proclaim rather than conceal this paradox.[54] The hymns are parallel because, though every step on the ladder to God is a new beginning, it is also a repetition. The early hymns are images or reflections of the more complete truths of the second pair.[55]

If the *Fowre Hymnes* are not an exercise in self-negation, neither do they fail in another way—because Spenser encountered irresolvable paradoxes in both imagery and argument and could not accomplish the recantation he promised. The paradoxes do not block his success; they *are* his success, reflecting his understanding that recantations are always partial and that genuine yeas include nays. What could be a better affirmation than an antithesis that progresses, a wandering that never goes astray, for a poet whose aim was not to retract, but, as he said in the dedication, "by way of retractation to reforme"?

We have wandered far from Cupid, but perhaps not astray. In the inconclusive recantation of the *Fowre Hymnes,* we can see an image of Spenser's characteristic blending of medieval and Renaissance. Like Conti, he joins the Renaissance theodicy of Cupid with the medieval concern for the abuse of fictional divinity. The heavenly hymns forestall the abuse mentioned in the dedication, much as the *Triumphus Pudicitiae* corrected the *Triumphus Cupidinis.* But Spenser does not deny Cupid's divinity by reducing him to an accident in a substance; his figurative divinity is subsumed within real divinity.

In *The Faerie Queene,* Cupid's divinity is circumscribed by the boundaries of Faeryland, and in that world apart he is one of the real gods, about whom opinions, rituals, and misrepresentations multiply. In reporting these appearances and in trying to see through them to Cupid's single deity, the narrator of *The Faerie Queene,* especially in Book 3, undertakes a theodicy different in mode but similar in concerns to that of the minor poems.

7

The Faerie Queene

Among the gods and goddesses who figure in *The Faerie Queene*, Cupid is the most active, as a glance at the Whitman *Subject-Index* will show. He appears or is mentioned in every book except Book 5 and in enough contradictory variety to make any reader despair of making sense of him. He can promote the frivolous lusts of Malecasta's courtiers and one canto later effect "the fatall purpose of divine foresight" (3.3.2). He appears as a capricious and cruel infant and as a "Great God of love" (4.7.1). He represents a principle of destruction akin to Mutabilitie, but looks like Life itself. *The Faerie Queene* would seem to confirm Bacon's opinion: "That which the Poets say of *Cupid* or *Love* cannot properly be attributed to one and the selfe same person."[1]

It is not, in fact, apparent that the reader of *The Faerie Queene* must make sense of these inconsistencies. Cupid intervenes in the action only in a few episodes and otherwise is not a protagonist, as he was in the *Roman de la rose* or the *Triumphus Cupidinis*. Characters and narrator regularly invoke Cupid, but their invocations lack the obvious structural importance that they had in *Colin Clouts Come Home Againe* or the *Fowre Hymnes*. Focusing upon Cupid does not produce a reading of the entire poem, then, but it does provide an approach to several major episodes and, more important, suggests several conclusions about how to read the entire poem. The most immediate of these conclusions is that the reader of *The Faerie Queene* must indeed make sense of Cupid because, despite appearances, his integrity as a figure is no less important than in the minor poems. Cupid's integrity, in turn, argues for the integrity of Spenser's narrative, in which even the ubiquitous god of love is neither an ornament nor a local device, but a figure that collects and communicates meanings, and in Book 3 even organizes the sequence of the plot. Unlike other Renaissance epics, *The Faerie Queene* does not merely use poetic theology intermittently; it is a poetic theology and therefore, although opinions about Cupid are legion, in the world of the poem he is one of the true gods.

In urging these arguments, I shall be controverting two of Spenser's best readers, C. S. Lewis and Paul J. Alpers. Toward the end of his life, Lewis began to implement his conviction that the "poetic theology" being studied by historians of Renaissance art could illuminate Spenser. Not surprisingly, therefore, in the posthumous *Spenser's Images of Life* he judged that Bacon's opinion holds for *The Faerie Queene*. What Spenser says of Cupid cannot properly be attributed to one and the self same person. To make sense of Cupid, Lewis would distinguish two persons, a true and a false Cupid.[2] Alpers, on the other hand, though not concentrating on Cupid, urges a view of the poem that renders trying to make sense of Cupid unnecessary and mistaken. *The Faerie Queene*, in Alpers's reading, has only intermittent rhetorical consistency and does not attempt to create a fictional world either in the sense of fully visualized space in which the poem's incidents occur or in the larger sense of an integral cosmos in which, for instance, a distinction between nature and supernature is sustained and significant. Unless *The Faerie Queene* represents such a cosmos, Cupid cannot have either fixed or evolving significance. If the reader's eyes are fixed before, lacking power to look backward, Cupid must lack the integrity that he had in the minor poems, where each appearance implicitly alluded to previous appearances. Alpers's view would posit neither one Cupid nor two, but as many as there are independent references to him in the poem.[3]

Both Lewis and Alpers want to account for Spenser's inconsistencies, and their methods are perhaps comparable to those of the mythographers, who wanted to account for the inconsistencies in the pagan poets' presentation of their gods. Lewis, like Boccaccio and his ancient and medieval predecessors, rationalizes the inconsistencies by duplicating Cupids. Alpers, like Giraldi or Cartari, escapes inconsistency by embracing multiplicity. If the poetic tradition, whose purposeful inconsistencies we have studied, offers little encouragement to either of these methods, Spenser's minor poems offer even less. In them Spenser repeatedly figured his justification of human love as a theodicy of Cupid, thereby affirming both Cupid's divinity and his singleness. In *The Faerie Queene* also there is only one Cupid, whose divinity is not asserted as in the minor poems and has nothing to do with the Empedoclean, cosmogonic Eros. Cupid is a god in *The Faerie Queene* because he is omnipotent and benevolent, rather than because he made the world, but faith in him emerges only gradually from the incidents of the poem and from attempts by the narrator and his characters to understand them. These attempts nearly always involve the question, "What kind of god causes these effects?" and are related to tentative answers to the same question offered earlier in the poem. Though the book or legend is the basic unit of the poem, the theodicy of Cupid makes a kind of underplot spanning several books, sketched in 1 and 2, addressed directly in 3, reverted to briefly in 4, and achieved with a sad resignation in 6. This is a large claim and the success of my argument must be its justification. I want to offer as an initial defense, however, the references to Cupid in the proems to Books 1 and 4.

After invoking his muse, and before invoking the Queen, Spenser in the proem to Book 1 invokes Cupid:

And thou most dreaded impe of highest *Jove*,
Faire *Venus* sonne, that with thy cruell dart
At that good knight so cunningly didst rove,
That glorious fire it kindled in his hart,
Lay now thy deadly Heben bow apart,
And with thy mother milde come to mine ayde:
Come both, and with you bring triumphant *Mart*,
In loves and gentle jollities arrayd,
After his murderous spoiles and bloudy rage allayd.

(1.pr.3)

This stanza adumbrates two of the justifications Spenser will offer for Cupid. The first concerns effects: though Cupid's dart is "cruell," it kindles "glorious fire." The second concerns rewards: like Mars himself, fierce wars at last give way to faithful loves. Arthur's suffering, "the undeserved wrong" that Spenser rues in the preceding stanza, will be redeemed by the harmony figured here in the union of Mars and Venus.[4] Why should Cupid be invoked at the beginning of the poem, however? What kind of aid can he offer the poet? Because the poem is highly allusive, it may be fair to find an answer in a comparison with Ovid.

In the first of the *Amores*, Ovid prepares to sing of "arms and violent wars" in epic hexameters, but Cupid condemns the poet to elegiacs by stealing one foot from the second line. At first Ovid disputes Cupid's authority over poetry and then complains of a lack of fit matter for elegiacs. Cupid quickly remedies this lack:

> . . . pharetra cum protinus ille soluta
> legit in exitium spicula facta meum,
> lunavitque genu sinuosum fortiter arcum,
> "quod" que "canas, vates, accipe" dixit "opus!"[5]

(Forthwith he loosed his quiver, and chose from it shafts that were made for my undoing. Against his knee he stoutly bent moonshape the sinuous bow, and "Singer," he said, "here, take what will be matter for thy song.")

Cupid has now determined both matter and meter, and Ovid bids farewell to both "iron wars" and his epic ambitions. Spenser, in contrast, is beginning an epic whose matter will combine "Fierce warres and faithfull loves" (1.pr.1). Its faithful loves will not be his own, however, and he therefore invokes Cupid's aid while asking him to lay his "deadly Heben bow apart." The invocation of Cupid, like the invocation of the muse, helps to define both the genre and matter of Spenser's poem.

The Second Part of the Faerie Queene was published in 1596, and, renewing his poem, Spenser also audaciously renews his invocation of Cupid. A mighty statesman, apparently Lord Burleigh, has criticized Spenser

> For praising love, as I have done of late,
> And magnifying lovers deare debate;
> By which fraile youth is oft to follie led,
> Through false allurement of that pleasing baite,
> That better were in vertues discipled,
> Than with vaine poemes weeds to have their fancies fed.
>
> (4.pr.1)

The criticism is twofold. The matter of Spenser's "looser rimes" may corrupt his readers, but, whatever their matter, "vain poemes" do readers little good. In both the dedicatory sonnet to Burleigh (omitted in 1596) and the letter to Raleigh, Spenser had anticipated this general complaint that good discipline is better "delivered plainly in way of precepts."[6] In the proem to Book 4, therefore, one might expect him to defend his method rather than his matter. Instead, he defends his matter and tacitly continues his method. Burleigh's failing is not that he cannot read poetry, but that he cannot love:

> Such ones ill judge of love, that cannot love,
> Ne in their frosen hearts feele kindly flame:
> For thy they ought not thing unknowne reprove,
> Ne naturall affection faultless blame,
> For fault of few that have abusd the same.
> For it of honor and all vertue is
> The roote, and brings forth glorious flowres of fame. . . .
>
> (4.pr.2)

The imagery of the stanza also subsumes the general defense within the special; "vaine poemes weeds" punningly cloak the "roote" of all honor and virtue and the "glorious flowres" it brings forth.

A fit audience for *The Faerie Queene*, then, will be capable of love, and fittest of all will be the Queene, "In whose chast breast all bountie naturall, / And treasures of true love enlocked beene" (4.pr.4). To assure her acceptance, Spenser again appeals to Cupid:

> Which that she may the better deigne to heare,
> Do thou dred infant, *Venus* darling dove,
> From her high spirit chase imperious feare,
> And use of awfull Majestie remove;
> In sted thereof with drops of melting love,
> Deawd with ambrosiall kisses, by thee gotten
> From thy sweete smyling mother from above,
> Sprinckle her heart, and haughtie courage soften,
> That she may hearke to love, and reade this lesson often.
>
> (4.pr.5)

The audaciousness of this stanza is its own defense. The fourth line, for example, alludes to Ovid's tale of the rape of Europa, in which Jove, changed to a bull for love, exemplifies the maxim that majesty and love are incompatible.[7] The allusion demonstrates the flexibility of Spenser's poetic methods and demands a similar flexibility from the reader. Stoic censors, to whom Spenser no longer sings, may be outraged, but fitter, more flexible readers will see that the invocation works both ways. If Cupid makes the Queen "the better deigne to heare," the Queen shows that Cupid's significance extends to the civic love that Spenser opposes as a principle of social order to Burleigh's "grave foresight." The Queen is the paragon of civic love, because she "loveth best, / And best is lov'd of all alive I weene" (4.pr.4).

Where the proem to Book 1 concerns the composition of the poem, the proem to Book 4 concerns its reception. The Queen, for example, must inspire the poet in 1 and "deigne to heare" him in 4. Because the later proem concerns reception, Spenser does not reinvoke the muse. His reinvocation of Cupid, however, pointedly continues both the matter and method that Burleigh had objected to in Book 3 and also begins the second major installment of the poem with an appropriate, if partial, parallel to the first. The invocations of Cupid in these proems are hardly decisive, but they may at least suggest that Spenser considers him as a part of the machinery of the poem's presentation—a figure whose integrity makes his *reinvocation* significant—and not merely as an isolated mythological ornament.

Cupid is hardly a major figure in Books 1 and 2, but his appearances must be surveyed here because they lay the groundwork for later developments in Books 3 and 4. This relationship between the first pair of books and the second probably argues less for Spenser's prescience than for Cupid's integrity as a figure whose potential significances will unfold only in the more appropriate contexts of the legends of chastity and friendship. It also illustrates the general truth that Spenser builds his effects cumulatively in *The Faerie Queene*. The poem teaches us which analogies among its manifold persons and incidents to attend to; it fashions us as readers while fashioning us as men and women. Indeed, it fashions us *by* fashioning us as readers in a virtuous and gentle discipline that encompasses both reading and living. To allow Spenser's didactic method to work, then, one must respect the sequence of details and episodes. This view of the proper way to read *The Faerie Queene*, fully implemented, would require here a plodding treatment, passage by passage, of those in which Cupid appears. Fortunately things group themselves by pairs in Books 1 and 2, so that it is possible to compromise, respecting the poem's sequence while proceeding topically through the three major issues introduced by Cupid's activities. These issues are the familiar abuse that deifies desire, an opposing faith in Cupid as an agent of Providence, and the relation between *eros* and *heros,* love and heroic endeavor. One further issue is really a narrative device— a form of indirect discourse by which the narrator records the opinions of figures like Redcrosse and Belphoebe in his own voice.

The first appearance of Cupid in Book 1 returns us to the medieval tradition, but now transformed. Amorous mortals, we remember, feigned love to be a god in the abuse of fiction that was a central issue in medieval appearances of Cupid. The nobleman of Andreas's dialogue used Cupid's unreal divinity to woo a lady, as would countless sonneteers, but in the *De planctu Naturae*, the *Vita Nuova,* and the *Trionfi,* the poet deified his own passion chiefly to deceive himself. These works both record and represent that self-deception and its undoing. In the first canto of *The Faerie Queene* Book 1, however, the old abuse of fiction is contained within a larger fiction whose characters, rather than the poet himself, are the illusionist and dupe.

Once the Redcrosse Knight and Una have retired to bed at Archimago's cottage, Archimago calls up two sprites "fittest for to forge true-seeming lyes" (1.1.38). The lies they forge are first a dream in which the Redcrosse Knight seems to see Venus bring Una to his bed, and then a false Una to carry on when he awakes. But why should Redcrosse believe that Una, "whom he waking evermore did weene / to be the chastest flowre, that ay did spring / On earthly braunch," has now become the "loose Leman" in his bed (1.1.48)? Archimago addresses this difficulty by schooling his sprites to plead heavenly compulsion. The lady in the dream complains "how that false winged boy / Her chast hart had subdewed, to learne Dame pleasures toy," and the lady in the bed elaborates:

> Ah Sir, my liege Lord and my love,
> Shall I accuse the hidden cruell fate,
> And mightie causes wrought in heaven above,
> Or the blind God, that doth me thus amate,
> For hoped love to winne me certaine hate?
> Yet thus perforce he bids me do, or die.
>
> (1.1.47, 51)

Venus leads the false Una to Redcrosse's bed and the Graces dance around hymning an antique epithalamion in order to indicate supernatural sanction like the omens that Dido thought had sanctified her "marriage" to Aeneas in the cave above Carthage.

Though this first spell fails to overthrow the Redcrosse Knight's virtue, Archimago is wrong to think it labor lost. The second spell builds upon the first, which has not only confirmed the self-righteousness that will lead the knight astray, but has also shaken his faith in Una. "Her doubtfull words made that redoubted knight / Suspect her truth"—that is, her fidelity.[8] Cupid is no respecter of vows; if he can force her to visit Redcrosse by night, he can force her to visit a convenient squire in a "secret part" of Archimago's cottage. Compulsion paradoxically liberates, as Redcrosse recognizes when he sees his lady "Now a *loose* Leman to vile service *bound,*" and he half-expects the ocular proof that Archimago shortly provides (1.1.48; emphasis added).

The reader who has watched Archimago rehearse his sprites will waste little belief on the divinity they invoke, but it is worth distinguishing Archimago's abuse of Cupid from the abuse anatomized by earlier poets. Cupid cannot be here a personification misrepresented as a divinity, for no lover justifies self-indulgence by deifying his own passion; the episode involves only the semblance of a lover and a pretended passion. Behind these "false shewes," however, stands their creator (1.1.46). Archimago imitates the earlier form of abuse, but his abuse is different, less like the delusion that makes desire a god than like the lies about Cupid in *Muiopotmos*. There the invidious lies of the nymphs and Arachne subtly commented upon the salutary lie of the poem itself. Here, as the language of the episode also suggests, Archimago's black magic reflects the dangerous potential of poetry to "abuse" its reader's "fantasy."

The nature of Archimago's abuse does not become clear until canto nine when Arthur describes the true dream-vision that Archimago has parodied. Arthur too dreams that a lady lay beside him and bad him love her dear, but when he awakes he finds only pressed grass where she had lain. On this scanty evidence, Arthur makes a leap of faith, vowing to seek out the lady who said she was the Faerie Queene, even though he cannot be sure "whether dreames delude, or true it were" (9.14). Redcrosse did just the opposite in response to his dream vision: he too feared that dreams delude, but proved his own lack of faith by trying to "prove his sense, and tempt her faigned truth" and ended up fleeing from his lady (1.50). Such detailed contrasts clinch the importance of pairing the episodes and extend also to a contrasting use of Cupid. Gloriana does not appeal to Cupid in Arthur's dream as the false Una did in Redcrosse's, nor does Arthur, though a rebel to Love, suffer an epic intervention in the fashion of the March eclogue. Instead, Arthur himself appeals to Cupid in a way that makes him once more a "sub-vicar" of God.

The episode began with Una asking Arthur to tell his name and nation and the adventure or high intent that brought him to Faeryland.

> Full hard it is (quoth he) to read aright
> The course of heavenly cause, or understand
> The secret meaning of th'eternall might,
> That rules mens wayes, and rules the thoughts of living wight.
>
> For whither he through fatall deepe foresight
> Me hither sent, for cause to me unghest,
> Or that fresh bleeding wound, which day and night
> Whilome doth rancle in my riven brest,
> With forced fury following *his* behest. . . .
>
> (1.9.6–7; emphasis added)

The ambiguous pronoun indicates that Arthur sees the wound of love as a means by which the eternal might rules men's ways. Arthur's suffering does not make him, like Colin in the *Shepheardes Calender*, doubt its providential purpose. But, pleading "Ah Love, lay downe thy bow, the whiles I may respire," he explains that his faith is new come by. Once, like Chaucer's Troilus or Poliziano's Giuliano, he was a scorner of love:

> That idle name of love, and lovers life,
> As losse of time, and vertues enimy
> I ever scornd, and joyd to stirre up strife,
> In middest of their mournfull Tragedy,
> Ay wont to laugh, when them I heard to cry,
> And blow the fire, which them to ashes brent:
> Their God himselfe, griev'd at my libertie,
> Shot many a dart at me with fiers intent,
> But I them warded all with wary government.
>
> (1.9.10)

A god whom human government can thwart might, as in many earlier poems, seem hardly a god at all, but Arthur concludes differently. His wary government, like Thomalin's courage in the March eclogue, has been "all in vaine." Cupid's inevitable victory proves the limitations of human government: "Nothing is sure that growes on earthly ground" (1.9.11). Una and Redcrosse should take example of Arthur, "Whose prouder vaunt that proud avenging boy / Did soone pluck downe, and curbd my libertie" (1.9.12). Where Cupid curbs Arthur's liberty, he "bound" Archimago's false Una to looseness, and the difference clarifies the earlier abuse. Archimago imitated the old abuse that feigns love to be a god "quoque liberior foret," in the tag from Seneca—"in order to enjoy greater liberty." But divine compulsion liberates only if one believes that the gods have power without goodness. Cupid curbs Arthur's liberty because Arthur, despite his earlier apostasy, now believes that Cupid is a god and that a god cannot be "vertues enimy." Cupid may inflict pain, but cannot cause evil; the pains of love, therefore, can only compel Arthur to do good while punishing his earlier hubris. Cupid's power binds the believer to loyalty rather than looseness. Arthur's belief in Cupid's divinity jibes with Spenser's in the proem and makes it clear that, although Archimago may imitate the abuse by which lust deifies itself, he also blasphemes a real god, like the courtiers of *Colin Clouts Come Home Againe*, who made Cupid "serve to them for sordid uses" (792).

If canto nine affirms Cupid's divinity, it hardly encourages attempts to distinguish between multiple Cupids. Several critics have followed Lewis in judging that the presence or absence of Cupid's bow and arrows identifies him "as a particular kind of Cupid." The arms are said to designate the false Cupid, enemy of chastity, "syre of lawlesse lust."[9] Lewis therefore dismisses as perfunctory the "cruell dart" with which Cupid roved at Arthur in the proem and ignores canto nine altogether. But Cupid's arms and their effects are more than perfunctorily mentioned in canto nine; they occupy a major portion of four stanzas. Arthur's plea, "Ah Love, lay downe thy bow," echoes the proem, "Lay now thy deadly Heben bow apart," and the conjunction thus underlined confirms the proem's introduction of Arthur as a victim of Cupid. If Cupid's arrows represent the pangs of "base desire," it follows that base desire motivates the poem's central quest. Actually, the association between Arthur and Cupid works in exactly the opposite way. If Cupid's wound rankles in Arthur's breast, then Cupid cannot be simply the sire of lawless lust. Lewis and his followers have reversed the process by which meaning attaches to Spenser's figures, reading their conclusions about the false Cupid in Busyrane's house back into earlier episodes. Instead, one ought to begin with Cupid's relation to both the hero and the poem, which Spenser seems concerned to establish in Book 1.

Book 2 runs a like race to Book 1, and Cupid, as we would expect if he is more than a rhetorical ornament, is part of the likeness. As in Book 1, linkages between episodes maintain Cupid's integrity, as do other linkages between references to Cupid in the two books. Context, not an iconographical code, continues to govern the meaning of references to Cupid, but, as linkages within and between books make clear, the context includes other, and potentially all other, references to Cupid in the poem.

Things come by pairs in Book 2. The first passage we have to consider mentions neither Cupid's name nor any identifying attribute, yet must be considered a reference to Cupid because it is paired with a later passage in which Cupid is mentioned. Arriving at the castle of Medina in canto two, Guyon naturally pays court to Medina herself. Her sisters Elissa and Perissa, the extremes of defect and excess, already have their knights, Sir Huddibras and Sansloy.

> These two gay knights, vowd to so diverse loves,
> Each other does envie with deadly hate,
> And dayly warre against his foeman moves,
> In hope to win more favour with his mate,
> And th'others pleasing service to abate,
> To magnifie his owne.
>
> (2.2.19)

When Guyon tries to pacify their strife, he finds himself in a three-way battle:

> Straunge sort of fight, three valiaunt knights to see
> Three combats joyne in one, and to darraine
> A triple warre with triple enmitee,
> All for their Ladies froward love to gaine,
> Which gotten was but hate. So love does raine
> In stoutest minds, and maketh monstrous warre;
> He maketh warre, he maketh peace againe,
> And yet his peace is but continuall jarre:
> O miserable men, that to him subject arre.
>
> (2.2.26)

By its nature, love is extreme, even love of the mean. Among the heroes of *The Faerie Queene*, only the knight of temperance is not, except in this stanza, a lover. His love for the *mean* here leads him to mistake the *means* for achieving it, and so he fights—entangled in paradoxes, making war to win love, admitting wrath to "pacifie" the wrathful.[10] The final paradox—that even Medina's love if gotten would be but hate—stems from her allegorical nature. She is not like Shakespeare's Hippolyta. Guyon woos her with his sword, but will not win her love by doing her injuries. Extremes can be tempered, but not conquered; if they could, the victory would be defeat.

This episode is not really about love—Medina does not mention it in her "pitthy words and counsel sad"—but the narrator's incidental mingling of Spenser's announced themes of love and war will dominate the references to Cupid in Book 2.[11] Here Spenser criticises the usual chivalric coupling of love and war through the intermediary, fame. Stanza 25 indirectly reports Guyon's opinion of the "triple warre":

> Wondrous great prowesse and heroick worth
> He shewed that day, and rare ensample made,
> When two so mighty warriors he dismade. . . .
> So double was his paines, so double be his prayse.
>
> (2.2.25)

Like Sir Huddibras and Sansloy, Guyon follows the chivalric creed that war produces praise and praise wins love. As Spenser reflects later, "It hath bene through all ages ever seene, / That with the praise of armes and chevalrie, / The prize of beautie still hath joyned beene" (4.5.1). Making peace among the knights, Medina attacks this creed's premise:

> Sad be the sights, and bitter fruits of warre,
> And thousand furies wait on wrathfull sword;
> Ne ought the prayse of prowesse more doth marre,
> Then fowle revenging rage, and base contentious jarre.
>
> (2.2.30)

Praise, Medina argues, is much more due to "lovely concord, and most sacred peace" (st. 31).

The episode clearly paired with this one rejoins the same issue and adds a mythological vocabulary. In canto six, Phaedria also separates battling knights, but advances a debased version of Medina's doctrine:

> Debatefull strife, and cruell enmitie
> The famous name of knighthood fowly shend;
> But lovely peace, and gentle amitie,
> And in Amours the passing houres to spend,
> The mightie martiall hands doe most commend;

Of love they ever greater glory bore,
Then of their armes: *Mars* is *Cupidoes* frend,
And is for *Venus* loves renowmed more,
Then all his wars and spoiles, the which he did of yore.

(2.6.35)

Phaedria rejects the same chivalric creed as Medina, but replaces it with one equally extreme. Love, she says, wins renown rather than rewarding it, but her "Amours" only appear to be "lovely peace, and gentle amitie." In fact, like the love that spurred the knights of canto two, they are a form of war:

Another warre, and other weapons I
Doe love, where love does give his sweet alarmes,
Without bloudshed, and where the enemy
Does yeeld unto his foe a pleasant victory.

(2.6.34)

Spenser will not work out a love that is a form of concord until Book 4. Phaedria's casual invocation of Mars, Cupid, and Venus—they are merely myths to her—parodies Spenser's invocation of them in the first proem, but her misapplication reflects little upon them, even upon their openness to abuse. She has already abused the Scriptural lilies of the field to urge that knights fulfill themselves by vegetating.

Between Medina's plea and its distorted echo on Phaedria's isle occurs a double reference that appears to challenge, but in fact confirms, the view of Cupid I have been proposing. The second and third stanzas of the long blazon of Belphoebe's beauty describe her eyes and forehead:

In her faire eyes two living lamps did flame,
Kindled above at th'heavenly makers light,
And darted fyrie beames out of the same,
So passing persant, and so wondrous bright,
That quite bereav'd the rash beholders sight:
In them the blinded god his lustfull fire
To kindle oft assayd, but had no might;
For with dredd Majestie, and awfull ire,
She broke his wanton darts, and quenched base desire.

Her ivorie forhead, full of bountie brave,
Like a broad table did it self dispred,
For Love his loftie triumphes to engrave,
And write the battels of his great godhed. . . .

(2.3.23–24)

At first these stanzas seem to demand a distinction between Cupid, patron of *base* desire, and Love, whose *loftie* triumphs might more appropriately be linked with Belphoebe.[12] But to make this distinction is precisely to miss the point. Through much of the blazon, Belphoebe seems consciously to cooperate with the poet. His art in describing her effect on a beholder reflects her self-conscious design (as several critics have noted).[13] In the lines on her eyes, the poet's words reflect Belphoebe's understanding of her own attractiveness and her design for combatting it. Although her resistance to Cupid echoes Arthur's, Cupid does not aim his darts at Belphoebe; she need not quench base desire within herself, but in "rash beholders." The tale of her miraculous conception, which Spenser relates in Book 3, makes the nature of Belphoebe's virtue clearer, as does the echo when Spenser describes Acrasia's eyes:

> And her faire eyes sweet smyling in delight,
> Moystened their fierie beames, with which she thrild
> Fraile harts, yet quenched not.
>
> (2.12.78)

But Belphoebe's resistance to Cupid is clear enough without appealing to later passages. Cupid's arrows normally strike from the eyes to the heart, and his victims never feel his fire in their eyes. The stanza reverses the allegory of enamorment familiar since the troubadours and at the same time nearly reduces Cupid to a personification of the spirit in Belphoebe's eyes and the desire kindled in the beholder. If the stanza reflects Belphoebe's self-awareness, then she sees herself as part of a triumph of chastity like Laura, who also broke Cupid's arrows in the mismatched conflict that exposed him as merely an accident given an imaginary substance and deity.

The incidents of canto three demonstrate, however, that Belphoebe overestimates her ability to control the effects of her beauty on beholders. Her beauty kindles Braggadocchio to "burne in filthy lust"; flight and her boar-spear must protect her rather than "dredd Majestie, and awfull ire" (2.3.42). Moreover, her understanding, as reflected in the lines on Cupid, is gravely simplistic, as she will show later, first when she does not recognize the wound she has given Timias "Through an unwary dart, which did rebound / From her faire eyes and gracious countenaunce" (3.5.42) and again when she mistakes his attentions to Amoret (4.7.35–6). Belphoebe both overestimates and oversimplifies her victory over Cupid, and Spenser signals her partial understanding with the next stanza's contradictory view that the "loftie triumphes" and battles of Love's "great godhed" might suitably be engraved in Belphoebe's face. Love is not a different god; he is a corrective view of Cupid.

The blazon of Belphoebe illustrates the use of a form of indirect address that allows the narrator to report in his own voice the opinions of his characters, or rather—to drop the convenient fiction that Spenser's figures are people—it allows the narrator to present the constitutive ideas of his figures in ironic simplicity or isolation. Another example of this technique was passed over in

Book 1: another blazon with another reference to Cupid. The last of the three sisters whom Redcrosse meets at the House of Holinesse is Charissa,

> a woman in her freshest age,
> Of wondrous beauty, and of bountie rare,
> With goodly grace and comely personage,
> That was on earth not easie to compare;
> Full of great love, but *Cupids* wanton snare
> As hell she hated, chast in work and will. . . .
>
> (1.10.30)

As in the stanzas on Belphoebe's beauty, an inconsistency points toward the status of these lines as indirect discourse. Three stanzas later Charissa instructs the Redcrosse Knight "hatred warely to shonne." Unless Charity is hypocritical, then, the condemnation of Cupid must reflect the awakened zeal of Redcrosse, who has just emerged from the ministrations of penance and repentance. As his imputation of hatred to her confirms, Redcrosse is still to Charity an "unacquainted guest" and has need of her lesson (1.10.29). Charity may condemn Cupid, though not *hate* him, just as Redcrosse must eventually renounce his love for Una, because "loose loves are vaine, and vanish into nought" (1.10.62). But, as the hermit Contemplation continues, teaching the doctrine we traced in the *Fowre Hymnes,* only through keeping faith with these loves do we come to renounce them.

These references to Cupid from canto ten of Book 1 through half of Book 2 are all in one way or another negative, representing, often in subtle indirect discourse, the views of figures who question or contradict or depart from the view of Cupid implied in Book 1 through his association with Arthur and with the poet. Cupid's divinity and his singleness, never explicitly established, would soon lose their force if the poem continued to wander in a labyrinth of opinion, and in the later cantos of Book 2 the poet therefore underprops Cupid's divinity and reiterates his singleness.

Both underpropping and reiteration begin in canto eight when an angel watches over Guyon, who has been overcome after emerging from Mammon's cave. The canto begins with two rhetorical questions which the angel's presence answers: "And is there care in heaven? and is there love / In heavenly spirits to these creatures bace. . . ?" (2.8.1). God's love, mentioned twice more in the opening stanzas, receives further emphasis in a stanza-long simile describing the angel:

> Like as *Cupido* on *Idaean* hill,
> When having laid his cruell bow away,
> And mortall arrowes, wherewith he doth fill
> The world with murdrous spoiles and bloudie pray,
> With his faire mother he him dights to play,

> And with his goodly sisters, *Graces* three;
> The Goddesse pleased with his wanton play,
> Suffers her selfe through sleepe beguild to bee,
> The whiles the other Ladies mind their merry glee.
>
>   (2.8.6)

"The pedant finds the comparison ludicrous," wrote Professor de Selincourt, "the more prosaic pietist finds it profane" (p. lvii). Recent critics find it neither, dividing into those who find it appropriate and those who find it ironic, although it ought to be seen as both.

To defend its appropriateness, the critic invokes Renaissance syncretism and identifies Cupido on Idaean hill as the Neoplatonic celestial Cupid, an appropriate figure for the "love in heavenly spirits to these creatures bace."[14] If the argument stopped here it would usefully suggest that the angel is like Cupid because both execute the designs of Providence, thus reiterating Arthur's faith in Cupid as an agent of Providence. But most defenders of the simile's appropriateness go on to exclude the armed or blind Cupid who, they say, signifies base desire and is therefore obviously inappropriate.[15] Spenser's lines, however, argue against this disjunction. Ida, of course, is a place in the mundane world, and the disarmed, angelic Cupid is the same being as the tyrannous, cruel Cupid, but at a different *time:*

> When having laid his cruell bow away,
> And mortall arrowes, wherewith he doth fill
> The world with murdrous spoiles and bloudie pray. . . .

Like the proem to Book 1, which it echoes, the simile implies that Cupid's kindness follows and perhaps compensates for his cruelty. "Lovers heaven must passe by sorrowes hell," as Glauce will say later (4.6.32). Armed and dangerous, Cupid may not look like an agent of divinity, but, unlike many of its defenders, Spenser's simile does not distinguish Cupids in order to preserve an easy decorum. We miss the meaning of the simile if we notice its syncretism, but do not see it as an oblique expression of the faith that Cupid employs his "mortall arrowes" in the service of Providence.

Even if Spenser *had* distinguished and banished a false Cupid, the simile would remain difficult, still in its context less than "a perfectly understandable and effective" comparison for an angel.[16] The best comment on its irony is Donald Cheney's: "The reader's sense that Guyon is protected by a merciful deity beyond his own comprehension is made the more ironic by the fact that he is watched over by an angel in the form of Cupid, the last figure to whom this knight of Maidenhead might expect to turn."[17] The literary relations of the simile further underline its ironies and the status of its Cupid, for it is the converse of a more famous simile. The god of love in the *Roman de la rose,* we remember, looked like "an angel come straight from heaven." In the *Vita*

Nuova, Dante recast this simile in Biblical detail, and Chaucer compressed it into the adjective "aungelyke" in the *Prologue to the Legend of Good Women* (F text, 236). Not only Spenser's simile, but the situation in which it appears is the converse of this tradition. The angelic Cupids of the *Roman*, Chapter 12 of the *Vita Nuova*, and the *Prologue to the Legend* all appear in dream-visions, framed by the form in which "many men say that there is nothing but fables and lies," as the *Roman* concedes in its first line. Spenser also has a figure "slumbring fast," but Guyon does not dream and, indeed, never sees the angel. Spenser's conversion of the old simile and its situation thus emphasizes the truth of the divine intervention he records and implicitly also of the Cupid he chooses for comparison.

The last Cupid of Book 2 appears in the House of Temperance and sorts out the book's earlier references to Cupid. Alma, the lady of the castle, is "a virgin bright; that had not yet felt *Cupides* wanton rage" (2.9.18), yet Cupid is a welcome visitor in her parlor:

> And in the midst thereof upon the floure,
> A lovely bevy of faire Ladies sate,
> Courted of many a jolly Paramoure,
> The which them did in modest wise amate,
> And eachone sought his Lady to aggrate:
> And eke emongst them litle *Cupid* playd
> His wanton sports, being returned late
> From his fierce warres, and having from him layd
> His cruell bow, wherewith he thousands hath dismayd.
>
> (2.9.34)

At its third repetition, this time in the authoritative *locus* of Book 2, this version of Cupid's warfare and disarming may seem to gather up and correct the earlier references, which were similarly attached to female figures. True, "he maketh warre, he maketh peace againe," but not true that "his peace is but continuall jarre." Phaedria misunderstands the truth of her own motto; Mars *is* Cupid's friend, but in several senses besides the one she means. Cupid sometimes lays his cruel bow aside, but no one, not even Belphoebe, disarms him or breaks his wanton darts. Alma's Cupid sums up these echoes from earlier cantos of Book 2, but its clearest parallel, enforced by the parallel structure of Books 1 and 2, is with the Cupid excluded from the House of Holinesse.[18] The later reference does not summarize or retract the earlier, but completes it, adding the affirmation without which renunciation seems both empty and easy.

Cupid's role in the parallelism between Books 1 and 2, though small, argues for his integrity, of course, but it is an integrity despite or within a multitude of invocations, opinions, and lies. Even the poet and Arthur, whose shared belief in Cupid Book 2 subtly sustains, pray to a god they have never seen. In the House of Temperance, however, Spenser begins to give substance to the name. Cupid is not merely mentioned in canto nine, he *appears* amongst the bevy of ladies in Alma's parlor: "And eke emongst them litle *Cupid* playd. . . ." The nature of the place explains why Cupid can appear here without the fanfare of the theophanies in Andreas Capellanus, the *Roman de la rose,* or the *Vita Nuova.* The House of Temperance images the organization and faculties of the human body. Its residents are traits and passions which are accidents in individual human beings, but essences or universals in Alma's house, an unfolded archetype of human beings. Spenser analyzes and calls attention to the nature of the place by introducing his heroes to Shamefastnesse and Prays-desire, which are from one point of view accidents within themselves and from another essences which they embody.[19] Like the bevy of passions amongst whom he plays, Cupid is a personification, but the medieval distinction between the god and the personification has no more meaning here than in the minor poems. For Spenser the distinction would be between Cupid's immanence and transcendence. In the House of Temperance, we see his immanence. The god himself will not appear in Faeryland until Book 6.

Cupid is talked about and even once appears in Books 1 and 2, but he is not an actor or a significant force. Except for Arthur, everyone in those books shares Alma's lot; no one has "yet felt *Cupides* wanton rage." Books 3 and 4, however, are pageants of Cupid's power, and the opening of canto five could stand as their motto:

> Wonder it is to see, in diverse minds,
> How diversly love doth his pageants play,
> And shewes his powre in variable kinds.

Interlaced tales on the model of Ariosto replace the single quests of the first two books, because chastity is only one of love's variable kinds, and Spenser cannot picture it without anatomizing love, its effects, its enemies, and its justifications. Cupid and Venus are not only actors in several of these interlaced tales, but also become important structural devices in each book, as several distinguished studies have shown.[20] Rather than reconsider their function in his *anatomy* of love, I want to suggest that they also function in a *theodicy* of Cupid that develops alongside the anatomy, though it is not complete until Book 6.

Colin Clout and the poet of the *Hymne in Honour of Love* defend Cupid's divinity explicitly, at the same time affirming their own experience, since both are lovers. The theodicy of Cupid in *The Faerie Queene* is less straightforward. As we saw in the first proem, the narrator has escaped Cupid's arrow and, though no Chaucerian naïf, speaks as a spectator rather than as a participant in Love's pageants. He neither prophesies Cupid's mighty mysteries nor justifies Cupid's ways, but rather comments upon the stories he is telling. In Books 3 and 4, far more palpably than in 1 and 2, he presents himself disposing and observing these stories, but the pose is disingenuous, of course, for he also invents them.[21] *The Faerie Queene*'s theodicy of Cupid is therefore double and indirect; the poet determines Cupid's actions and victims and then comments upon them. Obviously such a theodicy will be as facile as the poet wishes. Spenser, I will argue, is meditating in narrative on Love's power and wants so little to fudge the outcome that Book 3 ends, not with a god justified, but with a temple destroyed.

The easiest way for Spenser to fudge his justification of Cupid would be to unite his lovers in mutual bliss that would demonstrate the truth of Glauce's maxim: "Lovers heaven must passe by sorrowes hell" (4.6.32). But there are very few happy endings in *The Faerie Queene*. Only Marinell and Florimell marry; the reunion of Scudamour and Amoret is cancelled in the augmented edition; Merlin prophesies little bliss for Britomart before "secret foes" murder her husband. Spenser acknowledges the pains of love as unflinchingly in *The Faerie Queene* as in *Colin Clouts Come Home Againe* or the first *Hymne*. Thomalin's emblem from the March eclogue might serve for the whole *Faerie Queene:*

> Of Hony and of Gaule in love there is store:
> The Honye is much, but the Gaule is more.

The ability to choose Cupid's victims gives Spenser, however, a second and more subtle way to fudge his justification of Cupid, one which he does not fully acknowledge until Book 3, canto 10. It will be convenient to discuss it first.

Among all the lovers false and true of *The Faerie Queene*, Spenser reserves Cupid's darts, and in one case his bridle, for the true lovers, the heroes of the poem: Arthur, Britomart, Calidore, Marinell, Scudamour, Amoret.[22] Braggadocchio, the witch's son who moons for Florimell, the fisherman who assaults her, the faithless knights who fight all through Book 4 for love of one lady or another—none of these base lovers ever mentions Cupid, nor does the poet in connection with them. Cupid's associations with places in Faeryland follow the same pattern. He is present in the House of Temperance, the Garden of Adonis, and the Temple of Venus and absent from the Bower of Bliss, an absence, as C. S. Lewis said, "very remarkable to anyone well read in previous allegory."[23] Important exceptions to this pattern show Spenser worrying that its rationale may be arbitrary or facile, but, before turning to the exceptions, it is important to note that the pattern does have a rationale.

Spenser presents the rationale for his use of Cupid at the beginning of canto three:

> Most sacred fire, that burnest mightily
> In living brests, ykindled first above,
> Emongst th'eternall spheres and lamping sky,
> And thence pourd into men, which men call Love;

Not that same, which doth base affections move
In brutish minds, and filthy lust inflame,
But that sweet fit, that doth true beautie love,
And choseth vertue for his dearest Dame,
Whence spring all noble deeds and never dying fame:

Well did Antiquitie a God thee deeme,
That over mortall minds hast so great might,
To order them, as best to thee doth seeme,
And all their actions to direct aright. . . .

(3.3.1–2)

Spenser here follows Poliziano, who had also made Cupid a spur to public and heroic virtues, and, like Ficino, he elevates the familiar distinction between love and lust into a distinction between a god of love and an ambiguous force responsible for "base affections." Where Ficino had stated the negative—"the sacred name of Love is given falsely" to base affections—Spenser states the positive, and the "dread darts" of the next stanza make clear that the Love properly deemed a god is not to be distinguished from Cupid. Naturally, then, Cupid will stir up the "high intents" of the heroes of the poem and have nothing to do with the base desires of the villains. Guinizelli's famous line— "Al cor gentil ripara sempre Amore"—could serve as the motto for most of Cupid's doings in *The Faerie Queene*, for he inflames only the noble.

Ficino had made the divinity in the ancient double metaphor "god of love" control what kind of love could be signified. Realignment of Cupid so that he no longer stimulated human lust made Ficino's theodicy possible, even easy, just as it did Spenser's theodicies in *Colin Clouts Come Home Againe* and the first *Hymne*. But in *The Faerie Queene* the distinction between love and lust conflicts with Spenser's impulse to anatomize love in all its variable kinds. This impulse, whose motto might be "Omnia vincit Amor," appears explicitly in another canto opening already quoted:

Wonder it is to see, in diverse minds,
How diversly love doth his pageants play,
And shewes his powre in variable kinds:
The baser wit, whose idle thoughts alway
Are wont to cleave unto the lowly clay,
It stirreth up to sensuall desire,
And in lewd slouth to wast his carelesse day:
But in brave sprite it kindles goodly fire,
That to all high desert and honour doth aspire.

(3.5.1)

This stanza collapses the distinctions drawn at the beginning of canto three between the sources of love and lust. There is no longer a divine source of love and an unspecified, but certainly not divine, source of lust, but rather a single power whose effects vary according to the persons affected. This power has the same great might over mortal minds as the deified love of canto three, but it does not direct all their actions "aright," indeed, does not direct them at all. Lacking the moral justification, it cannot easily be deemed a god, and the stanza therefore uses no mythology and, with its neuter pronouns (*his* is the old neuter possessive), only minimal personification. The idea of love as a morally neutral force neatly unifies Book 3's anatomy of love, but conflicts with its theodicy. Or, more accurately, Spenser's anatomy of love leads him to question, as had Leone Ebreo and Natale Conti, the arbitrariness of realigning Cupid so that he is responsible only for "goodly fire." These questions appear in the exceptions to the pattern that Cupid wounds only the heroes of the poem, the true lovers "that to all high desert and honour [do] aspire."

An obvious exception is Spenser's imitation of the first Idyll of Moschus in canto six. Venus, searching for the runaway Cupid, finds court, city, and country all complaining of Cupid's tyranny. Few of these victims can be heroes, but Spenser emphasizes not the variable kinds of love in this passage, but its uniform pains.

A more important exception occurs in the first canto of Book 3. After describing the tapestry of Venus and Adonis that adorns the great chamber of Castle Joyous, Spenser describes the use to which that chamber is put:

> So was that chamber clad in goodly wize,
> And round about it many beds were dight,
> As whilome was the antique worldes guize,
> Some for untimely ease, some for delight,
> As pleased them to use, that use it might:
> And all was full of Damzels, and of Squires,
> Dauncing and reveling both day and night,
> And swimming deepe in sensuall desires,
> And *Cupid* still emongst them kindled lustfull fires.
>
> (3.1.39)

As Paul Alpers says, the last line of this stanza "does not describe something that is actually going on in Malecasta's chamber," but neither is it merely a stock formula.[24] Castle Joyous, with its mythological tapestry, its mimic orgy, and its Lydian harmony, is a deliberate imitation of "the antique worldes guize." Indeed, the transition between this stanza and the preceding one assimilates the orgy to the tapestries: the flower into which Adonis was transmuted "in that cloth was wrought, as if it lively grew. / *So* was that chamber clad in goodly wize . . ." (3.1.38–39). "So" refers to the whole tale of Venus and Adonis, but the parallelism between "that cloth" and "that chamber" with their passive verbs makes "so" for a moment identify the lively imitation in the cloth with the livelier imitation in the orgy. Cupid completes this assimilation; where the squires and damzels merge into the tapestries, he steps out of them. He is the deity which the neo-paganism of Castle Joyous requires, and Spenser catches their accent in the flat assertion: "And *Cupid* still emongst them kindled lustfull fires." But Malecasta's courtiers are acting out one of Love's pageants. How can we be sure that Cupid is not the god they take him for? Spenser does not seriously consider this question until canto ten, the episode of Malbecco and Helenore.[25]

When Britomart and Satyrane set out from Malbecco's castle leaving Paridell malingering behind, Malbecco redoubles his watch over his wife.

> But *Paridell* kept better watch, then hee,
> A fit occasion for his turne to find:
> False love, why do men say, thou canst not see,
> And in their foolish fancie feigne thee blind,
> That with thy charmes the sharpest sight doest bind,
> And to thy will abuse? Thou walkest free.
> And seest every secret of the mind;
> Thou seest all, yet none at all sees thee;
> All that is by the working of thy Deitee.
>
> (3.10.4)

This apostrophe to the god of Malecasta's courtiers, a pagan deity with power and omniscience, but without goodness, surprises the narrator in midstanza. It represents a sudden shift back to the unmoralized Cupid of the *Shepheardes Calendar,* a shift from Ficino to Leone Ebreo, who also gave to false love the title of a real divinity. We saw in the contrast between Arthur's faith in Cupid and Archimago's abuse of him that mortal fidelity is meaningless if Cupid has power without goodness, and here Spenser goes on to provide the divine sanction for Paridell that Archimago had provided for his false Una:

> So perfect in that art was *Paridell,*
> That he *Malbeccoes* halfen eye did wyle,
> His halfen eye he wiled wondrous well,
> And *Hellenors* both eyes did eke beguyle,
> Both eyes and hart attonce, during the whyle
> That he there sojourned his wounds to heale;
> That *Cupid* selfe it seeing, close did smyle,
> To weet how he her love away did steale,
> And bad, that none their joyous treason should reveale.
>
> (3.10.5)

The inconsistency between these stanzas shows, however, that the poet has not had a revelation of Cupid's true nature, but a realization of the arbitrariness of his use of Cupid. No one at all sees the working of Cupid's deity in stanza four, including the poet, who nevertheless can report Cupid's smile of approval in stanza five. The fact that only the poet mentions Cupid in this episode emphasizes his arbitrary power over what he chooses to report. Helenore sends at Paridell "one firie dart, whose hed / Empoisned was with privy lust, and gealous dred" (9.28). Paridell weeps and wails his wound, but in his "false laments" never mentions Cupid. Spenser has set out to present love's pageants, to reveal "all that is by the working of [Cupid's] Deitee," but he *sees* no more than other men and must make his own decisions about what is Cupid's work and what is not. Those decisions, he seems to realize here, can only demonstrate his own faith in Cupid, never Cupid's true nature. As in *Muiopotmos*, he comes upon the paradox that poetical gods are invented and disposed by mortal poets and, as in *Muiopotmos*, the paradox subverts his moral. At first it merely circumscribes his moral: a poetic theodicy can only justify the poet's ways with his fictions. Even Milton, to the extent that he adds to Genesis, might be said to justify his own art rather than God's ways. But a corollary follows that turns the pious fiction, once recognized as such, against itself. If Cupid really is a god, then he must escape all of the poet's fictions about him, including those that maintain his moral probity. Once Spenser concludes, "Thou walkest free," it follows that Cupid must wound villains like Paridell *because* Spenser has made him wound only heroes.

The episode of Malbecco, Helenore, and Paridell plays somewhat humorously with themes of possession, captivity, and mastery that dominate the second half of Book 3 and culminate in the next episode at the house of Busyrane. But if, as I have suggested, the incidents of the poem correspond to the narrator's meditation on his themes, then there is a closer connection between these episodes and another way in which the Busyrane episode is the climax of Book 3.[26] In fact, the House of Busyrane objectifies Spenser's assertion in canto ten that the final mastery is Cupid's; it is a temple to the capricious, cruel pagan god that Spenser there acknowledges and also his means of undoing that acknowledgement. If poetic self-consciousness has temporarily subverted his theodicy, it does not preclude iconoclasm, for in negative theology, though the true nature of a god can never be demonstrated, false ideas about him can be dispelled. Spenser, finding that he cannot make a religion in canto ten, ends Book 3 by rooting out an idolatry.

The other aspect of Spenser's theodicy of Cupid is justification of the gall in love; because it also culminates in Britomart's victory over Busyrane, I must turn to it before discussing the Busyrane episode itself. Chaucer's Troilus, echoing Petrarch, had asked, "If love be good, from whennes cometh my woo?" (1.402). In *The Faerie Queene,* the question becomes: If Love is a god, from whence comes my woe?" and is faced by Arthur in Book 1 and by nearly every major figure of Book 3. Spenser is still asking the question in Book 6, but in Book 3 he provides two kinds of answer. The first, and more important, is historical, Virgilian, and, one might say, arboreal; the second natural, Lucretian, and "floral."

In canto two, Britomart turns from the magic glass in which she has seen the image of Artegall, unaware that she has received a wound,

> But the false Archer, which that arrow shot
> So slyly, that she did not feele the wound,
> Did smyle full smoothly at her weetlesse wofull stound.
>
> (3.2.26)

Spenser has begun the tale of Britomart's enamorment in the same vein:

> But as it falleth, in the gentlest harts
> Imperious Love hath highest set his throne,
> And tyrannizeth in the bitter smarts
> Of them, that to him buxome are and prone:
> So thought this Mayd (as maydens use to done)
> Whom fortune for her husband would allot. . . .
>
> (3.2.23)

In the *Hymne in Honour of Love,* this same injustice had raised a doubt—

> How falles it then, that with thy furious fervour,
> Thou doest afflict as well the not deserver,
> As him that doeth thy lovely heasts despize,
> And on thy subjects most doest tyrannize?—

but here Spenser knows the answer. The archer is false only from Britomart's point of view. Her experience duplicates Arthur's to some degree, but she lacks Arthur's faith in Providence. *Fortune,* she believes, will alot her a husband; *misfortune* has subjected her "to loves cruell law."[27] In the next canto Merlin teaches otherwise:

> It was not, *Britomart,* thy wandring eye,
> Glauncing unwares in charmed looking glas,
> But the streight course of heavenly destiny,
> Led with eternall providence, that has
> Guided thy glaunce, to bring his will to pas:
> Ne is thy fate, ne is thy fortune ill,
> To love the prowest knight, that ever was.
> Therefore submit thy wayes unto his will,
> And do by all dew meanes thy destiny fulfill.
>
> (3.3.24)

The reader has already learned this lesson in the stanzas that open the canto, when Spenser explicitly links the providentiality of Britomart's love with the divinity of Cupid:

> Well did Antiquitie a God thee deeme,
> That over mortall minds hast so great might,
> To order them, as best to thee doth seeme,

And all their actions to direct aright;
The fatall purpose of divine foresight,
Thou doest effect in destined descents,
Through deepe impression of thy secret might,
And stirredst up th'Heroes high intents,
Which the late world admyres for wondrous moniments.

But thy dread darts in none doe triumph more,
Ne braver proofe in any, of thy powre
Shew'dst thou, then in this royall Maid of yore,
Making her seeke an unknowne Paramoure,
From the worlds end, through many a bitter stowre:
From whose two loynes thou afterwards did rayse
Most famous fruits of matrimoniall bowre,
Which through the earth have spred their living prayse,
That fame in trompe of gold eternally displayes.

(3.3.2–3)

The "fruits of matrimoniall bowre" echo the stanza that introduced the retrospective tale of Britomart's vision in the magic mirror, from which, says Spenser,

did grow her first engraffed paine;
Whose root and stalke so bitter yet did tast,
That but the fruit more sweetnesse did containe,
Her wretched dayes in dolour she mote wast,
And yield the pray of love to lothsome death at last.

(3.2.17)

But the fruit will be sweet only in contemplation; her destiny is not to taste this fruit, but to bear it, to *be* the bitter root or stalk, as Merlin explains:

Most noble Virgin, that by fatall lore
Hast learn'd to love, let no whit thee dismay
The hard begin, that meets thee in the dore,
And with sharpe fits thy tender hart oppresseth sore.

For so must all things excellent begin,
And eke enrooted deepe must be that Tree,
Whose big embodied braunches shall not lin,
Till they to heavens hight forth stretched bee.
For from thy wombe a famous Progenie
Shall spring, out of the auncient *Trojan* blood. . . .

(3.2.21–22)

Like Aeneas, whom she remembers in canto nine, Britomart bears as her burden the fame and fate of her children's children. In the long view of history,

which she must learn to take, she is not a helpless victim of a "false archer."
Cupid's arrow threatens to make her "languish as the leafe falne from the tree"
(3.2.39), but once engrafted will instead grow into the tree, the ancestral tree
whose height and glory must redeem the bitterness of its root.

The long view is not an easy one to maintain, and Britomart must be reminded that her suffering is necessary and has a divinely ordained end or *telos*.
The first of these reminders comes in the next canto where, "following the
guidance of her blinded guest," she comes to the seacoast. To have a blinded
guide, however, is to wander aimlessly, and Britomart, seeing her internal state
imaged in the tempestuous sea, once again allies Love with Fortune:

> . . .my feeble vessell crazd, and crackt
> Through thy strong buffets and outrageous blowes,
> Cannot endure, but needs it must be wrackt
> On the rough rocks, or on the sandy shallowes,
> The whiles that love it steres, and fortune rowes;
> Love my lewd Pilot hath a restlesse mind
> And fortune Boteswaine no assuraunce knowes,
> But saile withouten starres gainst tide and wind:
> How can they other do, sith both are bold and blind?
>
> (3.4.9)

Glauce must reprove her despair and give her good relief,

> Through hope of those, which *Merlin* had her told
> Should of her name and nation be chiefe,
> And fetch their being from the sacred mould
> Of her immortall wombe, to be in heaven enrold.
>
> (3.4.11)

"Hope" here has a secondary theological sense; she must trust to the Providence which both Cupid and Fortune serve. Glauce's words have no time to
take effect, however, for Marinell appears at this point, and, after wounding
him, Britomart rides out of the poem until canto nine.

Canto six presents Spenser's second answer to the question "If Love is a god,
from whence comes my woe?" and also introduces Amoret, who will later
exemplify the limitations of this answer. The canto begins with the miraculous
conception of Belphoebe and Amoret and then explains how they came to be
adopted by Diana and Venus. Venus has left "her heavenly hous" in search of
Cupid who has fled from her and "wandred in the world in strange aray, /
Disguiz'd in thousand shapes, that none might him bewray":

> First she him sought in Court, where most he used
> Whylome to haunt, but there she found him not;
> But many there she found, which sore accused

His falsehood, and with foule infamous blot
His cruell deedes and wicked wyles did spot:
Ladies and Lords she every where mote heare
Complayning, how with his empoysned shot
Their wofull harts he wounded had whyleare,
And so had left them languishing twixt hope and feare.

She then the Citties sought from gate to gate,
And every one did aske did he him see;
And every one her answerd, that too late
He had him seene, and felt the crueltie
Of his sharpe darts and whot artillerie;
And every one threw forth reproches rife
Of his mischievous deedes, and said, That hee
Was the disturber of all civill life,
The enimy of peace, and author of all strife.

Then in the countrey she abroad him sought,
And in the rurall cottages inquired,
Where also many plaints to her were brought,
How he their heedlesse harts with love had fyred,
And his false venim through their veines inspyred;
And eke the gentle shepheard swaynes, which sat
Keeping their fleecie flockes, as they were hyred,
She sweetly heard complaine, both how and what
Her sonne had to them doen; yet she did smile thereat.

                                          (3.6.11, 13–15)

The humor and complaisance of Spenser's version of Moschus's famous idyll should not be mistaken. Many seem to have bewrayed Cupid despite his disguises, and if Venus keeps her promises, she has been a busy goddess, for

> She promist kisses sweet, and sweeter things
> Unto the man, that of him tydings to her brings.
>
> (3.6.12)

In Moschus and his other imitators including Tasso in *Aminta*, Venus offers graduated rewards: a kiss for "tydings" about Cupid, "sweeter things" for his return.[28] Spenser eliminates the distinction because he is saying that Venus follows Cupid and rewards his victims. Her smile, and Spenser's tone, tell us that all the complainers about Cupid do not properly understand their pains.

   The second half of canto six, following Amoret to the Garden of Adonis, balances this picture of Cupid's fierce wars, but offers a glimpse behind the picture rather than an alternative to it. The Garden is not outside the world Cupid ransacks, but is less *in* it than *inside* it, the seedplot of the world from which all things "doe their first being fetch" (3.6.37). In the mythological

argument of Book 3, the Garden serves chiefly to answer Malecasta's sentimen-
talized and death-fixated tapestries of Venus and Adonis with an affirmation
that death and decay are necessary parts of the process of life. But Cupid, too,
shares in the affirmation and plays unarmed in the Garden. Revived, Adonis
now lives there in everlasting joy,

> With many of the Gods in company,
> Which thither haunt, and with the winged boy
> Sporting himselfe in safe felicity:
> Who when he hath with spoiles and cruelty
> Ransackt the world, and in the wofull harts
> Of many wretches set his triumphes hye,
> Thither resorts, and laying his sad darts
> Aside, with faire *Adonis* playes his wanton parts.
>
> (3.6.49)

As in Book 2, the temporal disjunction between Cupid's "safe felicity" and his
"spoiles and cruelty" rules out a disjunction between two Cupids, one "good,"
one "bad."[29] *Inside* the world where courtiers and citizens and rustics complain
of Cupid's doings, at its natural source, the pains of love, like those of time and
death, are necessary and benignant. This affirmation complements the earlier
one. Though trees grow there, the Garden of Adonis is a flower garden. An
individual's experience of love transcends itself there, not in ancestral trees
spreading toward heaven in historical time, but in endless generations of flowers which grow and bloom and die in the cyclical time of natural process.

Cupid lays his sad darts aside in the Garden to play with Adonis, but he also
has another playmate:

> And his true love faire *Psyche* with him playes,
> Faire *Psyche* to him lately reconcyld,
> After long troubles and unmeet upbrayes,
> With which his mother *Venus* her revyld,
> And eke himselfe her cruelly exyld:
> But now in stedfast love and happy state
> She with him lives, and hath him borne a chyld,
> *Pleasure*, that doth both gods and men aggrate,
> *Pleasure*, the daughter of *Cupid* and *Psyche* late.
>
> (3.6.50)

Psyche's history is treated so briefly that it may be better to see it rather than as
an epitome of all the painful histories of Book 3 than the archetype for them as
A. C. Hamilton does.[30] It recapitulates the movement of the canto: from a
world in which love has more gall than honey to the garden of the world where
the gall is redeemed by Pleasure herself. The Platonic allegory in Apulieus and
Boccaccio seems not to be relevant to Spenser's use of the myth.[31] Psyche is the

human soul "reconcyld" to Love rather than purged and finally deified by him. The myth of Cupid and Psyche also serves to suggest the human relevance of the mysteries of natural generation, already partially anthropomorphized in Venus and Adonis, and to return the description of the Garden to its narrative function. Venus brings her foundling Amoret to the Garden and commits her to Psyche to be "trained up in true feminitee" and "lessoned / In all the lore of love, and goodly womanhead" (51). When we next hear of Amoret in canto eleven, however, her story has begun to look like Psyche's in reverse. She has been "brought . . . forth into the worldes vew" where, despite her lessons and firsthand knowledge of Cupid's benevolence (or perhaps because of them), she has become Busyrane's victim.

The Busyrane episode joins together the three strands of Spenser's theodicy of Cupid that we have been tracing. Its triumphant Cupid takes up the dilemma that surfaces in the previous episode when Cupid walks free of Spenser's moral constraints and smiles at Paridell's seductive arts. Amoret brings with her to Busyrane's house the lessons of the Garden of Adonis that the gall in love is all on the outside. Britomart brings with her the lessons of Merlin's cave that her burden of pain is divinely ordained, teleological, and must be endured. Readers who may have forgotten Britomart's destiny since she rode out of the poem in canto four are reminded in canto nine when, in contrast to Paridell, she feels the pathos of "mans wretched state" in the fall of Troy, but also predicts the renewed glory of Troynovant (3.9.39–46). Even Paridell has heard of her ancestral tree:

> Indeed he said (if I remember right,)
> That of the antique *Trojan* stocke, there grew
> Another plant, that raught to wondrous hight,
> And far abroad his mighty branches threw,
> Into the utmost Angle of the world he knew.
>
> (3.9.47)

Providence and its connection with lovers' pains are further emphasized in what might be called the prologue-scene to the Busyrane episode. Britomart comes upon Scudamour, disarmed, "all wallowed," and questioning Providence:

> At last forth breaking into bitter plaintes
> He said; O soveraigne Lord that sit'st on hye,
> And raignst in blis emongst thy blessed Saintes,
> How suffrest thou such shamefull cruelty,
> So long unwreaked of thine enimy?
> Or hast thou, Lord, of good mens cause no heed?
> Or doth thy justice sleepe, and silent ly?
> What booteth then the good and righteous deed,
> If goodnesse find no grace, nor righteousnesse no meed?

> If good find grace, and righteousnesse reward,
> Why then is *Amoret* in caytive band,
> Sith that more bounteous creature never far'd
> On foot, upon the face of living land?
> Or if that heavenly justice may withstand
> The wrongfull outrage of unrighteous men,
> Why then is *Busirane* with wicked hand
> Suffred, these seven monethes day in secret den
> My Lady and my love so cruelly to pen?
>
> (3.11.9–10)

Britomart's presence is, of course, the answer to Scudamour's prayer, but she also responds verbally to his complaint, underscoring her progress since she too lamented her fate and forgot Providence in canto four:

> Ah gentle knight, whose deepe conceived griefe
> Well seemes t'exceede the powre of patience,
> Yet if that heavenly grace some good reliefe
> You send, submit you to high providence,
> And ever in your noble hart prepense,
> That all the sorrow in the world is lesse,
> Then vertues might, and values confidence,
> For who nill bide the burden of distresse,
> Must not here thinke to live: for life is wretchednesse.
>
> (3.11.14)

Yet if Britomart's submission to Providence is a source of her strength in this episode, it is also a potential source of weakness. In the second half of the prologue-scene, she and Scudamour come to Busyrane's castle gate where they find "A flaming fire, ymixt with smouldry smoke, / And stinking Sulphure, that with griesly hate / And dreadfull horrour did all entrance choke" (3.11.21). Thinking it "daunger vaine . . . to have assayd / That cruell element," she asks:

> What monstrous enmity provoke we heare,
> Foolhardy as th'Earthes children, the which made
> Battell against the Gods? so we a God invade.
>
> (3.11.22)

Submission to Providence begins to express itself as submission to the appearance of the supernatural, but Britomart takes second thought. Perhaps this only looks like a god:

> Perdy not so; (said she) for shamefull thing
> It were t'abandon noble chevisaunce,
> For shew of perill, without venturing. . . .
>
> (3.11.24)

She passes through the enchanted fire "as a thunder bolt / Perceth the yielding ayre," in other words like the weapon with which Jove defeated the giants "the which made / Battell against the Gods," rather than like the giants themselves.[32] The "shew of perill" has an effect, however; Scudamour is "scorcht" attempting to follow her. The preliminaries outside the House of Busyrane establish for the reader and for Britomart two ideas essential to interpreting what follows: that the adventure inside the house will challenge faith in the gods and that it may involve a "shew of perill" without substance.

In the first hall of Busyrane's house, Britomart finds tapestries depicting "all *Cupids* warres . . . / And cruell battels, which he whilome fought / Gainst all the Gods, to make his empire great" (11.29). Not only gods appear in these tapestries, but

> Kings Queenes, Lords Ladies, Knights and Damzels gent
> Were heap'd together with the vulgar sort,
> And mingled with the raskall rablement,
> Without respect of person or of port,
> To shew Dan *Cupids* powre and great effort.
>
> (3.11.46)

At the upper end of this room stands an altar with an image of Cupid and the inscription "Unto the Victor of the Gods this bee" (11.49). In a second room, the walls record in massy gold reliefs the "thousand monstrous formes . . . / Such as false love doth oft upon him weare . . ." (11.51).

As Paul Alpers says, we do not see Busyrane's house through Britomart's eyes, but neither are her responses merely devices to intensify ours as he suggests.[33] Britomart's responses appear only after Spenser has described Busyrane's decor with a tour guide's admiring commentary ("O wondrous skill, and sweet wit of the man . . ." 11.32), and they serve to measure and correct our response. She is "amazed"—impressed, but also puzzled (11.49). The inscriptions "Be bold, be bold, be not too bold" make Busyrane's rooms a riddle which seems to figure some "sence" that she cannot "construe" (11.50, 54). She marvels "that no footings trace, / Nor wight appear'd"; "Straunge thing it seem'd, that none was to possesse / So rich purveyance . . ." (11.53). Her reactions include the aesthetic wonder that Spenser's description encourages, but go well beyond it; she wants to know who owns all this and what he means by it. Moreover, as at Castle Joyous, she has a moral response:

> And underneath his feet was written thus,
> *Unto the Victor of the Gods this bee:*
> And all the people in that ample hous
> Did to that image bow their humble knee,
> And oft committed fowle Idolatree.
>
> (3.11.49)

There are no people in that ample house, however. Spenser uses the inconsistency to show that Britomart sees in the image of Cupid the idolatry it implies. The reader who does not see this has just had an ambiguous warning: "Ah man beware, *how* thou those darts behold" (11.48; emphasis added).

Britomart, suspicious and "stedfast" waits in the second room until, in imitation of Biblical theophanies, a stormy whirlwind, thunder and lightning, an earthquake, and a shrilling trumpet announce the beginning of the masque of Cupid. But, instead of a god, there "forth issewd, as on the ready flore / Of some Theatre" the presenter Ease, followed by a musical prelude of "wanton Bardes, and Rhymers impudent," and a procession of personifications from the tradition of the *Roman de la rose* (12.2–5). Busyrane's decor and entertainments seem about to duplicate the witty mock-religion of poems like Marot's *Temple de Cupido* when in the midst of the procession stumbles Amoret, her heart "drawne forth" and "transfixed with a deadly dart." And "after her the winged God himselfe / Came riding on a Lion ravenous" (12.21–22). The sadism replaces suspiciousness with horror absent even in the Petrarchan original of this triumph of Cupid.

Britomart watches the spectacle until it retires into the inner room. Thinking it vain to force the wicket, she resolves to wait for the masque to reappear and spends the day "in wandering, / And gazing on that Chambers ornament" (12.29). When the next night the brazen door to the inner room flies open,

> in went
> Bold *Britomart,* as she had late forecast,
> Neither of idle shewes, nor of false charmes aghast.
>
> (3.12.29)

Again Britomart's reactions measure the reader's, and subsequent events prove her right. In the third room, the figures of the masque "streight were vanisht all and some" (12.30). After Busyrane has reversed his charms, the ornaments of those goodly rooms are "vanisht utterly, and cleane subverst" (12.42). Even "that *fained* dreadfull flame, / Which chokt the porch of that enchaunted gate / . . . / Was vanisht quite" (12.43; emphasis added). All of Busyrane's retinue and decor were deceptive appearances, mere illusions, but not, as in Marot or the *Trionfi,* only accidents in a substance. But how does Britomart know that Busyrane's house and his masque are merely "idle shewes" and "false charmes"?

She may, of course, merely have applied the lesson of the "shew of perill" in Busyrane's gate. But, in taking the decor as "idle shewes," she also asserts her belief in Providence against the challenge they present. The tapestries and gold reliefs teach a doctrine more drastic than "Omnia vincit Amor." Cupid does not play his pageants diversely in Busyrane's decor, which illustrates another adage: "amor omnibus idem."[34] As in Petrarch's first triumph, Cupid crushes all human uniqueness—

Kings Queenes, Lords Ladies, Knights and Damzels gent
Were heap'd together with the vulgar sort,
And mingled with the raskall rablement,
Without respect of person or of port—

but Busyrane outdoes Petrarch in degrading the gods, showing them in bestial transformations rather than merely chained before Cupid's chariot. The hierarchy of heaven is confounded. What Britomart thinks that the giants were foolish to attempt Cupid achieves with ease:

Whiles thus on earth great Jove these pageaunts playd,
The winged boy did thrust into his throne,
And scoffing, thus unto his mother sayd,
Lo now the heavens obey to me alone,
And take me for their *Jove*, whiles *Jove* to earth is gone.

(3.11.35)

History, according to Busyrane, has no "faithfull loves," no "destined descents," no *telos* or even progression, but only endlessly repeated victories of Cupid represented in the nightly repetition of Busyrane's triumphal masque. The god who others believe stirs up "th'Heroes high intents, / Which the late world admyres for wondrous moniments" (3.2) here treads all such moniments under foot:

Their swerds and speres were broke, and hauberques rent;
And their proud girlonds of tryumphant bayes
Trodden in dust with fury insolent,
To shew the victors might and mercilesse intent.

(3.11.52)

The masque presents the necessary course of individual histories in this cosmos: idleness and fancy lead through dissemblance and grief to reproach and shame and end at last in "death with infamie" (12.25). Amoret is the victim of this vision because her lessons in the Garden of Adonis have taught her the benignant function of love in natural generation, but not prepared her for the pains she encounters in the world where Cupid goes armed. Britomart can see Busyrane's artifice as "idle shewes" and as "fowle Idolatree" because she has learned Merlin's lesson that a beneficent deity guides history, at least partially, by means of human loves.

The Busyrane episode has most often been read from Amoret's point of view.[35] I have been reading it mostly from Britomart's, but should now like to return to my suggestion that it marks the climax of the underplot of Book 3, Spenser's theodicy of Cupid. In canto ten, poetic self-consciousness forced Spenser to acknowledge a pagan Cupid, powerful and omniscient but without the goodness that would prevent him from smiling at Paridell's deception of

Malbecco and Helenore. Cantos eleven and twelve present a temple to that god and the rites appropriate to his worship, but now Busyrane is responsible for them. Spenser has projected the self-consciousness that blocked his theodicy into the fiction in the form of Busyrane and associated him, even more clearly than Archimago, with poetry. In the inner room, Britomart finds him "figuring straunge characters of his art" and forces him to overthrow his "wicked bookes" and to measure back "many a sad verse" and bloody line (12.31–32, 36). Theatrical imagery surrounds the masque; Amoret's torture grotesquely literalizes a poetic commonplace; Cupid's triumph combines the *Roman de la rose* tradition, Petrarch, and a popular emblem illustrating an epigram from the *Greek Anthology*.[36] Busyrane's tapestries depict stories judged in Antiquity, the Middle Ages, and the Renaissance alike to be lies told by the poets.[37]

In the House of Busyrane, Spenser makes nearly the whole tradition of Cupid's poetic theology into an idolatry and places it in the poem where it can be defeated, not by the poet himself, but by the lady knight in whom he expresses chastity. Busyrane's defeat is a fitting climax for the legend of chastity not only because it exposes as illusory a view of love in which women are helpless and hopeless victims, their fidelity rewarded with torture, their emotional integrity destroyed by compulsion.[38] It is a fitting climax also because Cupid walks free of it. The Busyrane episode is Spenser's *Triumphus Cupidinis* and also his *Triumphus Pudicitiae*, but the differences from Petrarch are as significant as the likenesses. Where Laura encountered Cupid himself in a mismatched battle that exploded his pretended divinity, Britomart contends only with Busyrane. Laura leads Cupid bound to the temple of chastity; Britomart binds an enchanter and leads him out of the false temple which his art has framed. Her opponent is not Cupid, but the abuse of Cupid that we have seen repudiated in earlier poems, except that here, as in *Colin Clouts Come Home Againe* and the first canto of Book 1, the abuse is also blasphemy.[39] Like Cynthia's courtiers and like Archimago, Busyrane makes a real god serve him "for sordid uses"; like Arachne, whose tapestry he copies, he tells lies about the gods. By attempting to master Amoret through misrepresenting the mastery of Cupid, he only exemplifies the truth that Britomart tells Malecasta's knights in canto one:

> Ne may love be compeld by maisterie;
> For soone as maisterie comes, sweet love anone
> Taketh his nimble wings, and soone away is gone.
>
> (3.1.25)

Busyrane's house is a false temple but, as the later books of *The Faerie Queene* make explicit, it is a false temple to a real god. The Busyrane episode alludes to and incorporates almost all of the tradition we have been surveying, including the poetic self-reflexiveness prompted regularly by Cupid's figurative divinity. The episode thus represents both a culmination of Cupid's literary career and an undoing of that career, but it is an undoing, unlike earlier ones, that the god of love himself survives. Chastity for Spenser is a broad concept, perhaps indefinable except in the narrative terms he provides, but the Busyrane episode affirms paradoxically that chastity requires faith in Cupid.

If the iconoclasm that ends Book 3 reflects Spenser's realization that the poetic theology of love can never be more than either a pious fiction or an enthralling idolatry, then it is not surprizing that Cupid plays only a diminished and disconnected part in the last three books. Some of the looseness of the later books may also reflect Spenser's loss of confidence in his own mythopoeia, in the idea that poetry can be a kind of scripture with gods of its own yet not clashing with Christianity—that it can be a health-giver and shaper of both individuals and culture. The Busyrane episode, then, though Spenser's analogue of earlier demythologizations like Alain de Lille's "Descriptio Cupidinis," Chapter 25 of the *Vita Nuova*, or Petrarch's *Triumphus Pudicitiae*, has the opposite effect. Instead of controlling abuse of Cupid's poetic theology by exposing him as only a figurative divinity and thus allowing new chastened uses, the Busyrane episode leaves Cupid free from the poet's mythopoeic powers, but also leaves those powers without their major subject. Mirabella's trial in Book 6 is an exception, perhaps not a wholly compelling one; but for the most part the social and civic concerns of the later books engage Cupid only marginally and sometimes mechanically. He is no longer the center of an underplot.

As if the bonds that secure Busyrane also bind the self-consciousness that had subverted Spenser's theodicy, the earlier rationale determining Cupid's victims plays itself out in Book 4. Britomart still makes blind love her guide, now blind because she cannot see that the Salvage knight is the object of her quest. In canto twelve Marinell's enmity to Cupid reaches an emblematic end, but even in Proteus's bower we will not imagine it as an actual divine intervention:

> Thus whilst his stony heart with tender ruth
> Was toucht, and mighty courage mollifide,
> Dame *Venus* sonne that tameth stubborne youth
> With iron bit, and maketh him abide,
> Till like a victor on his backe he ride,
> Into his mouth his maystring bridle threw,
> That made him stoupe, till he did him bestride:
> Then gan he make him tread his steps anew,
> And learne to love, by learning lovers paines to rew.
>
> (4.12.13)

Paridell reappears in Book 4 and meets Blandamour and several other knights for whom love is a game, but no one suggests that their actions are among "All that is by the working of [Cupid's] Deitee."

Spenser's one address to Cupid in Book 4 confirms this pattern with its retrospective glance at the heroines of Books 3 and 4:

> Great God of love, that with thy cruell dart
> Doest conquer greatest conquerors on ground,
> And setst thy kingdome in the captive harts
> Of Kings and Keasars, to thy service bound,
> What glorie, or what guerdon hast thou found
> In feeble Ladies tyranning so sore;
> And adding anguish to the bitter wound,
> With which their lives thou lanchedst long afore,
> By heaping stormes of trouble on them daily more?
>
> So whylome didst thou to faire *Florimell;*
> And so and so to noble *Britomart;*
> So doest thou now to her, of whom I tell,
> The lovely *Amoret,* whose gentle hart
> Thou martyrest with sorrow and with smart,
> In salvage forrests, and in deserts wide,
> With Beares and Tygers taking heavie part,
> Withouten comfort, and withouten guide,
> That pittie is to heare the perils, which she tride.
>
> (4.7.1–2)

The word "martyrest" inevitably recalls the Masque of Cupid, but only now is Amoret to be martyred, and in the same way as Florimell and Britomart—by wandering alone and "withouten guide" in the forests and deserts of the chivalric world. In the first stanza, the narrator questions the divinity that Busyrane had abused, but the doubt no longer seems urgent. Britomart is hardly a feeble lady. In the second stanza, the doubt of the first resolves into a neat "transition in the manner of Ariosto," which is also a kind of prospectus.[40] Britomart has just been affianced; the process of reconciliation has begun that will, by the end of Book 4, redeem the anguish of Amoret and Florimell.

The Temple of Venus is the major doctrinal place of Book 4, even though it appears only in Scudamour's recital of his adventure there. Venus and her portress Concord embody the major themes of the book, but Cupid, though absent, is not excluded from the Temple. As a respite from his cruel work in the world, we remember, Cupid resorted to Alma's House of Temperance, to Ida, and to the Garden of Adonis. In the Temple of Venus, conversely, Cupid is absent because he is at work. His younger brothers, "A flocke of litle loves, and sports, and joyes," fly about the idol of Venus,

> The whilest their eldest brother was away,
> *Cupid* their eldest brother; he enjoyes
> The wide kingdome of love with Lordly sway,
> And to his law compels all creatures to obay.
>
> (4.10.42)

Elsewhere in the Temple, a "thousand payres of lovers walkt, / Praysing their god, and yeelding him great thankes" (25). If the Garden of Adonis is the "place" inside the visible processes of nature where matter joins with form, the Temple of Venus is that place inside visible social processes where men fetch their wives and friends join in friendship. Social processes are human institutions, part convention and part instinct, and therefore in the Temple art and nature cooperate. The idol of Venus at the center of the Temple embodies this cooperation. Venus herself, present in the Garden of Adonis, is not present here, but mysteriously animates her idol. Cupid's role precedes the social processes imaged in the Temple. He is what compels men to come here and women to leave, and therefore, though not present, he is represented on the shield of love and by the eponymous knight who bears it. When the idol laughs at Scudamour's sacrilege in robbing her church, it reaffirms Venus's smile in Book 3 at the ubiquitous complaints about her fugitive son. The goddess laughs and smiles at the concord in which mortals see only discord.

In Book 3, sober citizens complained to Venus that her son "Was the disturber of all civill life, / The enimy of peace, and author of all strife" (3.6.14). Both Boccaccio and Conti gave precedent for this accusation, but in Book 5 of *The Faerie Queene*, where civil life is the center of concern, Cupid is never mentioned.[41]

Cupid has been absent from the poem for eighteen cantos when the narrator begins the tale of scornful Mirabella and her trial before Cupid. Mirabella has been more than an aloof Petrarchan mistress; she has been a female Don Juan, glorying that

> her beautie had such soveraine might,
> That with the onely twinckle of her eye,
> She could or save, or spill, whom she would hight.
> What could the Gods doe more, but doe it more aright?
>
> But loe the Gods, that mortall follies vew,
> Did worthily revenge this maydens pride;
> And nought regarding her so goodly hew,
> Did laugh at her, that many did deride,
> Whilest she did weepe, of no man mercifide.
> For on a day, when *Cupid* kept his court,
> As he is wont at each Saint Valentide,
> Unto the which all lovers doe resort,
> That of their loves successe they there may make report;
>
> It fortun'd then, that when the roules were red,
> In which the names of all loves folke were fyled,
> That many there were missing, which were ded,
> Or kept in bands, or from their loves exyled,
> Or by some other violence despoyled.
> Which when as *Cupid* heard, he wexed wroth,
> And doubting to be wronged, or beguyled,

He bad his eyes to be unblindfold both,
That he might see his men, and muster them by oth.

(6.7.31–33)

In the civil world of the later books, Cupid must proceed by law. Infamy and
Despight give evidence, a warrant is issued, Mirabella attached and sentenced.
Arthur, who at first offers to free her from her punishment, perhaps remembers
his own rebellion and submission to Cupid, as described in Book 1, when he
affirms Cupid's judgment:

> Certes (sayd then the Prince) the God is just,
> That taketh vengeaunce of his peoples spoile.
> For were no law in love, but all that lust,
> Might them oppresse, and painefully turmoile,
> His kingdome would continue but a while.[42]

(6.8.23)

"Like other incidents in Book VI," writes Harry Berger,

> the Mirabella episode (vii.27–viii.30) has the air of being a reprise: in a kind
> of miniature compass it recalls the erotic atmosphere of Books III and IV
> (especially Busirane's house), the Cruel Fair sonnets among the *Amoretti*,
> passages from *Colin Clouts Come Home Againe* and the *Hymn of Love*.[43]

It is, in fact, an anti-reprise of the Busyrane episode. Mirabella's judge, "the
sonne of Venus who is myld by kynd" (7.37) and acts as the agent of other
gods, in every way contrasts with Busyrane's tyrannical deity. In the masque,
for example, Cupid unblinds himself for a sadistic thrill; in his court, to ad-
minister justice. More importantly, Mirabella meets Cupid himself, where
Amoret and Britomart met only the "false shewes" of Busyrane's art. The
Mirabella episode records a real divine intervention, at last transforming Cupid
into a fully epic figure present in the world of the poem. But despite its
assertion of Cupid's justice, the episode does not reveal the true religion which
Busyrane distorted into an idolatry. It reveals, if anything, the impossibility of
revealing a religion in such a fiction. Colin Clout reported a similar incident in
his prophecy against Cynthia's courtiers:

> . . . *Cupid* selfe of them ashamed is,
> And mustring all his men in *Venus* vew,
> Denies them quite for servitors of his.

(768–70)

Colin wisely let Cupid's muster hover between fact and figure of speech. If he
had elaborated it, he would have begun to make fictions about Cupid, compromising his own faith and his testimony against others' apostasy.

In the Mirabella episode, Spenser knows too well the paradox that surfaced toward the end of Book 3: if a poet invents and disposes his gods, then any theodicy he offers can be only a pious fiction. The Mirabella episode, with its oversophisticated imitation of old models, presents itself as merely that—a pious fiction. Its materials are the same as Busyrane's—literalized sonnet motifs—but, beside Busyrane's dangerous mythopoeia, Mirabella's trial appears paradoxically as a disillusioned wish-fulfillment of prayers for divine intervention like that of *Amoretti* 10:

> Unrighteous Lord of love, what law is this,
> That me thou makest thus tormented be:
> the whiles she lordeth in licentious blisse
> of her freewill, scorning both thee and me.

A theodicy of poetical gods will be as facile as the poet permits, and the Mirabella episode is perhaps meant, like the anacreontics between the *Amoretti* and *Epithalamion*, to show how judiciously Spenser has exercised his sway over the gods in the rest of the poem. The episode certainly leads forward, with the other "flat" episodes of Book 6, to the vision on Mount Acidale, which Colin Clout sees but cannot preserve in song and which Calidore destroys, as Britomart destroyed Busyrane's "idle charmes," by wanting to *know* whether the vision is an "enchaunted show."[44]

But Cupid is not so easily reduced to a poetic figure, a medieval fiction permitted to warm up Spenser's audience for the real show. He has been one of the true gods of *The Faerie Queene*, and the facileness of the Mirabella episode therefore produces a reaction. In the last address to Cupid in the poem, Spenser's theodicy returns to its beginning. In Book 1, Arthur saw his fall to Cupid as an exemplum of the truth that "Nothing is sure that growes on earthly ground" (1.9.11). At the end of Book 6, Spenser returns to this expression of faith, radical because minimal; the gods are gods and they are beneficent if only in reminding us that we are mortal:

> The joyes of love, if they should ever last,
> Without affliction or disquietnesse,
> That worldly chaunces doe amongst them cast,
> Would be on earth too great a blessednesse,
> Liker to heaven, then mortall wretchednesse.
> Therefore the winged God, to let men weet,
> That here on earth is no sure happinesse,
> A thousand sowres hath tempred with one sweet,
> To make it seeme more deare and dainty, as is meet.

(6.11.1)

Epilogue

CUPID appears twice in the Mutabilitie Cantos, both times in the pageant of the months, but between them the two references seem to summarize the breakdown of Spenser's mythopoeia. Dressed all in green, Cupid flutters about May (7.34), triumphing once again in springtime as he had in the *Shepheardes Calender* (March and May) and twice in the *Amoretti* (19 and 70). He is part of the natural and emblematic visibilia that Mutabilitie places in evidence, but the second reference to Cupid, in the last stanza of the pageant, reflects upon the illusoriness of all such visibilia:

> And after all came *Life*, and lastly *Death;*
> *Death* with most grim and griesly visage seene,
> Yet is he nought but parting of the breath;
> Ne ought to see, but like a shade to weene,
> Unbodied, unsoul'd, unheard, unseene.
> But *Life* was like a faire young lusty boy,
> Such as they faigne *Dan Cupid* to have beene,
> Full of delightfull health and lively joy,
> Deckt all with flowres, and wings of gold fit to employ.
>
> (7.7.46)

Because Death is nothing, he cannot be imaged or named except deceptively. Death is not "he" or even "it," so that the truthful poet can only advance and then retract the traditional image, the poetic "shade." Life, on the other hand, is almost everything, presence itself, and so he can be imaged, but only retrospectively by a potentially infinite regress of likenesses. Life itself escapes the poet's figurations twice over; it only *looked like* a boy such as Cupid was *feigned* to have been. Yet even here Cupid is closer to the poet than the other gods, for all of them are feigned, as the poet will soon acknowledge when he turns from the insufficient consolations of poetic theology to the God of Sabbaoth.

As Dante discovered in the *Vita Nuova*, the god of love finally leads to a dead end for poets ambitious to do more than recreate their muse. Literary history recapitulates that discovery. Cupid does not disappear from seventeenth-century literature, of course, but his importance clearly wanes after Spenser, lasting longest in the court masque, a form whose very premises exalt art as the image of royal government and which therefore concedes little to the iconoclastic component of poetic theology. Ben Jonson, for instance, can combine the fugitive Cupid of Moschus with the Statius-Claudian form of epithalamion to make his wedding masque for Viscount Haddington. In other masques, other exploits or associations of Cupid—Eros and Anteros, Ausonius's Cupid crucified, Neoplatonic cosmogonies—have more or less central roles.

Lyric poets continue to play with Cupid, but, whether metaphysical or cavalier, most lyrics have the levity and self-enclosure of earlier Renaissance Alexandrianism, even if their spirit becomes less precious, more rigorous or domesticated. Even poems like Donne's "Loves Deitie" that reanimate the old religion of love preserve a witty equanimity:

> But every moderne god will now extend
> His vast prerogative, as far as Jove.
> To rage, to lust, to write to, to commend,
> All is the purlewe of the God of Love.
> Oh were wee wak'ned by this Tyrannie
> To'ungod this child againe, it could not bee
> That I should love, who loves not mee.[1]

A bland exception might be the short song by Aphra Behn, which tries to revive the old tension between Love as a god and as a personification:

> Love in Fantastique Triumph satt,
> Whilst Bleeding Hearts around him flow'd.
> . . . .
> From me he took his sighs and tears,
> From thee his Pride and Crueltie;
> From me his Languishments and Feares,
> And every Killing Dart from thee;
> Thus thou and I, the God have arm'd,
> And set him up a Deity;
> But my poor Heart alone is harm'd,
> Whilst thine the Victor is, and free.[2]

No poet after Spenser made Cupid's problematical divinity and the dangerous old religion of love a sustaining and integral fiction. The affirmation of love ceases to figure itself in divinities of love and finds its mundane form in the novel. The abuse that masks self-indulgence as compulsion no longer appeals to Cupid: "Est-ce ma faute? O mon Dieu! non, non, n'en accusez que la fatalité! (Voilà un mot qui fait toujours de l'effet, se dit-il.)" (Am I to blame? No, by Heaven; blame only Fate!—"Always an effective word," he said to himself.) So Rodolphe Boulanger writing to Emma Bovary.[3]

Unlike many other mythological figures, Cupid still awaits a second renaissance. Even a poet like Shelley, who loved and imitated Dante and Petrarch and Spenser and whose experience approximated a triumph of Cupid, finds no place for Cupid in his mythmaking. Perhaps, like some actors, Cupid finally ruined his career by playing the decorative, facile, or trivial parts that in every age outnumbered the serious ones. Or perhaps the array of experiences and ideas that Cupid can represent is simply so central to our culture that we have filled his place too well with new myths, new myths especially intolerant of the old because they present themselves as the discoveries of the human sciences. A future age may see some literary uses of Freudian psychology as a new poetic theology, one whose gods are not transcendent but still deviously omnipotent.

The mythological figures who have survived and been born again in modern times are the heroes and demigods—Ulysses, Prometheus, Orpheus, Agamemnon, Helen. That the gods have remained dormant may testify to our confident modern humanism, untroubled by its possible relation to antique paganism and seldom, in its literary manifestations, worried by the authority of Scripture. The most complex and compelling uses of Cupid's poetic theology occured at times of literary and religious transition. Dante and Petrarch at the beginning of the Renaissance and Spenser in the middle of the Reformation shared a poetic self-consciousness produced in part by conflict between their own ambitions for poetry and contemporary religious or practical detraction of poetry. The conflict forced poetry to measure itself against Scripture and ruled out a simple or superficial use of poetic theology. With the resolution of that conflict, Cupid has perhaps lost the context that made him a figure useful not only for men's experience of love but also for the perplexities and dangers of figuring that experience in poetry. It has been possible to write love poetry without Cupid, not only because the experience of love has gradually divorced itself from religion, but also because poetry has given up its anxious alliance with Scripture.

Keats can provide the epilogue to this history. Though too late for the fond believing lyre, he consecrates himself as priest to Psyche, the latest born and loveliest of all Olympus's faded hierarchy. But Cupid, her companion, has had his prophets, and of him Keats says only, "The winged boy I knew."

Notes

Chapter 1. The Poetic Theology of Love

1. "Icones Symbolicae," rev. ed., in Gombrich, *Symbolic Images*, p. 127. See also his "Personification," in R. R. Bolgar, ed., *Classical Influences on European Culture, A.D. 500–1500*.

2. Tuve, *Allegorical Imagery*, p. 252; Fletcher, *Allegory: The Theory of a Symbolic Mode*, chap. 1; see also Paul Piehler, *The Visionary Landscape*, p. 45 and Michael Murrin, *The Veil of Allegory*, chaps. 1–3.

3. *Consolatio Philosophiae* 2. met. 8.

4. *Hippolytus* 196–98.

5. Auden, "Postscript: Christianity and Art," in *The Dyer's Hand*, pp. 456– 57.

6. Whitman, *Homer and the Heroic Tradition*, pp. 223, 227, 229.

7. Gombrich, *Symbolic Images*, p. 3.

8. *Canones et decreta*, p. 203 (session 25).

9. See Rona Goffen, "Icon and Vision: Giovanni Bellini's Half-Length Madonnas."

10. St. Antonio, *Summa theologia*, par. 11 (3:321C). On negative or aniconic imagery, see Gombrich, *Symbolic Images*, pp. 150–52.

11. See Joseph Antony Mazzeo, "St. Augustine's Rhetoric of Silence," in his *Renaissance and Seventeenth-Century Studies*, p. 27.

12. I am using the Padua edition of 1621 in the Garland reprint, pp. 73–4. In the first edition of 1531 and other editions, the illustrators depict the conventional image of Cupid instead of trying to follow the implications of the verses.

13. *Rime dubbie* 29, ll. 9–10 in *Le opere di Dante*, ed. Michele Barbi et al.

14. Ludwig Wittgenstein, *Philosophical Investigations*, 563.

Chapter 2. Medieval Developments

1. Gombrich, "Personification," pp. 251–52 and Roger Hinks, *Myth and Allegory in Ancient Art*, p. 17.

2. For a list of negative moralizations of Cupid's attributes ranging from antiquity to the Renaissance, see Erwin Panofsky, "Blind Cupid," in his *Studies in Iconology*, pp. 104–8. Many might be added, including Origen, *Commentary on Song of Songs*, Prol. (*PG* 13:67A); Augustine, *Contra Faustum* 20.9; Arnulf of Orléans, ed. Fausto Ghisalberti, p. 12; *Carmina Burana* 154; Theodulph of Orléans, *Carmina* 4.1 (*PL* 105:332C–D).

3. See Henri de Lubac, *Exégèse médiéval*, 2.2:182–208; Jean Pépin, *Mythe et allégorie*, part 3; M.-D. Chenu, "The Symbolist Mentality," in her *Nature, Man, and Society in the Twelfth Century*, pp. 99–145.

4. "Itidemque Amores duo; alter bonus et pudicus, quo sapientia et virtutes amantur; alter impudicus et malus, quo ad vitia inclinamur" (3.11.18) in Georg H. Bode, ed., *Scriptores rerum mythicarum Latini tres*, p. 239. On the identity of mythographus 3, see Eleanor Rathbone, "Master Alberic of London." The distinction between two loves derives ultimately from Plato's *Symposium*, and appears also in Latin works, including ones by Plautus, Apuleius, Servius, and Martianus Capella. Occasionally the two loves are distinguished genealogically as well as ethically and aligned with a distinction between Amor and Cupid, most influentially by John Scotus Erigena and

Remigius of Auxerre in commentaries on the *De nuptiis Mercurii et Philologiae*. See Peter Dronke, "L'Amor che move il sole e l'altre stelle," and Arthur Groos, "Amor and his Brother Cupid: The 'Two Loves' in Heinrich von Veldeke's 'Eneit,'" pp. 241–46, both of whom give extensive references.

5. For Barbarino's *Documenti d'Amore*, see Panofsky, *Iconology*, pp. 116–20; *Ovide moralisé*, 1.3297–3326 (ed. de Boer, 15:131); Ridewall's *Fulgentius metaforalis*, ed. Hans Leibeschutz, p. 81.

6. See Panofsky, *Iconology*, p. 95–97.

7. See the Vatican mythographers, 1.127; 2.48; and Ridewall, *Fulgentius metaforalis*, p. 81.

8. *Commentary on Song of Songs*, which survives only in Rufinus's Latin translation, Prol. (*PG* 13:62A–70B). For Augustine on *cupido*, see *Civ. Dei.* 14.7. Other exegetes on ambiguous vocabulary of love in Scripture: pseudo-Dionysius the Areopagite, *De celestibus nominibus* 4.11–14; Isidore of Seville, *Differentiarum* 1.2.5 and 2.37; Alain de Lille, *Distinctionum dictionum theologicalium*, s.v. "amor."

9. Instances are conveniently collected in the appendix to James J. Wilhelm, *The Cruelest Month*.

10. William of St. Thierry, *De natura et dignitate amoris*, 1.1; see R. Freyhan, "The Evolution of the Caritas Figure in the Thirteenth and Fourteenth Centuries," pp. 72–75.

11. *PL* 176. 974C–D. For the history of the *vulnus amoris* image, see *Dictionnaire de spiritualité*, s.v. "Blessure d'amour" (Dom. A. Cabassut).

12. Hans Robert Jauss discusses the subversive potential of these myths in "Allegorese, Remythisierung und neuer Mythus," an article that came to my attention after my manuscript was complete.

13. In Benoit de St-Maure's *Roman de Troie*, Amors utters a long speech (20704–74), and in the *Enéas* (8922–60) he is Cupido, Enéas's brother, and has the golden and leaden arrows of *Metam.* 1. 468–71, but even in these elaborations of ancient poems, Amors is generally less a mythical character than a figure of speech.

14. A few late twelfth and thirteenth–century troubadours do refer to Amors as the god of love (e.g. Folquet de Marseille, Peire Guilhem de Toulouse, Peire Vidal, and Rambaut de Vaqueiras), probably showing influence from northern France. See René Nelli, *L'Érotique des troubadours*, p. 165, n. 8; Edmond Faral, *Recherches sur les sources latines des contes et romans courtois du Moyen Age*, pp. 9–12; and Léopold Constans's appendix in his edition of Benoit de St-Maure, *Roman de Troie*, 6:346–52.

15. Amors's sex is inconsistent in the text and miniatures of even an allegorical poem like the *Cort d'Amor* (see Lowanne E. Jones, ed. and trans., pp. 13, 17–21, 210, n.48). Cf. the slightly earlier allegory by Guiraut de Calanso, "Celeis cui am de cor a de saber"—no. 132 in Hill and Bergin, eds., *Anthology of the Provençal Troubadours*, 2nd rev. ed.

16. "Cortezamen mou en mon cor mesclansa," in Francois M.-C. Raynouard, *Choix des poésies originales des troubadours*, 3:315, 5–8; translation by Maurice Valency (*In Praise of Love*, p. 151).

17. See Plotinus, *Enneads* 3.5.3; Nelli, *L'Érotique*, pp. 164–69; J. L. Lowes, "The Loveres Maladye of Hereos"; and Bruno Nardi, "L'Amore e i medici medievali."

18. The lady could be seen as the archer, as in Rigaut de Barbezieux, "Be volria saber d'Amor," quoted by Valency, p. 150. Peire Vidal's lady's eyebrows and nose formed a crossbow in "Tant an ben dig del marques"—no. 35 in Joseph Anglade, ed., *Poésies*. For an extreme example, see Chrétien's *Cligés*, 770–860, where the heroine's body is Amors' dart, her face the barb, her legs the notch, etc.

19. "Anc mais de joy ni de chan," 19–23—no. 8 in Shepard and Chambers, eds., *The Poems of Aimeric de Peguilhan*; my translation.

20. See Valency, p. 143 and Donald K. Frank, "On the Troubadour *Fin'Amors*." The variety and evolution of troubadour ideas about love are impressively surveyed by L. T. Topsfield, *Troubadours and Love*.

21. In poems by Peire Cardenal and Guilhem de Montanhagol; see Nelli, *L'Érotique*, p. 155.

22. See Valency, p. 126, 297 n. 30; Leo Spitzer, "L'Amour lointain de Jaufré Rudel et le sens de la poésie des troubadours"; Nelli, p. 107. Marcabru's stanza ("Pus mos coratges s'es clarzitz," st. 6—no. 40 in Dejeanne, ed.) is one of many about which scholars cannot agree. See, for example, D. W. Robertson, "Five Poems by Marcabru," pp. 557–59; Guido Errante, *Marcabru e le fonti sacre dell'antica lirica romanza*, pp. 206–9; A. Roncaglia, "'Trobar clus': discussione aperta"; Nelli, *L'Érotique*, pp. 152–57; Moshé Lazar, *Amour courtois et "Fin'Amors" dans la littérature du XIIe siècle*, p. 78–80.

23. The explicit normativeness of troubadour poetry has helped to foster arguments linking troubadour love and heresy, e.g., Denis de Rougemont, *Love in the Western World*, pp. 76–122.

24. *The Art of Courtly Love*, trans. John J. Parry, p. 28. The Latin text is *De amore libri tres*, ed. E. Trojel, 1.1.

25. Trojel, p. 89. The fifth dialogue appears on pp. 68–83 in Parry, pp. 80–110 in Trojel.

26. *The Allegory of Love*, pp. 38–9.

27. Later versions are assembled by William Allan Neilson in "The Purgatory of Cruel Beauties."

28. *An Apology for Poetry*, in G. Gregory Smith, ed., *Elizabethan Critical Essays*, 1:184. On the provenance of the distinction, see William Nelson, *Fact or Fiction*, pp. 11–37.

29. Deut. 13:2; for the anonymous translator, see Pio Rajna, "Tre studi per la storia del libro di Andrea Capellano," p. 209; for Drouart, see Barbara Nelson Sargent, "A Medieval Commentary on Andreas Capellanus." The condemnation of 1277 cites Andreas's book as "De amore sive de Deo amoris," suggesting that the bishop objected particularly to the poetic theology of dialogue 5; see Martin Grabmann, "Das Werk *De amore* des Andreas Capellanus und das Verurteilungsdekret. . . ."

30. The literature on Andreas and "courtly love" is immense. The good bibliography in F. X. Newman, ed., *The Meaning of Courtly Love* gives references to Lewis, Denomy, Robertson, and Donaldson, whose views I am epitomizing. See also Roger Boase, *The Origin and Meaning of Courtly Love*.

31. Latin text in Thomas Wright, ed., *Anglo-Latin Satirical Poets* 2:464–65. Translations are my own except where I cite Douglas Moffat's.

32. The other speakers of Cicero's *De natura deorum* accept the Epicurean Velleius's classing of the stories of the gods' lusts, passions, unions with mortals, etc. among "the errors of the poets" (1.42–43). In his threefold scheme of theology known to us from *Civ. Dei* 6.5, Varro classes these myths as the fabulous theology of poets, and Augustine reports a similar classification by Scaevola (*Civ. Dei* 4.27; see also 2.14, 3.3–4, 18.13). Seneca complained repeatedly about these myths (e.g. *De brev. vit.* 16), as did Christian apologists like Arnobius (*Ad. gent.* 5; *PL* 5:1030–1129) and Lactantius (*Div. instit.* 1.11; *PL* 6:165–76). See also Macrobius *Somn. Scip.* 1.2.11; Martianus Capella, *De nupt.* 1.3; Chalcidius, on *Timaeus*, chap. 128. At least one twelfth-century reader dissented from this general repudiation of these myths, William of Conches (see Peter Dronke, *Fabula*, pp. 26–29), but even William's figurative readings could be turned to amorous persuasion. Addressing a company of nuns, the carefully anonymous cleric who wrote "Profuit ignaris" interprets the amours of the gods as figures for affairs between clergy and laity and concludes: "When we are joined with you in a pact of love, those are the sacred unions of the high gods" (11.88–89; text in Peter Dronke, *Medieval Latin and the Rise of the European Love Lyric*, 2:454).

33. Abelard approves Plato's banishing poets who lie in order to incite men to offenses "as if imitating the deeds of gods" (*Theol. Christ.* 2.53–55); Albricus (the third Vatican mythographer), 5.2 (Bode, ed., pp. 171–72); "Imitemur superos" begins stanza 3 of *Carmina Burnana* 75, the famous "Omittamus studia." For examples of Jupiter as precedent, see "Veneris prosperis"— "Jupiter, / arbiter / rerum, instituit / nichil dum libuit / fieri turpiter" (11. 23–27 in Dronke, *Love Lyric*, 2:393)—as well as Serlo of Wilton, "Cipre, timent dii te,". 11. 45–47 (ibid., 2:498); "Amor habet superos," *Carm. Bur. 88).* "Primo veris tempore" depicts Jupiter himself inspired to seduce Danae by tales of his own and other gods' amours (ed. W. Wattenbach, *Zfd* 18 (1875):457–60). These poems may all be indebted to the incident in Terence's *Eununchus* discussed below (pp. 62–63).

34. For the analogy between linguistic and sexual vices in the *De planctu*, see Richard Hamilton Green, "Alan of Lille's *De Planctu Naturae*" and Winthrop Wetherbee, "The Function of Poetry in the *De Planctu Naturae* of Alain de Lille."

35. See Augustine, *On Christian Doctrine*, 3.29: "When the sense is absurd if it is taken verbally, it is to be inquired whether or not what is said is expressed in this or that trope which we do not know; and in this way many hidden things are discovered" (trans. Robertson); M. C. Beardsley, *Aesthetics*, chap. 3; also the traditional theory of aniconic imagery, e.g. Dionysius Ps-Areopagite, *De coel. hier.* 2 (*PG* 3:135–46).

36. Compare, for example, *Metam.* 3.426 ("Dumque petit, petitur"), also 434–36, 458–59. Alain's rhetorical mirroring also recalls James 4:7–8; "Resistite auto diablo, et fugiet a vobis. Appropinquate Deo, et appropinquabit vobis." The likeness points to the difference required to suggest that Love is a mirror image—Alain's use of the present tense.

37. *Le Roman de la rose*, ed. Ernest Langlois, 28–33, 2073–76).

38. See 3505–10 and L. T. Topsfield, "The *Roman de la rose* of Guillaume de Lorris and the Love Lyric of the Early Troubadours."

39. Rosemond Tuve, *Allegorical Imagery*, p. 253.

40. "Pour cui mort ma mere ploura / Tant que près qu'el ne s'acoura," 10517–18. The god of love's questionable immortality is reflected, too, in his garden, which, despite Lewis's identification of it as "the same garden which we have met in Andreas," is not the locus of souls after death, but the symbolic setting for a thoroughly mundane erotic farce (see *Allegory of Love*, p. 119).

41. The acute reader of MS Collins made the connection between the god of Love and Amant, noting that the god's finery corresponds to that of the voluptuous young man (no. 7 in Maxwell Luria, "A Sixteenth-Century Gloss on the *Roman de la Rose*"). Within the fiction the connection had to remain implicit in order to sustain the genre of the allegorical *debat* and to stay within the frame of the poem as dream vision and as "Le Mirouer aus Amoureus" (10651). Amant, of course, is not an *individual;* "his own passion" is as typical as Amant himself.

42. *De natura et dignitate amoris* 1.2 (*PL* 184:382A–B).

Chapter 3. The *Vita Nuova* and the *Trionfi*

1. See *Enciclopedia dantesca*, s.v. "Fiore" (by Gianfranco Contini); Contini, "Un nodo della cultura medievale: la serie *Roman de la rose-Fiore-Divina Commedia*"; and also Luigi Vanossi, *Dante e il "Roman de la rose*," who cites particular echoes on pp. 292–307. My text for Dante is *Opere di Dante*, Michele Barbi et al., eds., and I refer below to the edition of the *Vita Nuova* by M. Scherillo and of the *Rime* by K. Foster and P. Boyde.

2. See especially Marianne Shapiro, "Figurality in the *Vita Nuova*" and Giuseppe Mazzotta, "The Language of Poetry in the *Vita Nuova.*"

3. See Guido Cavalcanti, "O tu, che porti nelli occhi sovente / Amor tenendo tre saette in mano," "O donna mia, non vedestù colui" (where Love appears "in guisa d'arcier"—.7), "S'io fosse quelli che d'amor fu degno"; Lapo Gianni, "Amor, nova ed antica vanitate" (a mythographical canzone); Cino da Pistoia, "Io guardo per li prati ogni fior bianco" (where Amor is Cupid). Except where otherwise noted, I cite these and all Dante's contemporaries from Gianfranco Contini, ed., *Poeti del Duecento*, vol. 2. Amore has arrows in *Purg.* 31.117, in "La dispietata mente" (Barbi no. 50), in "Tre donne intorno al cor mi son venute" (no. 104), and in the Montanina canzone, "Amor, da che convien" (no. 116). In "Così nel mio parlar" (no. 103), Amore holds over Dante the sword with which he slew Dido.

4. At several points in the *V.N.*, Dante speaks of Amore's power over his *spiriti*, but does not call Amore a god (4.2; 11.2; 14.5, 12; 16.8; 23.22; 27.4). For examples of Amore as a god in the *stilnovisti*, see Guido Guinizelli, "Gentil donzella" 6, where he speaks of "la deïtà de l'alto deo d'amore"; Lapo Gianni, "Angelica figura" 4 echoes Guinizelli: "l'alto dio d'amore"; Cecco Angiolieri in "Dante Allaghier, Cecco, tu' serv' amico," prays Dante "per lo dio d'Amore, / il qual è stat' un tu' signor antico."

5. For Cavalcanti, see "Donna mi prega" 29–34.

6. See Ezekiel 2:2 or 2:10 and the formula which introduces many chapters: "Et factus est sermo Domini ad me, dicens. . . ."

7. "Il sembloit que ce fust uns anges / Qui fust tot droit venuz dou ciel," *Roman de la rose* 902–3. The many illustrated manuscripts of the *Roman* keep before readers' eyes the angelic appearance of the god of love (grownup, clothed, and with wings not mentioned in the text itself). On the influence of this image of the god of love, see Panofsky, *Iconology*, pp. 101–3.

8. As many commentators have noticed, the *Convivio* (4.22.14–15) uses almost the language of *V.N.* 12 to describe the angel in the sepulchre: "uno giovane vestito de bianco" and "uno giovane . . . in bianchi vestimenti."

9. See Charles S. Singleton, "*Vita Nuova* XII: Love's Obscure Words." This interpretation is now the consensus; see Domenico de Robertis, *Il libro della "Vita Nuova,"* pp. 68–70.

10. Colin Hardie, "Dante and the Tradition of Courtly Love," p. 32. Singleton would seem to agree; see "*V.N.* XII," p. 94.

11. Most commentators accept this interpretation as a forecast of Chapter 24 and on the basis of Dante's explanation of the occasion of the poem: "Anzi piangendo mi propuosi di dicere alquante parole de la sua morte, in guiderdone di ciò che alcuna fiata l'avea veduta con la mia donna. E di ciò

toccai alcuna cosa ne l'ultima parte de le parole che io ne dissi, sì come appare manifestamente a chi lo intende" (8.2–3). This "ultima parte," the *divisione* tells us, begins with "Audite. . . ." It is to be noted that Beatrice is not actually among the ladies lamenting over the dead woman.

12. Robert Hollander, "*Vita Nuova:* Dante's Perceptions of Beatrice," p. 6; Margherita de Bonfils Templer, "Amore e le visioni nella *Vita Nuova,*" pp. 21, 28.

13. Critics of the *Aeneid* give precedent for this sort of "translation." Brooks Otis judges the "divine machinery" to be superfluous: "Venus and Cupid but mark, so to speak, the result of the encounter which has already taken place" (*Virgil: A Study in Civilized Poetry,* p. 67). See also Richard Heinze, *Virgils epische Technik,* pp. 304–6.

14. "Platonic Love in Some Italian Poets," in *Selected Critical Writings of Santayana,* 1:56.

15. Singleton, "The Irreducible Dove," p. 129. See also Robert Hollander, "Dante: *Theologus-Poeta,*" pp. 100–102.

16. *Lives of the English Poets,* 1:102.

17. See *V.N.* 14.13 where the *divisione* exists in order to "aprire la sentenzia de la cosa divisa," or 25.8 where one may use rhetorical figures, "non sanza ragione alcuna, ma con ragione la quale poi sia possibile d'aprire per prosa."

18. See Hollander, "*V.N.:* Dante's Perceptions." Amore appears four times in the *V.N.,* in dreams in Chapters 3 and 12, in *imaginazioni* or waking dreams in Chapters 9 and 24.

19. *V.N.,* 3.3., 24.2. See also 9.5 and 12.3. Ovid may have given a hint for this device: "Is mihi sic dixit (dubito, verusne Cupido, / An somnus fuerit: sed puto, somnus erat) . . ." (*Remedia amoris* 555–56).

20. See Ernst Robert Curtius, *European Literature in the Latin Middle Ages,* p. 353; de Robertis, *Il libro,* p. 138; and Hardie, "Courtly Love," p. 41.

21. Singleton, *An Essay on the Vita Nuova,* p. 57.

22. For some examples of the old topic, see Giacomo da Lentini, "Tenzone con Jacopo Mostacci e Pier della Vigna" in Contini, *Poeti del Duecento,* 1:88–90; the lyric sometimes ascribed to Dante, "Molti volendo dir" ("Io dico che Amor non è sustanza, / Nè cosa corporal ch'abbia figura . . .") printed by Barbi among the *rime dubbie* (no. 29); and especially Guido Orlandi's sonnet "Onde si move e donde nasce Amore" often prefixed to Cavalcanti's "Donna mi prega" as well as "Donna mi prega" itself: "E non si pò conoscer per lo viso: / compriso—bianco in tale obietto cade; / e, chi ben aude,—forma non si vede: / dunqu' elli meno, che da lei procede. / For di colore, d'essere diviso, / assiso—'n mezzo scuro, luce rade" (63–68).

23. Singleton, *An Essay,* p. 74.

24. J. E. Shaw, *Essays on the Vita Nuova,* p. 85.

25. Ernest Hatch Wilkins, trans. *The Triumphs of Petrarch,* p. v; Carl Appel, ed., *Die Triumphe Francesco Petrarcas,* p. xviii; E. H. Wilkins, "The Quattrocento Editions of the *Canzoniere* and the *Trionfi,*" in *The Making of the "Canzoniere" and other Petrarchan Studies,* p. 379.

26. D. D. Carnicelli, "Renaissance Editions and Translations of the *Trionfi,*" in *Lord Morley's Tryumphes of Fraunces Petrarcke,* pp. 31–33. For the other arts, see Victor Masséna, prince d'Essling and Eugène Müntz, *Pétrarque: ses études d'art, son influence sur les artistes, ses portraits et ceux de Laure,* pp. 101–276 and Raimond van Marle, *Iconographie de l'art profane au Moyen-Age et à la Renaissance,* 2:111–131. See also Calcaterra's edition of the *Trionfi,* pp. lxi–lxiv.

27. See Carnicelli, pp. 29–35. An autobiographical interpretation has been urged against the allegorical reading in this century, but the two approaches have been convincingly joined by Calcaterra.

28. C. S. Lewis, *The Discarded Image,* p. 199.

29. *TAe* 145. My text is *Le Rime sparse e i Trionfi,* ed. Ezio Chiòrboli. I abbreviate the titles of the *Trionfi* with the first letters of Petrarch's Latin titles.

30. E. H. Wilkins, "The First Two Triumphs of Petrarch," pp. 14, 7. See also "On the Chronology of the *Triumphs,*" in Wilkins, *Studies in the Life and Works of Petrarch,* pp. 254–72.

31. *Epistolae metricae* 3.30, trans. David Thompson in *Petrarch: A Humanist Among Princes,* p. 42. On Petrarch's knowledge of the *Roman* and possible debts to it in the *Trionfi,* see Luigi Foscolo Benedetto, *Il "Roman de la Rose" e la letteratura italiana,* pp. 168–70.

32. See Petrarch's letter on the ascent of Mt. Ventoux (*Fam.* 4.1).

33. *Confessions* 1.16, trans. William Watts, slightly modernized. Petrarch refers to the *Eununchus* in *Secretum* 3; see *Opere latine,* ed. Antonietta Bufano, 1:200–202.

34. *City of God* 6.5. For Petrarch's knowledge of Varro, see *Fam.* 24.6 ("To Marcus Varro") and Pierre de Nolhac, *Pétrarque et l'humanisme,* 2nd ed., 2:110–15.

35. *Divinae institutiones* 1.11 (*PL* 7:165–66), trans. Alexander Roberts and James Donaldson, *The Ante-Nicene Fathers*, 7:20, slightly altered. The allusion was noticed as early as 1553; see *Il Petrarcha con l'espositione di M. Giovanni Andrea Gesualdo*, p. 554. Gesualdo did not notice it in his 1533 edition. On Petrarch's knowledge of Lactantius in general, see de Nolhac, 2:211–12.

36. *Invective contra medicum* 3 in *Opere latine*, ed. Bufano, 2:920: "Quis enim nisi amens adulteros aut fallaces veneraretur deos? . . . Cui preterea dubium esse posset, quin peccata que humanitatem ipsam hominibus ereptura essent, eadem multo magis diis talibus preriperent deitatem?"

37. *Trionfi. Sonetti e canzoni* (Venice, 1488), p. 8rH. I read "numinis" for "minimis" in the text as do contemporaries like Boccaccio and modern editors (see pp. 16, 89). Gesualdo quoted the same passage (p. 561), and Petrarch echoed it again in *Secretum* 3 (ed. Bufano, 1:194).

38. Wilkins, "First Two Triumphs," p. 16; Calcaterra, ed., *Trionfi*, pp. xlix–l.

39. Wilkins, "First Two Triumphs," p. 14.

Chapter 4. Renaissance Poetry

1. Praz, *Studies in Seventeenth-Century Imagery*, p. 98.

2. The best survey of medieval love allegories remains William Allan Neilson, *The Origins and Sources of the Court of Love*, but see also Doris Ruhe, *Le Dieu d'Amours avec son paradis*.

3. Lines 323–26 in *Oeuvres poétiques*, ed. Yves Giraud.

4. No. 360, 137–39; text and translation by Robert M. Durling, *Petrarch's Lyric Poems*.

5. See Janet Espiner-Scott, "Les Sonnets Élisabéthains: Cupidon et l'influence d'Ovide."

6. *Les Amours*, ed. Henri and Catherine Weber, p. 209.

7. François Habert, "D'un jeune Gentilhomme à une Damoyselle pour l'avoir en Mariage" in *Les Epistres héroïdes tressalutaires pour servir d'example à toute âme fidèle* (1550), quoted in Guy Demerson, *La Mythologie classique dans l'oeuvre lyrique de la "Pléiade,"* p. 251.

8. Thomas Sebillet, *Contramours* (1581), also quoted in Demerson, p. 252.

9. Lines 30–37 in *Oeuvres poetiques de Remy Belleau*, ed. Charles Marty-Laveaux, 1:171–72.

10. Son. 16 of the *Nouvelle continuation*, 9–14.

11. *Sonets pour Helene* (Livre 1), 8.

12. No. 44, 103–8 in *Premier Livre des Amours*, ed. Mathieu Augé-Chiquet, p. 78.

13. The minor tradition of short poetic descriptions of Cupid's image forms an exception to this rule. These usually take a skeptical attitude toward their subject, treating Cupid as an invention of human art or illusion. Propertius's elegy is a classical example. A selective list of later examples would include Guittone d'Arezzo's "Trattato d'Amore" (nos. 240–51 in Egidi's edition), Lapo Gianni, "Amor, nova ed antiche vanitate" (no. 14 in Contini, *Poeti del Duecento*, 2); Michele Marullo's epigram "De Amore" (no. 59 in Perosa's edition); Alciati's emblem "In Statuam Amoris" discussed in Chapter 1 above; and Sir Philip Sidney, "Poore Painters oft with silly Poets joyne" (no. 8 in the first eclogues of the *Old Arcadia*).

14. Text and translation from David Quint, *The Stanze of Angelo Poliziano*.

15. See *TC* 4: "ch'ogni maschio pensier de l'alma tolle" (105), "ozio / lento" (128–29), "diletti fugitivi" (116).

16. On these two anecdotes, see James Hutton, "Cupid and the Bee" and "The First Idyl of Moschus in Imitations to the year 1800;" also J. G. Fucilla's two articles, "Additions" to Hutton and "Materials for the History of a Popular Classical Theme."

17. See Guido Mazzoni, "Un capolavoro del Poliziano. Tra la canzon di Maggio, il canto carnascialesco e la festa mitologica."

Chapter 5. Renaissance Mythographers and Neoplatonists

1. On the date of the first edition of Conti, see Barbara C. Garner, "Francis Bacon, Natalis Comes and the Mythological Tradition," p. 264, n. 3.

2. The best account of the *trattati* is in Nesca A. Robb, *Neoplatonism of the Italian Renaissance*. See also Eugenio Garin, "Platonismo e filosofia d'amore," in his *L'umanesimo italiano*, pp. 146–72. Tireless summaries of these and several other *trattati* appear in John C. Nelson,

Renaissance Theory of Love. For dates of publication and influence, see Lorenzo Savino, "Di alcuni trattati e trattatisti d'amore italiani della prima metà del secolo XVI."

3. The phrase is Petrarch's, applied to Boccaccio by Jean Seznec, *The Survival of the Pagan Gods,* p. 220.

4. See, for example, Fulgentius (*Mitologiarum libri tres,* 3.6) or the second and third Vatican mythographers, ed. Bode, pp. 86, 239.

5. *Genealogia,* 2.13. I am using the first printed edition (Venice: Wendelin von Speyer, 1472) which I have checked against the edition of Boccaccio's MS edited by Vincenzo Romano. For books 14 and 15, I cite the translation by Charles G. Osgood, *Boccaccio on Poetry.*

6. See Panofsky, *Iconology,* pp. 104–5.

7. The Silenus was a favorite image of Erasmus. See his adage *Sileni Alcibiadis* translated by Margaret Mann Phillips, *Erasmus on his Times,* pp. 77–97. See also Edgar Wind, *Pagan Mysteries in the Renaissance,* 2d ed., pp. 172–73, 222, and A. B. Giamatti, "Spenser: From Magic to Miracle," p. 79, n. 17.

8. Boethius, *Consol.,* 2. met. 8; 4. met. 6.

9. Bode, ed., 231 (pp. 71–72); Don Cameron Allen, "On Spenser's *Muiopotmos,*" pp. 147–48.

10. See, for example, Seznec, *Survival,* p. 220.

11. On poetic theology, see Wind, *Pagan Mysteries,* pp. 17–25, and Eugenio Garin, "Le favole antiche."

12. *Allegorical Imagery,* chap. 4.

13. See Osgood, pp. xxiii n. 25, 46; Wind, *Pagan Mysteries,* pp. 1–25; Charles Trinkaus, *In Our Image and Likeness,* 2:689–704; Allen, *Mysteriously Meant.*

14. See also Osgood, p. xx, and Coluccio Salutati, *De laboribus Herculis,* 1:85–86.

15. See, for example, Lactantius, *Div. instit.* 1.11 (*PL* 7:175–76): "Hoc errore decepti etiam philosophi, quod ea, quae de Jove ferentur, minime in Deum convenire videbantur, duos Joves fecerunt, unum naturalem, alterum fabulosum." On Boccaccio's concern to provide for future poets, see Osgood, pp. xiv, 104–5.

16. See above, chap. 2, note 4.

17. The Cupid in 2.13 is the son of the second Mercury and the first Diana, for example.

18. Boccaccio's genealogies are taken up by Leone Ebreo in the *Dialoghi d'amore,* ed. Caramella, pp. 288–89, and by the English Neoplatonist mythographer Alexander Ross. See *Mel Heliconium,* pp. 101–104.

19. Paul Oscar Kristeller, *The Philosophy of Marsilio Ficino,* trans. Conant, p. 287. The *Commentary* was first printed in Ficino's translation of Plato (1484) and reprinted in every subsequent edition, of which there were 23 before 1603. Ficino himself made an Italian translation, published in 1544. See James A. Devereux, "The Textual History of Ficino's *De Amore.*"

20. See Ernst Cassirer, *The Individual and the Cosmos in Renaissance Philosophy,* pp. 131–35. Treatments of Ficino's philosophy in addition to Kristeller may be found in Robb, *Neoplatonism;* Jean Festugière, *La Philosophie de l'amour de Marsil Ficin;* and Panofsky, *Iconology,* chap. 5. There is a useful introduction and bibliography in Raymond Marcel, ed., *Marsile Ficin sur le Banquet de Platon ou "De l'Amour."*

21. 2.3; 3.3; 2.2; text and translation by Sears Reynolds Jayne, *Marsilio Ficino's Commentary on Plato's Symposium.*

22. *Epistolae* 1, fol. 632, quoted in Cassirer, *Individual and Cosmos,* p. 131.

23. Kristeller, *Philosophy of Ficino,* p. 287.

24. Pico della Mirandola shifted Venuses and Cupids differently from Ficino (see Panofsky, *Iconology,* pp. 144–45).

25. This clear formulation is Leone Ebreo's (*Dialoghi,* ed. Caramella, p. 155). E. H. Gombrich argues that Neoplatonism encouraged the view that every personification was the "grosser material form of an invisible entity." See "Icones Symbolicae," rev. ed., in *Symbolic Images,* pp. 123–91; here p. 153.

26. See Wind, *Pagan Mysteries,* p. 56.

27. Pico, in his commentary on Benivieni's versification of Ficino's doctrines, noted that the "Canzone d'amore" also mirrors its doctrine in its form (*Opera omnia,* 1:733, 754–55).

28. Robb, *Neoplatonism,* p. 176. See Panofsky, *Iconology,* pp. 144–46.

29. Robb, *Neoplatonism,* p. 188.

30. *The Philosophy of Love,* trans. F. Friedeberg-Seeley and Jean H. Barnes, pp. 191, 448–53. I cite this translation, except where noted.

31. Leone, pp. 339–42; see also 155.
32. My translation: "Cosí l'amore prima e piú essenzialmente si truova nel mondo intellettuale" (Caramella, ed., p. 155); see also p. 105: "E per questo fra li dèi sono nominati fama, amore, grazia, cupiditá, voluttá, litigio, fatica, invidia, fraude, pertinacia, miserie, e molte altre di quella sorte, per ciò che ognuna ha la sua propria idea e principio incorporeo (come t'ho detto), per il quale è nominata dio o dea."
33. Robb, *Neoplatonism*, p. 202.
34. See T. Anthony Perry, "Dialogue and Doctrine in Leone Ebreo's *Dialoghi d'amore.*"
35. See Robert Ellrodt, *Neoplatonism in the Poetry of Spenser*, chap. 11.
36. Robb, *Neoplatonism*, pp. 181–82.
37. *Pietro Bembo's "Gli Asolani,"* trans. Rudolf B. Gottfried, p. 153. I cite this translation except where noted. The Italian text is *Opere in volgare*, ed. Mario Marti.
38. Thomas Frederick Crane, *Italian Social Customs of the Sixteenth Century*, p. 278.
39. Except where noted, I cite the translation by Sir Thomas Hoby, first published in 1561, with some repointing; here p. 301.
40. On the relevance of Bembo's speech, see Lawrence Lipking, "The Dialectic of *Il Cortegiano*," also Wayne A. Rebhorn, "Ottaviano's Interruption: Book IV and the Problem of Unity in *Il Cortegiano.*"
41. Nelson, *Renaissance Theory of Love*, p. 119.
42. Giraldi, *Opera omnia*, 1:407E. The quotation is an "arbitratu excerpta" from Alexander of Aphrodisias. See also 408G, where, commenting upon "geminus Cupido," Giraldi confirms Alexander's opinion: "Quin et alii non Geminos, sed (ut diximus ante) tres et quinque, et plures." For a survey of Giraldi, Cartari, and Conti, see John Mulryan, "Venus, Cupid, and the Italian Mythographers."
43. Francesco Marcolini in the first edition (Venice: Marcolini, 1556), p. 3. My text for Cartari is the facsimile of the 1647 Venice edition, which I have checked against the first edition.
44. "L'error de ciechi, e miseri mortali / Per coprir il suo stolto, e van desio / Finge che Amor sia Dio. / . . . / Amor è vitio de la mente insana. / . . . / L'ocio il nodrisce, e lascivia humana. / . . . / Ma se questa vien meno, / Onde il Cieco desir al mal consente. / . . . / tosto perde amor ogni sua forza" (p. 258). "L'ocio il nodrisce, e lascivia humana" echoes *TC* 1.82–84. Cartari expands to thirty lines the nine from the pseudo-Senecan *Octavia* 557–65.
45. Cartari introduces this abrupt shift with the sentence: "Ma non più di molti, ma ragioniamo hora divino Amore solamente" (263), but the subsequent discussion does not bear out the adjective "divino." See p. 266: "Dipingesi Amore fanciullo, perche non è altro, che un pazzo desiderio, mentre che alla libidine solamente è intento." For the most part in these pages, Amore is "intento alla libidine."
46. My text is that of 1619 (Hanover: Typis Wechelianis); this passage, p. 402. Conti's name often appears in its Latin form, Natalis Comes.
47. Bacon, *The Wisedom of the Ancients*, chap. 17. For Bacon's debt to Conti, see Garner, note 1 above.
48. Berger, "The Renaissance Imagination," p. 43.

Chapter 6. Spenser's Minor Poems

1. *Astrophil and Stella*, 5, 5–7.
2. My text of Spenser is *Poetical Works*, ed. Smith and de Selincourt; here the Dedicatory Epistle, p. 416.
3. W. W. Greg noted the architectonic importance of the eclogues in which Colin appears and those in which his songs are sung by others; see *Pastoral Poetry and Pastoral Drama*, p. 91.
4. *Iliad*, 24. 525–26, trans. Lattimore.
5. *Dec.*, 7–12; E. K.'s general argument, p. 420; veiled Christianity appears in the moral eclogues *May, July,* and *September.*
6. In 1.15 ("De Amore primo herebe filio"), Boccaccio identifies Amor as a passion of the mind and describes its effects, concluding: "We therefore, having considered carefully all of these things, will not call him Love, but rather more accurately Hate." William Nelson notes that Spenser added the theme of love the destroyer to his major source for *December*, Marot's *Eclogue au Roy*; see *The Poetry of Edmund Spenser*, p. 41.

7. The general gloss on *March*. E. K. mistakenly attributes the model to Theocritus; it is rather Bion, *Eidyllion* 1. A. C. Hamilton places *March* among those eclogues that "exist in the poem as fragments of an earlier pastoral tradition"; see "The Argument of Spenser's *Shepheardes Calender*," p. 175. Hamilton's view is strengthened by the fact that Wyllie appears only in *March* and *August*, which is the other eclogue having a conspicuous classical model.

8. Study of the sources of *March* led Leo Spitzer to conclude: "We find here no moral formulated, as with Bion ('keep away from Love!')"; see "Spenser, *Shepheardes Calender, March* (Lines 61–114) and the Variorum Edition," p. 186.

9. Spitzer agrees with E. K.'s argument. Don Cameron Allen, arguing from comparison of Spenser's sources and from Thomalin's religious zeal in *July*, defends the gloss in which Thomalin's scorn for love leads to incapacity to love rather than to the conventional sudden fall into love. See "Edmund Spenser, 'The March Eclogue' of *The Shepheardes Calender*." Thomalin's excessive and nervous watch over his sheep (*August*, 20: "Never knewe I lovers sheepe in good plight") and the otherwise extraneous tale of Thomalin's ewe with its analogous wound in an extremity may argue for Allen's view.

10. This counsel appears in Andreas Capellanus (trans. Parry, p. 198), in Alain de Lille (see pp. 40–41 above), in the *Roman de la rose* (4358), and in Petrarch (see p. 63 above).

11. *Table Talk*, May 31, 1830 in *Table Talk and Omniana*, p. 87.

12. Dodds, *The Greeks and the Irrational*, Chap. 2, esp. pp. 28–32.

13. Spitzer, "*March*," p. 186.

14. *Jan.*, 64; see also *Aprill*, 9–22, *June*, 41–48, *Nov.*, 3–4.

15. *October*, 97–99; see Richard F. Hardin, "The Resolved Debate of Spenser's 'October.' " The editor's comment appears in *Variorum 7* (*MP*, pt. 1):372.

16. The separate title page of *Muiopotmos* is dated 1590 and the poem, unlike some of the *Complaints*, was probably written not more than a few years earlier; see *Variorum 8* (*MP*, pt. 2):598–99. Franklin E. Court ("The Theme and Structure of Spenser's *Muiopotmos*") gives a convenient survey of attempts to read the poem either as a political-historical allegory or as a moral one. Of the latter, the most impressive, yet still strained, is Don Cameron Allen, "On Spenser's *Muiopotmos*." See also Ronald B. Bond, "*Invidia* and the Allegory of Spenser's 'Muiopotmos.' "

17. The distinction between the goddesses forms the core of Allen's allegorical reading of the poem.

18. Court, "Theme and Structure," p. 5.

19. Idleness was portress of the love garden in the *Roman de la rose* (582) and, we may remember, is said with "lascivia umana" to have engendered Amore in the *Trionfi* and in *Gli Asolani*. The association goes back to Ovid, *Remedia amoris* 139–40.

20. Charles E. Mounts, who made some of these same points, was reprimanded by a prominent scholar for suggesting that Spenser had adopted his own brand of paganism. See "Colin Clout: Priest of Cupid and Venus" and "The Evolution of Spenser's Attitude toward Cupid and Venus."

21. Robert Ellrodt, *Neoplatonism*, pp. 92–93. For the evidence that Spenser did revise the poem before publication and for the date of the poem, see *Variorum 7* (*MP*, pt. 1):450–51.

22. Lines 875–76, omitting the comma that Smith and de Selincourt print following *fynd*.

23. See Ficino, *Commentary on the Symposium*, 1.3 and 5.10; Equicola, *Libro di natura d'amore*, pp. 93v–95r; Giraldi, *Historia de deis gentium*, col. 405; Conti, *Mythologiae*, pp. 402–5.

24. Lotspeich, *Classical Mythology in the Poetry of Edmund Spenser*, p. 49.

25. Empedocles: see G. S. Kirk and J. E. Raven, *The Presocratic Philosophers*, frag. 424 (pp. 327–28). Orpheus: see "To Love," no. 58 in Thomas Taylor, trans., *The Mystical Hymns of Orpheus*. Boethius: see *Consol.*, 2, met. 8. Chaucer: *Troilus*, 3. 1744–71.

26. See John Huntington, "Philosophical Seduction in Chapman, Davies, and Donne."

27. Lines 808, 812–13, 803, 799, 883 (my emphasis).

28. In the following discussion I have drawn upon John W. Moore, Jr., "How the Theme of Love Structures *Colin Clouts Come Home Againe*."

29. I have omitted the period that Smith and de Selincourt print following *he*.

30. See *Variorum 8* (*MP*, pt. 2):631–38, 647–52.

31. Renwick cites Petrarch no. 121, "Or vedi Amor," and Wyatt's version, "Behold, Love, thy power how she despiseth"; see *Variorum 8* (*MP*, pt. 2):423.

32. *The Hekatompathia or Passionate Centurie of Love*, no. 70. Watson is imitating, "some what a farre off," a Neolatin ode by Gervase Sepinus. On Spenser's knowledge of Watson, see William Ringler, "Spenser and Thomas Watson."

33. Sidney's conceit goes back to Peire Vidal, lacking, of course, the mythological anecdote. See chap. 2, n. 18 above.

34. Lever, *The Elizabethan Love Sonnet*, p. 65.

35. Lewis, *English Literature in the Sixteenth Century*, p. 372.

36. *Col.*, 789–90. *Am.* 8, which associates Cupid with "base affections," I consider an anomaly. It reverses *FQ*, 3. 3.1–3 while echoing 3.4.6 where Britomart, the knight of chastity, follows the guidance of her "blinded guest." See also Jon A. Quitslund, "Spenser's *Amoretti* VIII and Platonic Commentaries on Petrarch."

37. See *Variorum* 8 (*MP*, pt. 2):455–56.

38. Viglione, *La poesia lirica di Edmondo Spenser*, pp. 299–300. Spenser's anacreontics perhaps serve the same function as the two mythological sonnets that end Shakespeare's sequence.

39. Hutton, "Cupid and the Bee" (excerpted in *Variorum* 8 [*MP*, pt. 2]:456–58).

40. "Let mother earth now decke her self in flowers," 55–59 (Ringler, ed., p. 92).

41. Marriage is "Cupid's yoke" in *Col.*, 434–35, 566. Cupid appears also in *Prothalamion*, 96–97.

42. Thomas M. Greene, "Spenser and the Epithalamic Convention," p. 223.

43. See Dale Byron Billingsley, "Pageants and the Vision of Order in Spenser's Poetry," pp. 88–89.

44. Josephine M. Bennett, "The Theme of Spenser's *Fowre Hymnes*," p. 53. I shall abbreviate the titles of the hymns *HL, HB, HHL, HHB*.

45. As in *Col.*, conflation of Cupids has been discounted as evidence of revision. See Sears Jayne, "Attending to Genre: Spenser's *Hymnes*." C. S. Lewis called the conflation of genealogies a "dreadful blunder" (*English Lit. in 16th Century*, p. 374). John Mulryan argues that the mysteries of Cupid's nativity parallel those of Christ's ("Spenser as Mythologist: A Study of the Nativities of Cupid and Christ in the *Fowre Hymnes*").

46. Ellrodt, *Neoplatonism*, p. 128.

47. Sidney, *Apology*, ed. Smith, p. 187; *HB*, 157–58. In the Proem to Book 4 of the *Faerie Queene*, published in the same year as the *Hymnes*, Spenser argues that neither love nor by implication his poem should be blamed "For fault of few that have abusd the same" (4. proem. 2). Poison as an image for abuse was commonplace, of course, but Conti had applied it to literary abuse of Cupid (see p. 108 above).

48. E.g. Padelford cited in *Variorum* 7 (*MP*, pt. 1):661 and Einar Bjorvand, "Spenser's Defense of Poetry: Some Structural Aspects of the *Fowre Hymnes*," p. 14.

49. Cf. *Il Cortegiano*, 4. 67: "Whereupon being made dimme with this greater light, he shall not passe upon the lesser, and burning in a more excellent flame, he shall litle esteeme it, that hee set great store by at the first" (trans. Hoby, p. 318).

50. Critics like Ellrodt (chap. 8) and Bjorland (p. 14), drawing a false dichotomy between ascents and conversions, have therefore given a partial view of the relation between the pairs of hymns.

51. For impatience and anger, see *HHL*, 218–21 and *HHB*, 267–80, 288–91.

52. See Matt. 22:37–39: "You shall love the Lord your God with all your heart, and with all your soul, and with all your mind. This is the great and first commandment. And a second is like it, You shall love your neighbor as yourself."

53. *Opere latine*, ed. Bufano, 1:186. See also Petrarch, *Rime sparse*, no. 360, and Dante, *Convivio*, 4.12.15–19.

54. Bennett noticed parallels in 1931 ("The Theme of *Fowre Hymns*," pp. 36–37) and they are exhaustively surveyed by Bjorvand.

55. See Nelson, *Poetry of Edmund Spenser*, p. 110; A. Leigh DeNeef, "Spenserian Meditation: The *Hymne of Heavenly Beautie*;" and the important article by Jon A. Quitslund, "Spenser's Image of Sapience."

Chapter 7. *The Faerie Queene*

1. *The Wisedom of the Ancients*, chap. 17.

2. *Spenser's Images of Life*, pp. 11–35. Lewis alluded to the importance of art-historical studies for the critic of Spenser in his review of Ellrodt, "Neoplatonism in the Poetry of Spenser."

3. Paul J. Alpers, *The Poetry of the Faerie Queene*, esp. pp. 19–35, 111.

4. See A. C. Hamilton, *The Structure of Allegory in the Faerie Queene*, p. 138 and Wind, *Pagan Mysteries*, pp. 85–96.

5. *Amores*, 1.1.21–24, ed. Showerman; translation slightly altered.

6. Letter to Raleigh, ed. Smith and de Selincourt, p. 407. The dedicatory sonnet appears on p. 410.

7. *Metam.*, 2.846–7: "Non bene conveniunt nec in una sede morantur / maiestas et amor." The opposition became a commonplace; see Praz, *Studies in Seventeenth Century Imagery*, 1:103.

8. 1.1.53; see Tuve, *Allegorical Imagery*, p. 121. The secondary meaning of *veritas* is implied throughout the episode, however. What Redcrosse ought to do is doubt the veracity of appearances. "False" has a similar double meaning; see 1.2.4: "Come see, where your false Lady doth her honour staine." See Alpers, *Poetry of FQ*, p. 91.

9. Lewis, *Spenser's Images of Life*, pp. 21, 33. Others who have accepted a distinction between Cupids are William Nelson (*Poetry of Edmund Spenser*, pp. 236, 247), Robert Kellogg and Oliver Steele (in their edition of Books 1 and 2, e.g., on 2.8.6), Roger Sale (*Reading Spenser;* pp. 71ff.), and Douglas Brooks-Davies (*Spenser's Faerie Queene: A Critical Commentary on Books I and II,* e.g. on 2.8.6).

10. Spenser uses the pun on *mean* in stanza 21.

11. See Kathleen Williams, *Spenser's World of Glass*, p. 46.

12. A. C. Hamilton draws this distinction, for example, in his edition of the *Faerie Queene*.

13. Harry Berger, Jr., *The Allegorical Temper*, pp. 137–40 and Williams, *Spenser's World of Glass*, pp. 48–50. For Spenser's "ventriloquism" by which the narrator presents the thoughts or attitudes of his figures in a kind of indirect discourse, see Alpers, *Poetry of FQ*, pp. 331–33 and especially Judith H. Anderson, *The Growth of a Personal Voice*, p. 23 *et passim*.

14. See James E. Phillips, "Spenser's Syncretistic Religious Imagery," pp. 109–10, and R. M. Cummings, "An Iconographical Puzzle," p. 317. Rosemond Tuve argues for the simile's appropriateness on narrower grounds—Spenser has in mind manuscript illustrations of angelic Cupids. See "Spenser and Some Pictorial Conventions," pp. 164–66, and *Allegorical Imagery*, p. 377–78n.

15. For example, Hamilton and Kellogg and Steele in their editions; Brooks-Davies, *Critical Commentary.*

16. Phillips, "Syncretistic Imagery," p. 110.

17. Cheney, *Spenser's Image of Nature*, p. 67.

18. Both references occur in the major "temple" or doctrinal place of the books; both are attached to a woman in "her freshest age" (1.10.30 and 2.9.18).

19. Aquinas explains the points of view from which essences can be seen as accidents and vice versa in *Summa theologia*, 1, Q 77, Art. 1, especially Reply Obj. 5. See also Isabel MacCaffrey, *Spenser's Allegory: The Anatomy of Imagination*, p. 84.

20. See Kathleen Williams, "Venus and Diana: Some Uses of Myth in *The Faerie Queene*"; Hamilton, *Structure of Allegory*, pp. 138–69; Thomas P. Roche, Jr., *The Kindly Flame;* Elizabeth Story Donno, "The Triumph of Cupid: Spenser's Legend of Chastity"; and the excellent monograph by William V. Nestrick, *Spenser and the Renaissance Mythology of Love.*

21. Anderson, *Personal Voice*, pp. 99–100.

22. See 1.9.8–12; 3.2.23, 26, 35; 6.9.11; 4.12.13; 4.10.1; 4.7.1–2.

23. Lewis, *Allegory of Love*, p. 339.

24. Alpers, *Poetry of FQ*, p. 47.

25. Other obvious similarities encourage comparison of Castle Joyous to Malbecco's house. At both, Britomart is entertained with another knight or knights. At both, imitation is at issue, though Malecasta's courtiers imitate a generalized "antique worldes guize" while Paris's descendant rapes a "second Hellene."

26. I would not argue that *all* of the incidents of the poem answer to the narrator's meditation as revealed in stanzas of commentary. There is truth in the general view, of which Roger Sale is representative, that "Spenser's few apostrophes are allowed to dwindle away in their force before one stanza is over, and stand not as guideposts to the 'meaning' but as momentary responses to the immediate situation" (*Reading Spenser*, p. 87). Alpers argues something similar when he writes of "Spenser's failure to maintain a dramatic identity in relation to his poem" (*Poetry of FQ*, p. 332). Much remains to be learned about the relation between commentary and incident in the *Faerie Queene*. Judith Anderson has made a start *(Personal Voice)*, and see also Alpers, "Narration in *The Faerie Queene*," which discusses several other articles on the issue.

27. Fortune is emphasized throughout the episode; see stanzas 22, 23, 26, 38, 43, 44, 45.

28. See Nestrick, *Mythology of Love*, p. 38. E. K. in the gloss on *March* cites Poliziano's Latin translation of Moschus and reports that Spenser also translated it.

29. Cf. the opposite disjunction in *Colin Clouts Come Home Againe*, where Venus "nurst" Cupid in the "gardens of *Adonis*," but "Then got he bow and shafts of gold and lead . . ." (803–807).

30. Hamilton, *Structure of Allegory*, pp. 138–50.

31. See Ellrodt, *Neoplatonism*, p. 62, and Nestrick, *Mythology of Love*, p. 56.

32. Nestrick, *Mythology of Love*, p. 63.

33. Alpers, *Poetry of FQ*, pp. 14–19.

34. Virgil, *Georgics*, 3.244.

35. Roche makes the most convincing statement of this interpretation; see *The Kindly Flame*, pp. 72–88. See also A. Kent Hieatt, "Scudamour's Practice of *Maistrye* Upon Amoret," commenting upon an earlier version of Roche's chapter. A. C. Hamilton reads the episode this way (*Structure of Allegory*, pp. 166–67, 182), as does Alastair Fowler (*Triumphal forms*, pp. 47–58).

36. For the emblem in Alciati, Whitney, and others, see Arthur F. Marotti, "Animal Symbolism in the *Faerie Queene*," p. 74; for the epigram: *Greek Anth.* 9.221.

37. See above, pp. 38–39. In the *Dialoghi d'amore*, Sophia herself confidently applies the "common saying" to these stories, "many are the lies of the poets" (p. 110). Stephen Gosson made a similar denunciation in his *An Apologie of the Schoole of Abuse* (1579): "Whilest they [the poets] make Cupide triumphe in heaven, and all the gods to marche bounde like miserable captives, before his chariott, they belie God, and bewitch the reader with bawdie charmes" (ed. Arber, p. 67). Spenser mentioned the original *Schoole of Abuse* in a letter to Harvey (p. 635).

38. See Harry Berger, Jr., "Busirane and the War Between the Sexes."

39. Roche speculates that Busyrane's name signifies, among other things, *abuse* (*Kindly Flame*, p. 82).

40. A. H. Gilbert quoted in *Variorum* 4:203.

41. *Genealogia deorum*, 1.15 and *Mythologiae*, 4.14 (pp. 409–10).

42. Spenser encourages reminiscence of Book 1 by identifying the giant Disdain, who leads Mirabella, as "sib to great *Orgoglio*, which was slaine / By *Arthure*, when as Unas Knight he did maintaine" (6.7.41). James Nohrnberg mentions the detail (pp. 656, 711), as part of the general analogy between Books 1 and 6, in *The Analogy of the Faerie Queene*, which I obtained too late to make full use of.

43. Berger, "A Secret Discipline: *The Faerie Queene*, Book VI," p. 51. The episode reads like a reprise, and its detachability from the fragmented narrative of Book 6 and adherence to well-worn models have led some scholars to suspect that Spenser found a place in the *Faerie Queene* for the Court of Cupide mentioned by E. K. in the epistle dedicatory to the *Shepheardes Calender* (p. 418). See E. B. Fowler in *Variorum* 6:223.

44. 6.10.17. See Berger, "Secret Discipline," pp. 61–63.

Epilogue

1. Stanza 4; text: John Donne, *The Elegies and the Songs and Sonnets*, ed. Helen Gardner, p. 48.

2. "Song. Love Arm'd," (1–2, 9–16); text in Robin Skelton, ed., *The Cavalier Poets*, p. 35.

3. *Madame Bovary*, 2.13 (ed. Gothot-Mersch, p. 208; trans. Russell, p. 214).

Bibliography

Abelard, Peter. *Theologia Christiana. PL* 178:1123–1330.

Aimeric de Peguilhan. *The Poems of Aimeric de Peguilhan.* Edited by William P. Shepard and Frank M. Chambers. Evanston: Northwestern University Press, 1950.

Alain de Lille. *The Complaint of Nature.* Translated by Douglas M. Moffat. Yale Studies in English, 36. New York: Holt, 1908.

———. *Distinctiones dictionum theologicalium. PL* 210:685–1012.

———. *De planctu Naturae.* Edited by Thomas Wright in *The Anglo-Latin Satirical Poets and Epigrammatists of the Twelfth Century.* 2 vols. 1872. Reprint. London: Kraus Reprint, 1964.

Alciati, Andrea. *Emblemata.* Padua: Tozzius, 1621. Reprint. New York and London: Garland, 1976.

Allen, Don Cameron. "Edmund Spenser, 'The March Eclogue' of *The Shepheardes Calender.*" In *Image and Meaning: Metaphoric Traditions in Renaissance Poetry.* 2d enlarged ed., pp. 1–19. Baltimore: Johns Hopkins Press, 1968.

———. *Mysteriously Meant: The Rediscovery of Pagan Symbolism and Allegorical Interpretation in the Renaissance.* Baltimore and London: Johns Hopkins Press, 1970.

———. "On Spenser's *Muiopotmos.*" *Studies in Philology* 53 (1956):141–58. Reprinted in *Image and Meaning,* pp. 20–41.

Alpers, Paul J. "Narration in *The Faerie Queene.*" *ELH* 44 (1977):19–39.

———. *The Poetry of the Faerie Queene.* Princeton: Princeton University Press, 1967.

Alton, E. H. "The Medieval Commentators on Ovid's *Fasti.*" *Hermathena.* 20(1930):119–51.

Anderson, Judith. *The Growth of a Personal Voice: Piers Plowman and The Faerie Queene.* New Haven and London: Yale University Press, 1976.

Andreas Capellanus. *De amore libri tres.* Edited by E. Trojel. Copenhagen: Gadiana, 1892.

———. *The Art of Courtly Love.* Translated by John J. Parry. New York: Columbia University Press, 1941.

Antonio, Saint, Archbishop of Florence. *Summa theologia.* 4 vols. Verona: 1740. Reprint. Graz: Akademische Druck, 1959.

Arnobius. *Adversus gentes. PL* 5:713–1290.

Arnulf of Orléans. *Allegoriae super Metamorphosin.* Edited by Fausto Ghisalberti in "Arnolfo d'Orléans: un cultore di Ovidio nel secolo XII." *Memorie del reale Istituto Lombardo di scienze e lettere, classe di lettere, scienze morale e storiche* 24.4:194–229. Milan: Hoepli, 1932.

Auden, W. H. *The Dyer's Hand and Other Essays.* London: Faber, 1963.

Augustine, Saint. *Confessions.* Translated by William Watts. 1631. Reprint. 2 vols. LCL. London: Heinemann and New York: Putnam's, 1931.

———. *Contra Faustum. PL* 42 : 207–518.

———. *On Christian Doctrine.* Translated by D. W. Robertson. Indianapolis: Bobbs-Merrill, 1958.

Bacon, Sir Francis. *The Wisedom of the Ancients.* Translated by Arthur Gorges. London: John Bill, 1619.

Baïf, Jean-Antoine de. *Les Amours ou Les Amours de Méline.* Edited by Mathieu Augé-Chiquet. Paris: Hachette and Toulouse: Privat, 1909.

Beardsley, Monroe C. *Aesthetics.* New York: Harcourt Brace, 1958.

Belleau, Remy. *Oeuvres poétiques.* Edited by Charles Marty-Laveaux. 2 vols. Paris: Alphonse Lemerre, 1878.

Bembo, Pietro. *Opere in volgare.* Edited by Mario Marti. Florence: Sansoni, 1961.

———. *Pietro Bembo's "Gli Asolani."* Translated by Rudolf B. Gottfried. Bloomington: Indiana University Press, 1954.

Benedetto, Luigi Foscolo. *Il "Roman de la Rose" e la letteratura italiana.* Beihefte zur Zeitschrift für Romanische Philologie, 21. Halle: Niemeyer, 1910.

Bennett, Josephine W. "The Theme of Spenser's *Fowre Hymnes.*" *Studies in Philology* 28 (1931) : 18–57.

Benoit de Sainte-Maure. *Roman de Troie.* Edited by Leopold Constans. 6 vols. Société des Anciens Textes Français. Paris: Firmin-Didot, 1904–12.

Berger, Harry, Jr. *The Allegorical Temper: Vision and Reality in Book II of Spenser's Faerie Queene.* Yale Studies in English, 137. New Haven: Yale University Press, 1957.

———. "Busirane and the War Between the Sexes." *English Literary Renaissance* 1(1971) : 99–121.

———. "The Renaissance Imagination." *Centennial Review* 9 (1965) : 36–78.

———. "A Secret Discipline: *The Faerie Queene,* Book VI." In William Nelson, ed., *Form and Convention in the Poetry of Edmund Spenser.* Selected Papers from the English Institute. New York and London: Columbia University Press, 1961.

———. "Two Spenserian Retrospects: The Antique Temple of Venus and the Primitive Marriage of Rivers." *Texas Studies in Language and Literature* 10 (1968) : 5–25.

Billingsley, Dale Byron. "Pageants and the Vision of Order in Spenser's Poetry." Ph.D. dissertation, Yale, 1977.

Bjorvand, Einar. "Spenser's Defense of Poetry: Some Structural Aspects of the *Fowre Hymnes.*" In Maren-Sofie Rostvig, ed., *Fair Forms: Essays in English Literature from Spenser to Jane Austen.* Totowa, N.J.: Rowman and Littlefield, 1975.

Boase, Roger. *The Origin and Meaning of Courtly Love: A Critical Study of European Scholarship.* Manchester: Manchester University Press, 1977.

Boccaccio, Giovanni. *Genealogia deorum gentilium.* Venice: Wendelin von Speyer, 1472.

———. Περι γενεαλογιασ *deorum libri quindecim, cum annotationibus Jacobi Micylli.* Basel: Joannes Hervagius, 1532.

———. *Genealogie deorum gentilium libri.* Edited by Vincenzo Romano. 2 vols. Bari: Laterza, 1951.

————. *Boccaccio on Poetry.* Translated by Charles G. Osgood. 1930. Reprint. Indianapolis: Bobbs-Merrill, 1956.

Bode, Georg H., ed. *Scriptores rerum mythicarum Latini tres.* 2 vols. Celle: Schulze, 1834.

Boethius. *Consolatio Philosophiae.* Edited by Ludovick Bieler. Corpus Christianorum, Ser. Lat. 94. Turnhout: Brepols, 1957.

Bolgar, R. R. *The Classical Heritage and its Beneficiaries.* Cambridge: Cambridge University Press, 1954.

Bond, Ronald B. "*Invidia* and the Allegory of Spenser's 'Muiopotmos.'" *English Studies in Canada* 2 (1976):144–55.

Brooks-Davies, Douglas. *Spenser's Faerie Queene: A Critical Commentary on Books I and II.* Manchester: Manchester University Press and Totowa, N.J.: Rowman and Littlefield, 1977.

Calcaterra, Carlo. *Nella selva del Petrarca.* Bologna: Licinio Cappelli, 1942.

Caraccio, Armand. "Note sur le mythe d'Eros et sur l'apparition d' 'Amour' en tant qu'allégorie extérieure à Dante dans la *Vita Nuova.*" In *Dante et les mythes: Tradition et renovation. Revue des Études Italiennes,* n.s. 11(1965):30–39.

Carmina Burana. Edited by Alfons Hilka and Otto Schumann. 2 vols. Heidelberg: Carl Winter, 1941.

Cartari, Vincenzo. *Le imagini colla sposizione degli dei degli antichi.* Venice: Marcolini, 1556.

————. *Imagini delli dei de gl'antichi.* Venice: Tomasini, 1647. Facsimile edited by Walter Koschatzky. Graz, Austria: Akademische Druk, 1963.

Cassirer, Ernst. *The Individual and the Cosmos in Renaissance Philosophy.* Translated by Mario Domandi. 1927. Reprint. New York: Harper Torchbooks, 1964.

Castiglione, Baldassare. *Il libro del cortegiano.* Edited by Bruno Maier. 2d ed. Classici italiani, 31. Turin: U.T.E.T., 1964.

————. *The Book of the Courtier.* Translated by Sir Thomas Hoby. 1561. Reprint. New York: Dutton and London: Dent, 1928.

Chalcidius. *Timaeus a Calcidio translatus commentarioque instructus.* Edited by Jan Hendrik Waszink. Corpus Platonicum Medii Aevi. General editor Raymond Klibansky. Leiden: Brill, 1975.

Chaucer, Geoffrey. *The Works of Geoffrey Chaucer.* Edited by F. N. Robinson. 2d ed. London: Oxford University Press, 1966.

Cheney, Donald. *Spenser's Image of Nature: Wild Man and Shepherd in The Faerie Queene.* Yale Studies in English, 161. New Haven and London: Yale University Press, 1966.

Chenu, M.-D. *Nature, Man, and Society in the Twelfth Century: Essays on New Theological Perspectives in the Latin West.* Edited and translated by Jerome Taylor and Lester K. Little. Chicago: University of Chicago Press, 1968.

Chrétien de Troyes. *Le Chevalier au Lion (Yvain).* Edited by Mario Roques. *Les Romans de Chrétien de Troyes,* 4. Les Classiques Français du Moyen Age, 89. Paris: Champion, 1967.

————. *Cligés.* Edited by Alexandre Micha. *Les Romans de Chrétien de Troyes,* 2. Classiques Français du Moyen Age, 84. Paris: Champion, 1968.

Cicero. *De natura deorum and Academica.* Translated by H. Rackham. LCL. London:

Heinemann and Cambridge, Mass.: Harvard University Press, 1933.

Coleridge, Samuel Taylor. *Table Talk and Omniana of Samuel Taylor Coleridge.* Edited by T. Ashe. London: George Bell & Sons, 1909.

Conti, Natale [Natalis Comes]. *Mythologiae sive explicationis fabularum libri decem.* Hanover: Typis Wechelianis, 1619.

Contini, Gianfranco. "Un nodo della cultura medievale: la serie *Roman de la Rose-Fiore-Divina Commedia.*" *Lettere italiane* 25 (1973):162–89.

———, ed. *Poeti del Duecento.* 2 vols. Milan and Naples: Riccardo Ricciardi, 1960.

Cort d'Amor. Edited and translated by Lowanne E. Jones. North Carolina Studies in the Romance Languages and Literatures, 185. Chapel Hill: University of North Carolina Department of Romance Languages, 1977.

Court, Franklin E. "The Theme and Structure of Spenser's *Muiopotmos.*" *Studies in English Literature* 10 (1970):1–15.

Crane, Thomas Frederick. *Italian Social Customs of the Sixteenth Century.* New Haven: Yale University Press, 1920.

Cummings, R. M. "An Iconographical Puzzle: Spenser's Cupid at *Faerie Queene,* VII [sic], viii." *Journal of the Warburg and Courtauld Institutes* 33 (1970):317–21.

Curtius, Ernst Robert. *European Literature in the Latin Middle Ages.* Translated by Willard R. Trask. London: Routledge, 1953.

Dante Alighieri. *Le opere di Dante.* Edited by Michele Barbi et al. Florence: Bemporad, 1921.

———. *Paradiso.* Translated by John D. Sinclair. New York: Oxford University Press, 1961.

———. *Vita Nuova.* Edited by Michele Scherillo. Milan: Hoepli, 1911.

———. *Vita Nuova.* Edited by Kenneth McKenzie. Boston: Heath, 1922.

———. *La Vita Nuova.* Translated by Barbara Reynolds. Harmondsworth: Penguin, 1969.

———. *Dante's Lyric Poetry.* Edited by Kenelm Foster and Patrick Boyde. 2 vols. Oxford: At the Clarendon Press, 1967.

Demerson, Guy. *La Mythologie classique dans l'oeuvre lyrique de la "Pléiade."* Travaux d'humanisme et Renaissance, 119. Geneva: Droz, 1972.

DeNeef, A. Leigh. "Spenserian Meditation: The *Hymne of Heavenly Beautie.*" *American Benedictine Review* 25 (1974):317–34.

De Nolhac, Pierre. *Pétrarque et l'humanisme.* 2d ed. 2 vols. Paris: Champion, 1907.

De Robertis, Domenico. *Il Libro della Vita Nuova.* 2d rev. ed. Florence: Sansoni, 1970.

Devereux, James A. "The Textual History of Ficino's *De Amore.*" *Renaissance Quarterly* 28 (1975):173–82.

Dictionnaire de spiritualité. 10 + vols. Paris: Gabriel Beauchesne, 1937–.

Dionysius the pseudo-Areopagite. *De coelesti hierarchia.* PG 3:119–370.

———. *Divine Names.* Translated by C. E. Rolt. London: Macmillan, 1920.

Dodds, E. R. *The Greeks and the Irrational.* Berkeley and Los Angeles: University of California Press, 1951.

Donne, John. *The Elegies and Songs and Sonnets.* Edited by Helen Gardner. Oxford: At the Clarendon Press, 1965.

Donno, Elizabeth Story. "The Triumph of Cupid: Spenser's Legend of Chastity." *Yearbook of English Studies* 4 (1974):37–48.

Dronke, Peter. *Fabula: Explorations into the Uses of Myth in Medieval Platonism.* Mittellateinische Studien und Texte, 9. Leiden and Cologne: Brill, 1974.

———. "L'amor che move il sole e l'altre stelle." *Studi medievali,* 3d series, 6 (1965):389–422.

———. *Medieval Latin and the Rise of the European Love-Lyric.* 2 vols. 2d rev. ed. Oxford: At the Clarendon Press, 1968.

Ellrodt, Robert. *Neoplatonism in the Poetry of Spenser.* Geneva: Droz, 1960.

Enciclopedia dantesca. Edited by Umberto Bosco et al. Rome: Istituto della enciclopedia italiana, 1970.

Enéas: A Twelfth-Century French Romance. Translated by John A. Yunck. New York: Columbia University Press, 1974.

Equicola, Mario. *Di Natura d'Amore.* Venice: Giovanni Battista Bonsadino, 1587.

Erasmus, Desiderius. *Erasmus on his Times: A Shortened Version of the Adages of Erasmus.* Edited and translated by Margaret Mann Phillips. Cambridge: Cambridge University Press, 1967.

Errante, Guido. *Marcabru e le fonti sacre dell' antica lirica romanza.* Florence: Sansoni, 1948.

Espiner-Scott, Janet. "Les Sonnets Élisabéthains: Cupidon et l'influence d'Ovide." *Revue de Littérature Comparée* 31 (1957):421–26.

Essling, Victor Masséna, prince d', and Eugène Müntz. *Petrarque: ses études d'art, son influence sur les artistes, ses portraits et ceux de Laure.* Paris: Gazette des Beaux-arts, 1902.

Faral, Edmond. *Recherches sur les sources latines des contes et romans courtois du Moyen Age.* Paris: Champion, 1913.

Festugière, Jean. *La Philosophie de l'amour de Marsil Ficin.* Études de philosophie médiévale, 31. Paris: Vrin, 1941.

Ficino, Marsilio. *Marsilio Ficino's Commentary on Plato's Symposium.* Edited and translated by Sears Reynolds Jayne. University of Missouri Studies, 19.1. Columbia, Mo.: University of Missouri Press, 1944.

———. *Marsile Ficin sur le Banquet de Platon ou "De l'Amour."* Edited by Raymond Marcel. Paris: Société d'edition "Les Belles Lettres," 1956.

Flaubert, Gustave. *Madame Bovary.* Edited by Claudine Gothot-Mersch. Paris: Garnier Frères, 1971.

———. *Madame Bovary.* Translated by Alan Russell. Harmondsworth: Penguin, 1950.

Fletcher, Angus. *Allegory: The Theory of a Symbolic Mode.* Ithaca and London: Cornell University Press, 1964.

Fliedner, Heinrich. *Amor und Cupido: Untersuchungen über den römischen Liebesgott.* Beiträge zur Klassischen Philologie, 53. Meisenheim am Glan: Anton Hain, 1974.

Fowler, Alastair. *Triumphal forms: Structural patterns in Elizabethan poetry.* Cambridge: Cambridge University Press, 1970.

Frank, Donald K. "On the Troubadour Fin'Amors." *Romance Notes* 7 (1966):209–17.

Frank, Grace. "The Distant Love of Jaufré Rudel." *MLN* 57 (1942):528–34.

———. "Jaufré Rudel, Casella, and Spitzer." *MLN* 59 (1944):526–31.

Freyhan, R. "The Evolution of the Caritas Figure in the Thirteenth and Fourteenth Centuries." *Journal of the Warburg and Courtauld Institutes* 11 (1948):68–86.

Fucilla, Joseph G. "Additions to 'The First Idyl of Moschus in Imitations to the Year 1800.'" *American Journal of Philology* 50 (1929):190–93.

———. "Materials for the History of a Popular Classical Theme." *Classical Philology* 26 (1931):135–52.

Fulgentius. *Opera.* Edited by Rudolf Helm. Leipzig: Teubner, 1898.

———. *Fulgentius the Mythographer.* Translated by Leslie George Whitbread. Columbus: Ohio State University Press, 1971.

Garin, Eugenio. "Le favole antiche." In *Medioevo e Rinascimento,* pp. 66–89. Biblioteca di cultura moderna, 506. Bari: Laterza, 1954.

———. "Platonismo e filosofia d'amore." In *L'umanesimo italiano: Filosophia e vita civile nel Rinascimento,* pp. 146–71. Bari: Laterza, 1952.

Garner, Barbara C. "Francis Bacon, Natalis Comes and the Mythological Tradition." *Journal of the Warburg and Courtauld Institutes* 33 (1970):264–91.

Gay-Crosier, Raymond. *Religious Elements in the Secular Lyrics of the Troubadours.* University of North Carolina Studies in the Romance Languages and Literatures, 111. Chapel Hill: University of North Carolina Press, 1971.

Giamatti, A. Bartlett. "Spenser: From Magic to Miracle." In *Four Essays on Romance,* edited by Herschel Baker, pp. 17–31. Cambridge, Mass.: Harvard University Press, 1971.

Giraldi, Lilio Gregorio. *Opera omnia.* 2 vols. Leiden: Lugduni Batavorum, 1696.

Goffen, Rona. "Icon and Vision: Giovanni Bellini's Half-length Madonnas." *Art Bulletin* 57 (1975):487–518.

Gombrich, E. H. "Personification." In *Classical Influences on European Culture A.D. 500–1500,* edited by R. R. Bolgar. Cambridge: Cambridge University Press, 1971.

———. "Icones Symbolicae," rev. ed. In *Symbolic Images: Studies in the Art of the Renaissance,* pp. 123–91. London and New York: Phaidon, 1972.

Gorra, Egidio. "La teorica dell'amore." In *Fra drammi e poemi,* pp. 201–302. Milan: Hoepli, 1900.

Gosson, Stephen. *The Schoole of Abuse* and *A Short Apologie of the Schoole of Abuse.* 1579. In *English Reprints,* Vol. 1. Edited by Edward Arber. Reprint. New York: AMS Press, 1966.

Grabmann, Martin. "Das Werk *De amore* des Andreas Capellanus und das Verurteilungsdekret des Bischofs Stephan Tempier von Paris vom 7 Marz 1277." *Speculum* 7 (1932):75–79.

The Greek Anthology. Edited and translated by W. R. Paton. 5 vols. LCL. London: Heinemann and New York: Putnam's, 1925.

Green, Richard Hamilton. "Alan of Lille's *De Planctu Naturae.*" *Speculum* 31 (1956):649–74.

Greene, Thomas M. "Spenser and the Epithalamic Convention." *Comparative Literature* 9 (1957):215–28.

Greg, W. W. *Pastoral Poetry and Pastoral Drama.* London: A. H. Bullen, 1906.

Groos, Arthur. "'Amor and his brother Cupid': The 'Two Loves' in Heinrich von Veldeke's 'Eneit.'" *Traditio* 32 (1976):239–55.

Guillaume de Lorris and Jean de Meun. *Roman de la rose.* Edited by Ernest Langlois. 5 vols. Société des Anciens Textes Français. Paris: Firmin-Didot, 1914–24.

Guittone d'Arezzo. *Le Rime.* Edited by Francesco Egidi. Scrittori d'Italia, 175. Bari: Laterza, 1940.

Hamilton, A. C. "The Argument of Spenser's *Shepheardes Calender.*" *ELH* 23 (1956):171–82.

⸻. *The Structure of Allegory in the Faerie Queene.* Oxford: At the Clarendon Press, 1961.

⸻, ed. *The Faerie Queene.* Longman Annotated English Poets. London and New York: Longman, 1977.

Hardie, Colin. "Dante and the Tradition of Courtly Love." In *Patterns of Love and Courtesy,* edited by John Lawlor, pp. 26–44. Evanston: Northwestern University Press, 1966.

Hardin, Richard F. "The Resolved Debate of Spenser's 'October.'" *Modern Philology* 73 (1976):257–63.

Heinze, Richard. *Virgils epische Technik.* Leipzig: Teubner, 1903.

Hieatt, A. Kent. "Scudamour's Practice of *Maistrye* upon Amoret." *PMLA* 77 (1962):509–10. Reprinted in *Essential Articles for the Study of Edmund Spenser,* edited by A. C. Hamilton, pp. 191–201. Hamden, Ct.: Archon Books, 1972.

Hill, R. T. and T. G. Bergin, eds. *Anthology of the Provençal Troubadours.* 2d rev. ed. 2 vols. New Haven and London: Yale University Press, 1973.

Hinks, Roger. *Myth and Allegory in Ancient Art.* London: Warburg Institute, 1955.

Hollander, Robert. "Dante *Theologus-Poeta.*" *Dante Studies* 94 (1976):91–136.

⸻. "*Vita Nuova:* Dante's Perceptions of Beatrice." *Dante Studies* 92 (1974):1–18.

Homer. *The Iliad.* Translated by Richmond Lattimore. Chicago and London: University of Chicago Press, 1961.

Huntington, John. "Philosophical Seduction in Chapman, Davies, and Donne." *ELH* 44 (1977):40–59.

Hugh of St. Victor. *De laude charitatis. PL* 176:969–76.

Hutton, James. "Cupid and the Bee." *PMLA* 56 (1941):1036–58.

⸻. "The First Idyl of Moschus in Imitations to the year 1800." *American Journal of Philology* 49 (1928):105–36.

Isidore of Seville. *Differentiarum. PL* 83:9–98.

Jauss, Hans Robert. "Form und Auffassung der Allegorie in der Tradition der *Psychomachia* von Prudentius zum ersten *Romanz de la Rose.*" In *Medium Aevum Vivum,* Festschrift für Walther Bulst, edited by H. R. Jauss and D. Schaller. Heidelberg, 1960.

⸻. "La Transformation de la forme allégorique entre 1180 et 1240: d'Alain de Lille a Guillaume de Lorris." In *L'Humanisme médiéval dans les littératures romanes du XIIe au XIVe siècle,* edited by Anthime Fourrier, pp. 107–46. Paris: Klincksieck, 1964.

⸻. "Allegorese, Remythisierung und neuer Mythus." Reprinted in *Alterität und Modernität der Mittelalterlichen Literatur,* pp. 285–307. Munich: Wilhelm Fink, 1977.

Jayne, Sears. "Attending to Genre: Spenser's *Hymnes.*" English section 1, MLA Convention, Chicago, 27–30 December 1971. As abstracted in *Spenser Newsletter* 3:1, 5–6.

Joannes Scotus Erigena. *Annotationes in Marcianum.* Edited by Cora E. Lutz. Cambridge, Mass.: Medieval Academy of America, 1939.

————, trans. *De divinis nominibus* by Dionysius the pseudo-Areopagite. *PL* 122:1111–71.

Johnson, Samuel. "Milton." *Lives of the English Poets.* 2 vols. 1780. Reprint. London and New York: Dent and Dutton, 1968.

Kirk, G. S., and J. E. Raven, eds. *The Presocratic Philosophers.* Cambridge: Cambridge University Press, 1957.

Kristeller, Paul Oscar. *The Philosophy of Marsilio Ficino.* Translated by Virginia Conant. New York: Columbia University Press, 1943.

Lactantius. *Divinae institutiones. PL* 6:111–822.

————. *Divine Institutes.* Translated by Alexander Roberts and James Donaldson. In *The Ante-Nicene Fathers,* vol. 7. New York: Christian Literature Co., 1896.

Lasserre, François. *La Figure d'Eros dans la poésie grecque.* Lausanne: Imprimeries Réunies, 1946.

Lazar, Moshé. *Amour courtois et "Fin'Amors" dans la littérature du XIIe siècle.* Paris: Klincksieck, 1964.

Leone Ebreo. *Dialoghi d'amore.* Edited by Santino Caramella. Bari: Laterza, 1929.

————. *The Philosophy of Love.* Translated by F. Friedeberg-Seeley and Jean H. Barnes. London: Soncino Press, 1937.

Lever, J. W. *The Elizabethan Love Sonnet.* 2d ed. London: Methuen, 1956.

Lewis, C. S. *The Allegory of Love: A Study in Medieval Tradition.* London: Oxford University Press, 1936.

————. *The Discarded Image: An Introduction to Medieval and Renaissance Literature.* Cambridge: Cambridge University Press, 1964.

————. *English Literature in the Sixteenth Century Excluding Drama.* Oxford History of English Literature, 3. Oxford: At the Clarendon Press, 1954.

————. "Neoplatonism in the Poetry of Spenser." *Études Anglaises* 14 (1961):107–16. Reprint in *Studies in Medieval and Renaissance Literature,* edited by Walter Hooper, pp. 149–63. Cambridge: Cambridge University Press, 1966.

————. *Spenser's Images of Life.* Edited by Alastair Fowler. Cambridge: Cambridge University Press, 1967.

Lipking, Lawrence. "The Dialectic of *Il Cortegiano.*" *PMLA* 81 (1966):355–62.

Lotspeich, Henry G. *Classical Mythology in the Poetry of Edmund Spenser.* Princeton: Princeton University Press, 1932.

Lowes, J. L. "The Loveres Maladye of Hereos." *Modern Philology* 11 (1913–14):491–546.

Lubac, Henri de. *Exégèse médiéval: les quatre sens de L'Ecriture.* 2 vols. Paris: Aubier, 1959–64.

Luria, Maxwell. "A Sixteenth-Century Gloss on the *Roman de la Rose.*" *Medieval Studies* 44 (1982):333–70.

MacCaffrey, Isabel G. *Spenser's Allegory: The Anatomy of Imagination.* Princeton: Princeton University Press, 1976.

Macrobius. *Commentarii in Somnium Scipionis.* Edited by Jacob Willis. Leipzig: Teubner, 1963.

Marcabru. *Poésies complètes du troubadour Marcabru.* Edited by Jean–M.–L. Dejeanne. Toulouse: Édouard Privat, 1909.

Marle, Raimond van. *Iconographie de l'art profane au Moyen-Age et à la Renaissance.* 2 vols. The Hague: Nijhoff, 1932.

Marot, Clément. *Oeuvres poétiques.* Edited by Yves Giraud. Paris: Garnier-Flammarion, 1973.

Marotti, Arthur F. "Animal Symbolism in *The Faerie Queene:* Tradition and the Poetic Context." *Studies in English Literature* 5 (1965):69–86.

Martianus Capella. *De Nuptiis Mercurii et Philologiae.* Edited by Adolf Dick. Leipzig: Teubner, 1925.

Marullo, Michele. *Carmina.* Edited by Alessandro Perosa. Zurich: Artemis, 1951.

Mazzeo, Joseph Antony. "St. Augustine's Rhetoric of Silence: Truth vs. Eloquence and Things vs. Signs." In *Renaissance and Seventeenth-Century Studies.* New York: Columbia University Press and London: Routledge and Kegan Paul, 1963.

Mazzoni, Guido. "Un capolavoro del Poliziano. Tra la Canzon di Maggio, il canto carnascialesco e la festa mitologica." *Lares* 1 (1930):9–12.

Mazzotta, Giuseppe. "The Language of Poetry in the *Vita Nuova.*" *Rivista di studi italiani* 1 (1983):3–14.

Moore, John W. Jr. "How the Theme of Love Structures *Colin Clouts Come Home Againe.*" Seminar 176 (Shorter Poetical Works of the English Renaissance), MLA Convention, San Francisco, 1975.

Mounts, Charles E. "Colin Clout: Priest of Cupid and Venus." *High Point College Studies* 3 (1963):33–44.

———. "The Evolution of Spenser's Attitude toward Cupid and Venus." *High Point College Studies* 4 (1964):1–9.

Mulryan, John. "Spenser as Mythologist: A Study of the Nativities of Cupid and Christ in the *Fowre Hymnes.*" *Modern Language Studies* 1 (1971):13–16.

———. "Venus, Cupid, and the Italian Mythographers." *Humanistica Lovaniensa* 23 (1974):31–41.

Murrin, Michael. *The Veil of Allegory: Some Notes Toward a Theory of Allegorical Rhetoric in the English Renaissance.* Chicago and London: University of Chicago Press, 1969.

Nardi, Bruno. "L'Amore e i medici medievali." In *Studi in onore di Angelo Monteverdi,* vol. 2, pp. 517–42. Modena: Società tipografica editrice modenese, 1959.

Neilson, William Allan. *The Origins and Sources of the "Court of Love."* [Harvard] Studies and Notes in Philology and Literature, 6. Boston: Ginn, 1899.

———. "The Purgatory of Cruel Beauties." *Romania* 29 (1900):85–93.

Nelli, René. *L'Érotique des troubadours.* Toulouse: Édouard Privat, 1963.

Nelson, John C. *Renaissance Theory of Love: The Context of Giordano Bruno's Eroici Furori.* New York and London: Columbia University Press, 1958.

Nelson, William. *Fact or Fiction: The Dilemma of the Renaissance Storyteller.* Cambridge, Mass.: Harvard University Press, 1973.

———. *The Poetry of Edmund Spenser.* New York and London: Columbia University Press, 1963.

Nestrick, William V. *Spenser and the Renaissance Mythology of Love.* Literary Monographs 6. Madison: University of Wisconsin Press, 1975.

Newman, F. X., ed. *The Meaning of Courtly Love.* Albany, N.Y.: State University of New York Press, 1968.

Nohrnberg, James. *The Analogy of the Faerie Queene.* Princeton: Princeton University Press, 1976.

Origen. *In Canticum Canticorum prologus.* Latin translation by Rufinus. *PG* 13:61–84.

Orpheus. *The Mystical Hymns of Orpheus.* Translated by Thomas Taylor. London: Dobell, Reeves, Turner, 1896.

Otis, Brooks. *Virgil: A Study in Civilized Poetry.* Oxford: At the Clarendon Press, 1964.

Ovid. *The Art of Love and Other Poems.* Edited and translated by J. H. Mozley. LCL. London: Heinemann and Cambridge, Mass.: Harvard University Press, 1939.

———. *Fasti.* Edited and translated by J. G. Frazer. 5 vols. London: Heinemann and New York: Putnam's, 1931.

———. *Heroides and Amores.* Translated by Grant Showerman. LCL. London: Heinemann and New York: Macmillan, 1914.

———. *Metamorphoses.* Translated by Frank Justus Miller. LCL. 2d ed. 2 vols. London: Heinemann and Cambridge, Mass.: Harvard University Press, 1921.

Ovide moralisé: poème du commencement du quatorzième siècle. . . . Edited by C. de Boer. Verhandelingen der Koninklijke Akademie van Wetenschappen te Amsterdam, Afdeeling Letterkunde, n. s. 15, 21, 30, 37, 43. Amsterdam, 1915–38.

Panofsky, Erwin. *Studies in Iconology:Humanistic Themes in the Art of the Renaissance.* New York: Harper and Row, 1962.

Patrologiae cursus completus. Series Latina. Edited by J.-P. Migne. 221 vols. Paris, 1844–65.

———. Series Graeca. Edited by J.-P. Migne. 161 vols. Paris, 1857–66.

Pépin, Jean. *Mythe et allégorie: Les origines grecques et les contestations judéo-chrétiennes.* Aubier: Editions Montaigne, 1958.

Perry, T. Anthony. "Dialogue and Doctrine in Leone Ebreo's *Dialoghi d'amore.*" *PMLA* 88 (1973):1173–79.

Petrarca, Francesco. *Lord Morley's "Tryumphes of Fraunces Petrarcke."* Edited by D. D. Carnicelli. Cambridge, Mass.: Harvard University Press, 1971.

———. *Opere latine.* Edited by Antonietta Bufano. 2 vols. Turin: U.T.E.T., 1975.

———. *Il Petrarcha con l'espositione di M. Giovanni Andrea Gesualdo. . . .* Venice: Gabriel Giolito de Ferari e Fratelli, 1553.

———. *Petrarch: A Humanist Among Princes.* Edited and translated by David Thompson. New York, Evanston, and London: Harper and Row, 1971.

———. *Petrarch's Lyric Poems: The "Rime sparse" and Other Lyrics.* Translated and edited by Robert M. Durling. Cambridge, Mass. and London: Harvard University Press, 1976.

———. *Le Rime sparse e i Trionfi.* Edited by Ezio Chiòrboli. Bari: Laterza, 1930.

———. *Trionfi. Sonetti e canzoni.* With commentary by Bernardo da Pietro Lapini da Montalcino et al. Venice: Bernardinus Rizus, 1488.

———. *Trionfi.* Edited by Carlo Calcaterra. Turin: U.T.E.T., 1927.

———. *Die Triumphe Francesco Petrarcas.* Edited by Carl Appel. Halle: Max Niemeyer, 1901.

————. *The Triumphs of Petrarch.* Translated by Ernest Hatch Wilkins. Chicago: University of Chicago Press, 1962.

Phillips, James E. "Spenser's Syncretistic Religious Imagery." *ELH* 36 (1969):110–30. Reprinted in *Critical Essays on Spenser from ELH,* pp. 95–115. Baltimore and London: Johns Hopkins Press, 1970.

Pico, Giovanni, della Mirandola. *Opera omnia.* 2 vols. Basel: Hemicpetrina, 1572. Facsimile reprint. Monumenta politica philosophica humanistica rariora, 1.12. Turin: Bottega d'Erasmo, 1971.

Piehler, Paul. *The Visionary Landscape: A Study in Medieval Allegory.* London: Arnold, 1971.

Plotinus. *Opera.* Edited by Paul Henry and Hans-Rudolf Schwyzer. 3 vols. Oxford: At the Clarendon Press, 1964–77.

Poliziano, Angelo. *The Stanze of Angelo Poliziano.* Translated by David Quint. Amherst: University of Massachusetts Press, 1979.

Praz, Mario. *Studies in Seventeenth-Century Imagery.* 2d rev. ed. Rome: Edizioni di storia e letteratura, 1964.

Propertius. Edited and translated by H. E. Butler. LCL. London: Heinemann and New York: Macmillan, 1912.

Quitslund, Jon A. "Spenser's Image of Sapience." *Studies in the Renaissance* 16 (1969):181–213.

————. "Spenser's *Amoretti* VIII and Platonic Commentaries on Petrarch." *Journal of the Warburg and Courtauld Institutes* 36 (1973):256–76.

Rajna, Pio. "Tre studi per la storia del libro di Andrea Capellano." *Studi di filologia romanza* 5 (1891):193–272.

Rathbone, Eleanor. "Master Alberic of London, 'Mythographus Tertius Vaticanus.'" *Medieval and Renaissance Studies* 1 (1941–43):35–38.

Raynouard, François M.-C. *Choix des poésies originales des troubadours.* 6 vols. Paris: Firmin-Didot, 1816–61.

Rebhorn, Wayne A. "Ottaviano's Interruption: Book IV and the Problem of Unity in *Il Cortegiano.*" *MLN* 87 (1972):37–59.

Remigius of Auxerre. *Commentum in Martianum Capellam.* Edited by Cora E. Lutz. 2 vols. Leiden: Brill, 1962.

Ridevallus, Joannes. *Fulgentius Metaforalis.* Edited by Hans Liebeschütz. Leipzig and Berlin: Teubner, 1926.

Ringler, William. "Spenser and Thomas Watson." *MLN* 69 (1954):484–87.

Robb, Nesca A. *Neoplatonism of the Italian Renaissance.* London: Allen and Unwin, 1935.

Robertson, D. W., Jr. "Five Poems by Marcabru." *Studies in Philology* 51 (1954):539–60.

————. *A Preface to Chaucer.* Princeton: Princeton University Press, 1962.

Roche, Thomas P., Jr. *The Kindly Flame: A Study of the Third and Fourth Books of Spenser's Faerie Queene.* Princeton: Princeton University Press, 1964.

Roncaglia, A. "'Trobar clus': discussione aperta." *Cultura Neolatina* 29 (1969):1–55.

Ronsard, Pierre de. *Les Amours.* Edited by Henri and Catherine Weber. Paris: Garnier, 1963.

Ross, Alexander. *Mel Heliconium.* London: L. N. and J. F. for William Leak, 1642.

Rougemont, Denis de. *Love in the Western World.* Translated by Montgomery Belgion. Rev. and enlarged ed. New York: Pantheon, 1956.

Rousselot, Pierre. *Pour l'histoire du problème de l'amour au Moyen Age.* Beiträge zur Geschichte der Philosophie des Mittelalters, 6.6. Münster: Aschendorff, 1908.

Ruhe, Doris. *Le Dieu d'Amours avec son paradis: Untersuchungen zur Mythenbildung um Amor in Spätantike und Mittelalter.* Beiträge zur romanischen Philologie des Mittelalters, 6. Munich: Wilhelm Fink, 1974.

Sale, Roger. *Reading Spenser: An Introduction to The Faerie Queene.* New York: Random House, 1968.

Salutati, Coluccio. *De laboribus Herculis.* Edited by B. L. Ullman. 2 vols. Zurich: Thesaurus Mundi, 1951.

Santayana, George. "Platonic Love in Some Italian Poets." In *Selected Critical Writings of George Santayana,* edited by Norman Henfrey, 1:11–59. 2 vols. Cambridge: Cambridge University Press, 1968.

Sargent, Barbara Nelson. "A Medieval Commentary on Andreas Capellanus." *Romania* 94 (1973): 528–41.

Savino, Lorenzo. "Di alcuni trattati e trattatisti d'amore italiani della prima metá del secolo XVI." *Studi di letteratura italiana* 9 (1909): 223–435; 10 (1914): 1–342.

Scheludko, Dimitri. "Religiöse Elemente in weltlichen Liebeslied der Trobadors." *Zeitschrift für französiche Sprache und Literatur* 59 (1935): 402–21; 60 (1935–37): 18–35.

Seneca. *Tragedies.* Edited and translated by Frank Justus Miller. LCL. 2 vols. London: Heinemann and New York: Putnam's, 1917.

Seznec, Jean. *The Survival of the Pagan Gods.* Translated by Barbara F. Sessions. New York: Harper, 1961.

Shapiro, Marianne. "Figurality in the *Vita Nuova:* Dante's New Rhetoric." *Dante Studies* 97 (1979): 107–27.

Shaw, J. E. *Essays on the Vita Nuova.* Princeton: Princeton University Press, 1929.

Sidney, Sir Philip. *An Apology for Poetry.* In *Elizabethan Critical Essays,* edited by G. Gregory Smith, 1:148–207. London: Oxford University Press, 1904.

———. *The Poems of Sir Philip Sidney.* Edited by William A. Ringler, Jr. Oxford: At the Clarendon Press, 1962.

Singleton, Charles S. *An Essay on the Vita Nuova.* Cambridge, Mass.: Harvard University Press, 1949.

———. "The Irreducible Dove." *Comparative Literature* 9 (1957): 129–35.

———. "*Vita Nuova* XII: Love's Obscure Words." *Romanic Review* 36 (1945): 89–102.

Skelton, Robin, ed. *The Cavalier Poets.* New York: Oxford University Press, 1970.

Spencer, Floyd A. "The Literary Lineage of Cupid." *Classical Weekly* 25 (1932): 121–27, 129–34, 139–44.

Spenser, Edmund. *The Faerie Queene.* Edited by A. C. Hamilton. Longman Annotated English Poets. London and New York: Longman, 1977.

———. *Books I and II of The Faerie Queene, The Mutabilitie Cantos, and Selections from the Minor Poetry.* Edited by Robert Kellogg and Oliver Steele. New York: Odyssey Press, 1965.

———. *Poetical Works.* Edited by J. C. Smith and E. de Selincourt. Oxford Standard Authors. London: Oxford University Press, 1912.

————. *The Works of Edmund Spenser: A Variorum Edition.* Edited by Edwin Green-law et al. 10 vols. Baltimore: Johns Hopkins Press, 1932–49.

Spitzer, Leo. "L'Amour lontain de Jaufré Rudel et le sens de la poésie des troubadours." University of North Carolina Studies in the Romance Languages and Literatures, 5. Chapel Hill: University of North Carolina Press, 1944.

————. "Spenser, *Shepheardes Calender, March* (Lines 61–114) and the Variorum Edition." In *Essays On English and American Literature,* edited by Anna Hatcher, pp. 180–192. Princeton: Princeton University Press, 1962.

Tasso, Torquato. *Aminta: Favola Boscareccia.* Edited by Pia Piccoli Addoli. Biblioteca Universale Rizzoli, 926. Milan: Rizzoli, 1955.

Templer, Margherita de Bonfils. "Amore e le visioni nella *Vita Nuova.*" *Dante Studies* 92 (1974): 19–34.

Theodolph of Orléans. *Carmina. PL* 105: 283–376.

Topsfield, L. T. "The *Roman de la Rose* of Guillaume de Lorris and the Love Lyric of the Early Troubadours." *Reading Medieval Studies* 1 (1975): 30–54.

————. *Troubadours and Love.* Cambridge: Cambridge University Press, 1975.

Trent, Council of. *Canones et Decreta.* . . . Rome: Manutius and Aldus, 1564.

Trinkaus, Charles. *In Our Image and Likeness: Humanity and Divinity in Italian Humanist Thought.* 2 vols. Chicago: University of Chicago Press, 1970.

Tuve, Rosemond. *Allegorical Imagery: Some Medieval Books and their Posterity.* Princeton: Princeton University Press, 1966.

————. "Spenser and Some Pictorial Conventions." *Studies in Philology* 37 (1940): 149–76. Reprinted in *Essays by Rosemond Tuve,* edited by Thomas P. Roche, Jr., pp. 112–38. Princeton: Princeton University Press, 1970.

Valency, Maurice. *In Praise of Love: An Introduction to the Love-Poetry of the Renaissance.* New York: Macmillan, 1958.

Vanossi, Luigi. *Dante e il "Roman de la rose": Saggio sul "Fiore."* Florence: Olschki, 1979.

Vidal, Peire. *Les Poésies de Peire Vidal.* Edited by Joseph Anglade. 2d rev. ed. Paris: Champion, 1965.

Viglione, Francesco. *La poesia lirica di Edmondo Spenser.* Genoa: Emiliano degli Orfini, 1937.

Virgil. *Virgil.* Edited and translated by H. Rushton Fairclough. LCL. Rev. ed. 2 vols. London: Heinemann and Cambridge, Mass.: Harvard University Press, 1935.

Watson, Thomas. *The Hekatompathia, or Passionate centurie of love.* London: 1582. Reprint. Gainesville, Florida: Scholars' Facsimiles and Reprints, 1964.

Wattenbach, W. "Jupiter und Danae" ["Primo veris tempore"]. *Zeitschrift für Deutsches Alterthum* 18 (1875): 457–60.

Wellek, Rene, and Austin Warren. *Theory of Literature.* 3d ed. New York: Harcourt-Brace, 1970.

Wetherbee, Winthrop. "The Function of Poetry in the *De planctu naturae* of Alain de Lille." *Traditio* 25 (1969): 87–125.

————. *Platonism and Poetry in the Twelfth Century. The Literary Influence of the School of Chartres.* Princeton: Princeton University Press, 1972.

Whitman, Charles Huntington. *A Subject-Index to the Poems of Edmund Spenser.* New Haven: Yale University Press, 1918.

Whitman, Cedric. *Homer and the Heroic Tradition.* New York: Norton, 1965.

Wilhelm, James J. *The Cruelest Month.* New Haven: Yale University Press, 1965.

Wilkins, Ernest Hatch. "The First Two Triump!.s of Petrarch." *Italica* 40 (1963):7–17.

———. *The Making of the "Canzoniere" and other Petrarchan Studies.* Rome: Edizioni di storia e letteratura, 1951.

———. *Studies in the Life and Works of Petrarch.* Cambridge, Mass.: Medieval Academy of America, 1955.

William of St. Thierry. *De natura et dignitate amoris. PL* 184:379–408.

Williams, Kathleen. *Spenser's World of Glass: A Reading of The Faerie Queene.* Berkeley and Los Angeles: University of California Press, 1966.

———. "Venus and Diana: Some Uses of Myth in *The Faerie Queene.*" *ELH* 28 (1961):101–20. Reprinted in *Essential Articles for the Study of Edmund Spenser,* edited by A. C. Hamilton, pp. 202–219, 609. Hamden, Ct.: Archon Books, 1972.

Wind, Edgar. *Pagan Mysteries in the Renaissance.* 2d ed. Harmondsworth: Penguin, 1967.

Wittgenstein, Ludwig. *Philosophical Investigations.* Edited and translated by G. E. M. Anscombe. 3d ed. Oxford: Blackwell, 1967.

Index

Abelard, Peter, 39
Aimeric de Peguilhan, 34
Alain de Lille: *De planctu Naturae*, 38–43, 45, 53, 55, 62–63, 93, 175
Albricus, 39
Alciati, Andrea, 22–23, 73
Alpers, Paul J., 143–44, 161, 171
Altercatio Phyllidis et Florae, 35
Ambacht van Cupido, Het, 73
Amor. *See* Cupid
Anacreontea, 26, 73, 75, 130
Andreas Capellanus: *De amore*, 35–37, 41, 45, 55, 67, 85
Aniconic representation, 21
Antony, Saint (archbishop of Florence), 21
Aphrodite. *See* Venus
Apollo and Daphne, 30
Apuleius, 107, 168
Aristotle, 30
Auden, W. H., 17–18
Augustine, Saint, 21, 31, 52, 139; and Petrarch, 62–64
Ausonius, 107, 181

Bacon, Sir Francis, 109, 143
Baïf, Jean-Antoine de, 78, 131
Barbarino, Francesco, 30, 89
Behn, Aphra, 181
Belleau, Remy, 76, 112
Bembo, Pietro: *Gli Asolani*, 87, 100–103, 115
Benivieni, Girolamo, 103
Berger, Harry, Jr., 110, 178
Bible: Acts, 49; 1 Corinthians, 44; Ezekiel, 48; 1 John, 31; Mark, 49; Psalms, 136; Romans, 91; Song of Songs, 31; use of, in *Vita Nuova*, 47–49, 54
Bion, 116
Boccaccio, Giovanni, 101, 105, 168, 177;

Genealogia deorum gentilium, 30, 88–92, 108–9, 111, 114; *Teseida*, 81
Boethius, 14, 125

Caravaggio, Michelangelo Merisi, 24
Cartari, Vincenzo: *Le imagine degli dei*, 87, 96, 105–7
Castiglione, Baldassare: *Il cortegiano*, 88, 102–4, 115, 120
Catullus, 79
Cavalcanti, Guido, 36–37, 47, 52, 58
Cecil, William, first baron Burleigh, 145, 147
Chalcidius, 93
Charles d'Orleans: *La Retenue d'Amours*, 74
Chaucer, Geoffrey: *Prologue to the Legend of Good Women*, 157; *Troilus and Criseyde*, 15, 44, 81, 114, 125, 150, 163
Cheney, Donald, 156
Chrétien de Troyes, 32–33; *Lancelot*, 47, 55
Cicero, 88
Claudian, 79, 181
Coleridge, Samuel Taylor, 115
Colonna, Francesco: *Hypnerotomachia Poliphili*, 73
Conti, Natale, 96, 111, 114, 125, 161, 177; *Mythologiae*, 87, 105, 107–10
Council of Love at Remiremont, The, 35
Council of Trent, 20
Courtly love, 30
Cupid (Amor, Dieu d'Amours, etc.): angelic, 48–49, 95, 155–56, 186 n.7, 193 n.14; attributes of, 13, 20–22, 26, 29–30, 33, 43, 47, 67, 72–74, 77, 89, 96, 101–2, 106, 108–9, 124, 134, 150, 156, 162, 172, 178, 184 n.18, 186 n.3; as demon or pagan deity, 31, 95, 112–15, 117, 161–63, 173; derivative power of, 34, 40–41, 47, 76, 101; distinguished from Amor, 98–100, 153, 160, 183 n.4; divinity of, 20, 37,

Cupid (Amor, Dieu d'Amours, etc.) *(continued)*
42, 67, 81, 98–99, 104, 109–10, 125, 150, 160,
178, 186 n.4; double nature of (god and
personification), 13, 29–30, 76, 78, 84, 88, 93,
95, 97, 107, 181; ecphrases of, 21–22, 76, 107,
188 n.13; epithets and exploits of, 73; Eros
and Anteros, 181; genealogies of, 72, 88–90,
92, 97, 101, 108, 123, 125, 134, 192 n.45; as
idol, 18, 57, 112, 171; inspirer of poetry, 77,
96, 104, 116, 123, 133, 145; and Jocus, 41,
118, 176; in lyric poems, 26, 33, 74–78, 127,
130, 181; as mirror image of lover, 40, 50–51,
58, 76, 89, 186 n.41; as mythological or fictive
deity, 47, 75, 78, 135; one or many, 88, 94, 97,
104–8, 110, 143; as personification, 46, 65, 68,
74, 76, 88, 101, 105, 109, 158; and Psyche, 72,
88, 90, 118, 168, 182; two Cupids, 30, 41, 92,
95, 98, 110, 124, 144, 150, 156; as unincarnated personification, 32–33, 35, 49, 51,
184 n.13; and Voluptas (daughter), 72, 90, 95,
168. *See also* Love
"Cupid and the Bee," 84, 131

Dante, 23, 52, 71; *Commedia*, 57, 60, 71; *In-
ferno*, 47–48, 55, 67–68; *Le fiore*, 45; *Paradiso*,
56, 125; *Purgatorio*, 56; *Vita Nuova*, 19, 31,
45–51, 53–60, 69, 72, 95, 156, 175
Davies, Sir John, 125
De Selincourt, Ernest, 156
Diacetto, Francesco Cattani da, 100
Dieu d'Amours. *See* Cupid
Dionysius the pseudo-Areopagite, 95
Dolce stil nuovo, 47, 100
Donation of Constantine, 17
Donne, John, 181
Dream visions, 53–54, 59–60, 148–49
Drouart la Vache, 37

Ebreo, Leone: *Dialoghi d'amore*, 88, 98–100,
110, 161–62
Ellrodt, Robert, 135
Emblems, 19, 73
Empedocles, 14, 125
Epithalamia, 79, 181
Equicola, Mario: *Labro di natura d'amore*, 87,
97–98
Euhemerism, 88

Ficino, Marsilio, 82, 102–3, 105, 110, 125, 160,
162; *Commentary on Symposium*, 87, 93–96,
104; *De Christiana religione*, 93

Flaubert, Gustave, 181
Fletcher, Angus, 14
Fulgentius, 90

Giraldi, Lilio Gregorio: *De deis gentium*, 87,
105
Gombrich, E. H., 13, 20
Greek Anthology, 26, 73, 75, 109, 130, 174
Greene, Thomas M., 132
Guillaume de Lorris. *See Roman de la rose*
Guinizelli, Guido, 52, 160

Hamilton, A. C., 168
Hesiod, 13
Homer, 17, 113, 115
Hugh of St. Victor, 31
Hutton, James, 20

Iconoclasm, 20

Jean de Meun. *See Roman de la rose*
Johnson, Samuel, 53
Jonson, Ben, 181
Judici d'amor, 35

Keats, John, 182

Lactantius: *Divinae institutiones*, 64, 67
Lapini dal Montalcino, Bernardo da Pietro, 65,
99
Lever, J. W., 129
Lewis, C. S., 13, 27, 36, 130, 143, 150, 159
Lotspeich, Henry Gibbons, 125
Love: arts of (literary genre), 34–35, 42, 45;
association of, with spring, 44, 60, 73, 127–
28; as desire for beauty, 33, 93–94, 96–98,
100, 103; and heroism in Spenser, 152–53,
160; hierarchy of, in theology, 18, 30, 44; and
Idleness, 15, 65, 101, 191 n.19; and integrity
of individual, 59, 68, 82–83, 174; Latin vocabulary for, 30–31, 97; versus lust, 95, 98–
99, 103, 137, 160; Platonic love, 100; as primal
force of Creation, 14, 76, 93, 97, 104, 109,
123, 125, 134–35; relationship of, with reason, 32, 42, 47–48, 55–56, 96, 99; religion of,
36–37, 42–43, 85, 122–27; and theme of youth
and age, 43–44, 70, 102–4, 139. *See also*
Cupid; Neoplatonism
Love imagery, conflation of pagan and Christian, 31, 34, 141
Love allegories, late medieval, 73

Marcabru, 34
Marot, Clement: *Le Temple de Cupido,* 73–74, 172
Mars (Ares). *See* Venus: and Mars
Milton, John, 131, 163
Moschus: *Amor fugitivus,* 20, 84, 161, 167, 181
Mythography: medieval, 29–32, 88; Renaissance, 87–92, 104–10
Mythology: *amores deorum* as lies of poets, 38–39, 81, 89, 174, 185 n.32; as iconographical language, 18–19, 31, 92. *See also* Poetic theology

Narcissus, 41, 98
Neilson, William Allen, 20
Neoplatonism, 76, 82, 85, 120, 181; divinization of love and beauty in, 93, 95, 97, 99, 103–4, 106, 127, 134–35, 137, 156; hierarchical cosmology in, 93–94, 96, 98–99; ladder of love in, 88, 94–96, 99, 102–4, 137–138. *See also* Cupid; Love; Poetic theology

Octavia, 15, 21, 31, 40
Origen, 31
Origins and Sources of the Court of Love (Neilson), 20
Orpheus, 125
Osgood, Charles Grosvenor, 90
Ovid, 34–35, 38, 41, 51; *Amores,* 43, 77, 145; *Ars amatoria,* 31–32; *Fasti,* 92; *Metamorphoses,* 30, 81, 117, 146
Ovide moralisé, 30

Pan and Syrinx, 30
Panofsky, Erwin, 20
Petrarch, 13, 77, 128; *Africa,* 61–62; *Rime sparse,* 58, 60, 68, 71, 74; *Secretum,* 60, 71, 140; *Trionfi,* 23, 58–72, 74, 77, 81, 100–103, 106, 115, 120, 172, 174, 175
Petrarchism, 40, 75, 130
Pico della Mirandola, Giovanni di, 29, 96, 100, 103, 110
Plato, 72, 105; *Symposium,* 100; *Timaeus,* 39, 93
Pléiade, 75–77
Plotinus, 13, 16, 18, 93, 111
Poet as *vates* or *theologus,* 28, 33–34, 72, 82, 123, 133
Poetic theology: abuse of, to justify lust, 15–18, 36–38, 40, 55–56, 59, 63–65, 76–77, 81, 88–89, 92, 95, 98, 101, 106–9, 121, 138, 148–50, 174, 181, 185 n.33, 192 n.47, 194 n.37; anag-

norisis or reversal in, 47, 60, 79, 81, 85, 87; defense of poetry, 72, 78, 85, 91, 93; as delusion, 42, 45, 55, 59, 81; demythologization or iconoclasm in, 16, 19, 23, 40, 42, 47, 54, 163, 172, 175; as fictive scripture, 36–37, 51, 91, 111, 175; fictive worlds in, 17–18, 29, 68, 75, 78, 112, 132, 142; hierarchical cosmology in, 39–40; as idolatry, 57, 76, 174–75; and literalized metaphor, 48, 52, 57, 101, 174, 179; paradox of gods as creatures of mortal poets in, 119–20, 122, 159, 163, 178; and *prisca theologia,* 91, 93; purposeful inconsistencies in, 39, 41–42, 51, 66, 123, 125, 134, 154–55, 162, 185 n.35; Silenus Alcibiadis as image for, 89–90, 95, 189 n.7; subjective turn in, 42, 45–46, 52, 59, 74, 77; truth claims of, 17, 35–38, 52–53, 55, 82; unstable semantic hierarchies in, 18, 32, 38, 42, 58, 108–9. *See also* Neoplatonism; Poetry; Mythology
Poetry, relation of, with Scripture, 28, 92, 182
Poliziano, Angelo: *Stanze per la giostra,* 19, 79–83, 85, 150, 160; and *Trionfi,* 79, 81–83
Ponsonby, William, 117
Praz, Mario, 73
Propertius, 21, 107
Psyche. *See* Cupid: and Psyche

Reni, Guido, 23
Ridewall, John, 30
Robb, Nesca, 99
Roman de la rose, 19, 40–45, 47–48, 53–54, 60, 63, 70, 73, 102, 115, 120, 156, 172, 174
Ronsard, Pierre de, 75, 77, 131
Rudel, Jaufré, 34

Scherillo, Michele, 48
Seneca, 88, 106, 150; *Hippolytus,* 16, 65, 89, 98
Shaw, J. E., 58
Shelley, Percy Bysshe, 182
Sidney, Sir Philip, 112, 129, 131
Singleton, Charles, 52, 54, 56
Spenser, Edmund, works of: theodicy of love in, 112, 123–27, 133–37, 144, 158–75, 179
—*Amoretti,* 127–30, 132, 137, 140, 178–79
—*Anacreontics,* 130–31, 179, 192 n.38
—*Colin Clouts Come Home Againe,* 116, 120–27, 174, 178
—*Epithalamion,* 130–32
—*Faerie Queene,* analogies among episodes of, 147, 149, 151, 178; Cupid's victims in, 159, 161, 173, 175; love and heroism in, 152–53,

Spenser, Edmund, works of (continued)
  160; love and Providence in, 147, 149, 156,
  166, 173; narrator's indirect discourse in, 147,
  154–55; reading and narrative sequence of,
  147, 151; relation of naration to incident in,
  163, 173–75; unarmed Cupid in, 145, 150,
  155–57, 160, 168
—Faerie Queene, episodes discussed:
  Letter to Raleigh, 146
  1.proem, 144–45, 147, 150–51, 153
  1.1.38–2.6 (Archimago's cottage), 148–49
  1.9.6–16 (Arthur and the Faerie Queene),
    149–51
  1.10.29–33 (Charissa), 155
  2.2.12–33 (Medina's castle), 151–52
  2.3.23–24 (Belphoebe), 153–54
  2.6.29–36 (Phaedria's Isle), 152–53
  2.8.1–6 (Guyon's angel), 155–57
  2.9.18–34 (Alma's House), 157–58
  3.1.38–39 (Malecasta's revels), 161–62
  3.2.17–26 (Britomart's enamorment), 163–
    65
  3.3.1–3, 159, 164–65
  3.3.24 (Merlin's prophecy), 164–65
  3.4.9–11 (Britomart on the Rich Strond),
    166
  3.5.1, 160
  3.6.11–15 (Venus's search for Cupid), 166–
    67
  3.6.49–50 (Cupid in Gardens of Adonis),
    167–69
  3.10.4–5 (Paridell and Helenore), 162–63
  3.11.7–12.45 (House of Busirane), 81, 169–
    75
  4.proem, 145–47
  4.7.1–2, 176
  4.10.21–48 (Temple of Venus), 176–77
  4.12.13 (Marinell's enamorment), 175
  6.7.28–38 (Mirabella), 177–78
  6.8.22–25 (Mirabella), 178–79
  6.11.1, 179
  7.7.34, 43 (Mutabilitie Cantos), 180

—Fowre Hymnes, 123, 132–42, 178
—Muiopotmos, 117–20, 122, 131, 163
—Shepheardes Calender, 112–17, 126–27, 131,
  149, 159, 162
Spitzer, Leo, 115
Statius, 79, 181
Stesichorus, 102, 126

Tasso, Torquato: Aminta, 83–85, 131, 167; and
  Trionfi, 84–85
Tempier, Stephan (bishop of Paris), 37
Terence, 67–68; Eununchus, 62–63
Troubadours, 13, 33–34, 47, 49, 53, 114
Tuve, Rosemond, 14, 91

Uc Brunec, 33

Van Eyck, Jan, 21
Varro, Marcus Terentius, 64, 91
Vatican Mythographers, 106; First, 90; Third,
  30
Venus (Aphrodite), 39, 56, 106; in Alain de
  Lille, 39–41; in Ficino, 94; island of, in Pet-
  rarch and Poliziano, 81–82; and Mars, 17, 89,
  129, 145, 153; in Spenser, 118, 121, 123–24,
  129, 134, 148, 155, 158, 161, 166, 167–68,
  173, 176
Vermeer, Jan van der, 25–26
Viglione, Francesco, 130
Virgil, 62, 67; Aeneid, 51–52; quoted, 31, 40
Visual arts, 19–26, 58, 81, 85, 105. See also
  Cupid: ecphrases of; Emblems
Voluptas. See Cupid: and Voluptas (daughter)

Watson, Thomas, 129, 131
Wellek, René and Austin Warren, 27
Whitman, Cedric, 17
Whitman, Charles, 143
Wilkins, Ernest Hatch, 68
William of St. Thierry, 44
Wind, Edgar, 20
Wyatt, Sir Thomas, 128